Anxiety in and about Africa

CAMBRIDGE CENTRE OF AFRICAN STUDIES SERIES

Series editors: Adam Branch, Emma Hunter, and Christopher Warnes

The University of Cambridge is home to one of the world's leading centers of African studies. It organizes conferences, runs a weekly seminar series, hosts a specialist library, coordinates advanced graduate studies, and facilitates research by Cambridge- and Africa-based academics. The Cambridge Centre of African Studies Series publishes work that emanates from this rich intellectual life. The series fosters dialogue across a broad range of disciplines in African studies and between scholars based in Africa and elsewhere.

Derek R. Peterson, ed.
Abolitionism and Imperialism in Britain, Africa, and the Atlantic

Harri Englund, ed.
Christianity and Public Culture in Africa

Devon Curtis and Gwinyayi A. Dzinesa, eds.
Peacebuilding, Power, and Politics in Africa

Ruth J. Prince and Rebecca Marsland, eds.
Making Public Health in Africa: Ethnographic and Historical Perspectives

Emma Hunter, ed.
*Citizenship, Belonging, and Political Community in Africa:
Dialogues between Past and Present*

Felicitas Becker, Joel Cabrita, and Marie Rodet, eds.
Religion, Media, and Marginality in Modern Africa

Jessica Johnson and George Hamandishe Karekwaivanane, eds.
Pursuing Justice in Africa: Competing Imaginaries and Contested Practices

Florence Brisset-Foucault
Talkative Polity: Radio, Domination, and Citizenship in Uganda

Andrea Mariko Grant and Yolana Pringle, eds.
*Anxiety in and about Africa:
Multidisciplinary Perspectives and Approaches*

Anxiety in and about Africa
Multidisciplinary Perspectives and Approaches

Edited by
Andrea Mariko Grant and Yolana Pringle

Ohio University Press • *Athens*

Ohio University Press, Athens, Ohio 45701
ohioswallow.com
© 2021 by Ohio University Press
All rights reserved

To obtain permission to quote, reprint, or otherwise reproduce or distribute material from Ohio University Press publications, please contact our rights and permissions department at (740) 593-1154 or (740) 593-4536 (fax).

Printed in the United States of America
Ohio University Press books are printed on acid-free paper ∞ ™

30 29 28 27 26 25 24 23 22 21 20   5 4 3 2 1

Library of Congress Cataloging-in-Publication Data

Names: Anxiety in and about Africa {Conference} (2016 : Cambridge, England), author. | Grant, Andrea, 1981- editor. | Pringle, Yolana, editor.
Title: Anxiety in and about Africa : multidisciplinary perspectives and approaches / edited by Andrea Mariko Grant and Yolana Pringle.
Other titles: Cambridge Centre of African Studies series.
Description: Athens : Ohio University Press, 2021. | Series: Cambridge Centre of African Studies series | "This edited volume stems from a two-day interdisciplinary conference, 'Anxiety in and about Africa,' held at the University of Cambridge in June 2016"--Page vii. | Includes bibliographical references and index.
Identifiers: LCCN 2020036851 (print) | LCCN 2020036852 (ebook) | ISBN 9780821424360 (paperback) | ISBN 9780821447284 (pdf)
Subjects: LCSH: Anxiety--Africa--Congresses. | Africa--Social conditions--1960---Congresses.
Classification: LCC HN773.5 .A68 2020 (print) | LCC HN773.5 (ebook) | DDC 306.096--dc23
LC record available at https://lccn.loc.gov/2020036851
LC ebook record available at https://lccn.loc.gov/2020036852

Contents

Acknowledgments
vii

INTRODUCTION
States of Anxiety in Africa
Perspectives, Approaches, and Potential
YOLANA PRINGLE AND ANDREA MARIKO GRANT
1

PART I: ANXIOUS SPACES

ONE
Misapprehensions
Outlaws and Anxiety in Southern Africa's Archaeological Past
RACHEL KING
33

TWO
Between the Anxiogenic and the Soothing
*Settlers' Engagements with Africans
in Dance in Colonial Africa, 1920s–30s*
CÉCILE FEZA BUSHIDI
65

THREE
Epidemics and Anxiety in Saint-Louis-du-Sénégal, from the Mid-Nineteenth to the Early Twentieth Century
KALALA NGALAMULUME
92

Contents

PART II: UNSETTLING NARRATIVES

FOUR
Anxiety over Masculinity
Gendered and Sexual Struggles in Mwanga II's Buganda, 1884–97
NAKANYIKE B. MUSISI
115

FIVE
No End to the Trouble
Decolonization Anxieties and the Evacuation of White Settlers from Kenya, 1963–64
WILL JACKSON AND HARRY FIRTH-JONES
144

SIX
Competing Development "Visions"?
State Anxieties and Church Closures in Rwanda
ANDREA MARIKO GRANT
167

PART III: ALTERNATIVE TEMPORALITIES

SEVEN
"Right Now, I Don't Know What the Future Might Bring"
Hope, Anxiety, and Despair in the Burundian Crisis
SIMON TURNER
195

EIGHT
"Obuganda Buladde"
Power, Anxiety, and Calm in Postcolonial Buganda
JONATHON L. EARLE
217

Contributors
241

Index
245

Acknowledgments

This edited volume stems from a two-day interdisciplinary conference, "Anxiety in and about Africa," held at the University of Cambridge in June 2016. We would like to thank all of the participants for their intellectually stimulating discussions, particularly on the themes of politics and anxiety; anxiety and lived experience; and anxiety, bodies, and borders. We would also like to thank the Centre of African Studies, CRASSH, the Smuts Memorial Fund, and the Wellcome Trust for generously supporting the conference. The editorial team at Ohio University Press has also been instrumental in getting this project off the ground; we thank them for their patience and expert guidance. Final thanks go to the anonymous reviewers of the volume for their helpful and encouraging comments, as well as to the series editors for their support of this project.

INTRODUCTION

States of Anxiety in Africa

Perspectives, Approaches, and Potential

YOLANA PRINGLE AND ANDREA MARIKO GRANT

WHAT DOES IT MEAN TO UNDERSTAND LIVED EXPERIENCES, behaviors, or even whole spaces through the lens of anxiety? Such a question immediately calls for consideration of what, precisely, is meant by "anxiety." As a term that in Western medical and philosophical thinking has roots in classical Greek moral discourse, as well as in the Freudian psychoanalytic theories of the early twentieth century, *anxiety* is difficult to pin down.[1] Is it a pathological or a natural state? A normal response to fear, uncertainty, vulnerability, or more diffuse feelings of being unsettled or out of place? Is it a cultural construct? A symptom of the modern era, as it is regarded in twentieth-century Western social and cultural discourse; a way of neatly characterizing the ache of uncertainty and distress about everything from the horrors of World War II to the threat of nuclear war, environmental degradation, public health crises, violence, and family breakdown?[2] Is it more than just an internal state—pathological or otherwise—being something that emerges in relation to the outer world, in particular to material objects such as borders and bodies? Should it be read as a confluence of inner and outer worlds, an affect caused by particular social, political, and historical circumstances? And how do we know that we are dealing with anxiety, particularly where the word itself is rarely used, when instead we need to read anxiety through local idioms or in the traces left by individuals and communities—in rituals, behaviors, ideas, theories, policies, and material culture?

Such questions reflect theoretical debates within the study of the emotions between social constructivism and biological universalism, as well as the question of whether there is any such thing as an inner self, or if we are dealing with primarily cognitive as opposed to physiological emotional states. Recent scientific research that locates anxiety in biological processes and highlights the role of neurochemicals and neural networks might offer a new perspective on the social constructivist/universalist dichotomy, but it nevertheless fails to explain what anxiety might mean to individuals or communities at any one place or point in time, and what the study of anxiety as both expression and embodied experience offers analytically.[3] This lack of definitional precision is particularly acute when considering what the study of anxiety could bring to African studies. So pervasive are notions of anxiety as a symptom of the (Western) modern era that the use of the concept requires us to question the appropriateness of imposing it on the past, or on the words or actions of others, and in doing so implicitly positing anxiety as universal. This might help explain why, despite a vast literature on anxiety in Europe and the United States, anxiety in Africa has received relatively little scholarly attention.[4] This has remained the case even as the "affective turn" has seen the publication of numerous historically, culturally, and ethnographically sensitive studies of other emotions on the continent—of anger, jealousy, love, and happiness, among others.[5] The exception to this lack of attention to anxiety has been among historians of empire, particularly of settler colonies, who have since the 1980s shown how "colonial anxieties" of sexuality, authority, modernity, climate, and race shaped attitudes and policies in colonial settings in Africa and help reveal the vulnerability of the colonial enterprise.[6]

Influenced in part by the growth of interest in the emotions and affect across disciplines, the literature on anxieties and empire has moved a long way from its original focus on colonial medicine to encompass violence, rebellion, and intimacy, among other themes.[7] It demonstrates that feelings of anxiety were not limited to the imperial elite, but shaped behaviors across the colonial divide, including in African contexts. The edited collections *Anxieties, Fear and Panic in Colonial Settings: Empires on the Verge of a Nervous Breakdown* (edited by Harald Fischer-Tiné, 2016), *Empires of Panic: Epidemics and Colonial Anxieties* (edited by Robert Peckham, 2015), and *Helpless Imperialists* (edited by Maurus Reinkowski and Gregor Thum, 2013), while predominantly focused on Asia, offer comparative insights into the multiple ways such "negative" emotions not only expressed social and cultural attitudes but guided political action, having real, lived consequences for colonizers and the colonized alike. In this sense, the study of anxieties in the context of empire is not just an intellectual exercise, but a political project. "The very suggestion that imperial overlords could ever be viewed as vulnerable, or even 'helpless' in some situations," as Mark Condos has noted, "is deeply unsettling because empires ultimately represented power and dominance, and were often remarkably durable even during times of crisis."[8]

Across disciplines, as the literature on anxieties and empire reflects, emotions and the affective—anxiety, fear, and panic, as well as feelings of love, hate, and happiness—are undergoing a particular "moment." Far from the "unfocused" emotion talk described by historian Barbara Rosenwein in 2006, much of this work now deals not only with overt expressions of emotions but with the ways we might uncover the meanings and experiences of subjective emotional states, changes in affective norms across time and space, and how emotions order worlds and worldviews.[9] This scholarship demonstrates that emotion or sentiment is not epiphenomenal to power—"a smokescreen of rule"—but rather "the substance of politics, the moralising self-presentation of the state as itself a genre of political authority."[10] Borrowing the concept of "affective states" from Ann Laura Stoler, anthropologists Mateusz Laszczkowski and Madeleine Reeves take up the concept to consider "a range of affects, feelings, and emotions for and about 'the state' and its agents, and explore how those contribute to the state's emergence, transformation, endurance, or erosion."[11] Here they build on both earlier anthropological work from the 1970s and 1980s that explored the cultural constructedness of emotions[12] and the more recent "affective turn" that takes affect as a prediscursive charge or intensity, as presubjective but not presocial, defined against emotion that is already "fix[ed] into place through a variety of discursive practices."[13] While this latter work has helpfully moved anthropological attention away from the human subject and has taken seriously the kind of energies or affects discharged by particular objects and spaces, in certain iterations it has flattened out questions of history and politics.[14] Joining this work with more historical approaches to the emotions, particularly anxiety, then, helps us sidestep this risk. Indeed, attending to anxiety from a multidisciplinary perspective allows for an exploration of the political in ways that move beyond simplistic dichotomies (rational/irrational)—and reified categories (subject, object, society, past, present). As William Mazzarella has pointed out, affect "implies a way of apprehending social life that does not start with the bounded, intentional subject while at the same time foregrounding embodiment and sensuous life."[15]

These more recent approaches see emotions as multidirectional and existing in multiplicities, and are attendant to the intersections of the emotions and power not only as related to the colonial project, but as related both to more recent histories, and the deeper past. Even work that focuses on singular emotional states pays careful attention to the multiple emotional registers that are framed within them. In the case of ethnographic work on uncertainty in Africa, for example, anthropologists explore how it is accompanied by feelings of "vulnerability, anxiety, hope and possibility."[16] Unpacking these lived affective experiences can tell us much about what it feels like to navigate diverse social, political, and economic contexts marked by marginalization, violence, and inequality in ways often ignored or pushed aside in more "traditional" studies of, say, politics or development.[17] This research makes clear that exploration of the emotions requires keen attention to material factors and wider structures of power, often tracing them not only to transnational forces such as the enduring effects of structural adjustment policies but also to local and regional histories of war and conflict, in addition to the "afterlives" of colonial rule. As feminist scholar Sara Ahmed has written of the "sociality of emotions," "emotions are not simply something 'I' or 'we' have. Rather, it is through emotions, or how we respond to objects and others, that surfaces or boundaries are made: the 'I' and the 'we' are shaped by, and even take the shape of, contact with others."[18]

Scholarly literature on the emotions nevertheless remains uneven, not only in different geographical contexts but between disciplines. While anthropologists have long been interested in the emotions, new research by archaeologists into complex human emotions in the deeper past is only now opening up new possibilities for expanding the historicity of emotions. Work by Sarah Tarlow, as well as an edited volume put together by Jeffrey Fleisher and Neil Norman, both archaeologists of Africa, shows how emotions are central to understanding the "before" and "after" of events, the composition and reach of social and political structures, and give meaning to concepts such as power, control, and resistance.[19] Among the various entry points into the materiality of anxiousness, worry, and fear, according to these initial theoretical and methodological explorations, are the reconstruction of emotional communities, attention to evocative spaces, and risks inherent in the performance of rituals. Rachel King (this volume) similarly sees the material remains of encounters between people as a way of recovering "a sense of how objects and people behaved." Anxiety, through this approach, is something that "'makes sense' of and orders the world, based on often-imperfect information and sensibilities related to past experiences and visions for the future."[20]

This volume brings together essays on anxiety in Africa from a variety of perspectives—history, archaeology, anthropology—in order to demonstrate the potential of anxiety as a tool for scholars within African studies. The approach calls us to consider anxiety not as a category of universal human experience, as hard-wired or even as completely socially constructed, but instead as an analytical lens that can be employed in multiple ways. Collectively, the chapters showcase not only how anxieties are revealing of individual and collective vulnerabilities, but how anxiety can be used to explore subjectivities and embodied experience. The contributors particularly call attention to ways of thinking about African spaces—physical, visceral, somatic, and imagined—as well as time and temporality. They all, in different ways, reinforce the historically and culturally situated nature of anxiety—how it is embedded in practices, language, and material culture, and how it emerges in relation to the outer world, in particular to material objects such as bodies. Through a multidisciplinary approach, the volume also brings histories of anxiety in colonial settings into conversation with work on the "negative" emotions in disciplines beyond history. While anxiety has long been acknowledged as a powerful tool for unsettling colonial narratives and revealing the vulnerability of the colonial enterprise, this volume shows anxiety can equally disrupt related narratives in the contemporary moment, such as those of sustainable development, migration, sexuality, and democracy. The contributors highlight the need to take emotions seriously as contemporary realities, but ones with particular histories that must be carefully mapped out.

There is power and potential in anxiety precisely because it can both unsettle otherwise dominant narratives and reveal the ways these narratives are themselves embodied, reproduced through actions, coproduced between individuals, and represented in material culture. Anxiety, whether about the body, the environment, or the state, or indeed as an internal state, is always about something else as well. In colonial settler societies, anxieties about sexuality, authority, modernity, and climate, among other concerns, were also anxieties about race and gender, connected by the perceived need to maintain white male prestige. For the psychiatrists who attempted to theorize about Africans "in transition" in the late colonial period, anxiety was an inevitable result of "culture contact," modernity, and urbanization, but revealed just as much about the vulnerability of the colonial enterprise.[21] For African intellectuals and writers of the 1950s and 1960s, writing about anxiety was a way of capturing concerns about decolonization, modernity, and state formation.[22] Chinua Achebe wrote of a sense of chaos in the Igbo cultural world, describing the "continual struggle, motion and change" and "fear of anarchy" weighing down on his characters as a "resonance of an immemorial anxiety."[23] Here, anxiety is useful because it allows us to keep various kinds of narratives in focus: individual narratives of lived affective experience (of colonial settlers and missionaries, of persecuted pastors, of refugees) alongside more collective narratives of colonization, decolonization, modernity, hegemonic masculinity and heterosexuality, and postconflict political transition.

The rest of this introduction maps out the themes that recur throughout the volume. In bringing together chapters from different disciplines, the volume suggests three main entry points for thinking about anxiety. The first is the ways that anxieties might be tied to distinct African spaces or places—whether real or imagined—and the ways these "anxious spaces" shape not only actions and policies but material culture, language, and physical and psychological expression. The second arises from the ways that the chapters, particularly when read alongside each other, so often invite reflections on the future. Thinking about anxiety and temporality opens up ways of exploring imaginations of the future, questions of unknowability, and alternative visions and realities. And the third, which runs through our discussion of both space and temporality, is the power of anxiety to destabilize commonsense or normative narratives. Throughout the volume, the literature on colonial anxieties is frequently taken as a historiographical and analytical starting point. This is unsurprising, considering that anxiety, as a concept, has been most productively employed by historians of empire. In the discussion that follows, the literature on colonial anxieties is similarly taken as a starting point. The aim is to explore what new questions and avenues for investigation arise when this literature is placed in conversation with that from other historical or disciplinary approaches. But it is also to highlight the ways anxiety continues to pose challenges, not least that of language (where anxiety does not have an obvious equivalent) and ontology (for a construct that appears to presume the existence of an inner sense or being). Africa has long been "reinvented" as a particular kind of place through the imaginaries of Western observers—as a place of "lack" and "failure"; as "irrational" yet as enticingly exotic, if not erotic; as a void upon which the West has been able to project its own desires.[24] Such challenges need to be addressed head on by researchers if anxiety is going to hold any analytical power.

Anxiety, Environments, and Spaces (Real and Imagined)

In the colonial setting, it seems, the very environment was inscribed with anxiety.[25] These were spaces that offered adventure, opportunity, and wealth, but also immense danger. Medico-scientific thinking about the "tropics" had since the seventeenth century linked environment with disease, and even death, feeding into fears about the white man's ability to acclimatize and exposing the vulnerability of any long-term colonial project. Fears about the environment were not unfounded. Until the mid-nineteenth century, mortality rates were often so high that certain regions—notably West Africa—were considered effectively uninhabitable by Europeans.[26] Even as the immediate threat of disease was diminished through improved prevention and control measures, anxieties about the negative physical and psychological effect of the environment remained, now more frequently refocused on the climate itself. Medical officers stressed the "unhealthiness" of life in tropical climates and advanced theories about "tropical neurasthenia," a diagnosis of "nervous exhaustion" that was reserved almost exclusively for white colonizers.[27] Humidity and the sun—with its heat, light, and rays—were linked to changes in body temperature, pulse rate, heart and respiratory function, and perspiration, leading to a weakening of the nervous system. Settlers and missionaries, too, complained about the depletion of energy or "nerve force" that accompanied prolonged periods in the tropics, agonizing over its effects on bodies and minds.[28]

As historians of empire have shown, protecting vulnerable European bodies from the negative effects of tropical climates became a major business of imperial health and hygiene. No European could be properly equipped for life in colonial settings without purchasing a potentially lifesaving kit of soap, specialized clothing, medicines, and bedding.[29] Regular assessments of mental and physical fitness became an essential part of administering empire, providing a useful way of managing the behavior of missionaries and colonial servants.[30] Indeed, anxieties about environment and climate were never just about individual bodies but reflected broader colonial anxieties about prestige, race, masculinity, and the vulnerability of colonial states. Use of the diagnosis of tropical neurasthenia for "policing the colonizers," Anna Greenwood has argued, persisted as medical officers in British East Africa continued to publish on neurasthenia and its relationship to environment and climate until well into the 1930s, long after such thinking had fallen out of fashion in Europe.[31] When people were invalided or removed from site, moreover, the action was taken not only for their own health but for the reputation of empire.

Anxieties about environment, race, and prestige were shaped by social and political dynamics in specific settings, but, for the colonizers at least, they were also transcolonial concerns. At their heart was a discomfort caused by the experience of difference and being different: the sense of having to constantly navigate uncertainties of environment and people, of alien encounters, and the feeling, as Ranajit Guha posits, of "indefiniteness" and of being "not at home in empire."[32] In this way, anxiety could be said to be indicative not only of a shared settler identity or experience, but of a colonial condition.[33] Certainly, the need to manage and understand difference underpinned cultures of imperial research and knowledge production on colonized peoples.[34] Medical, anthropological, and ethnopsychiatric knowledge in particular both articulated and offered explanations for stereotypes of natives as irrational, overemotional, and prone to sporadic outbursts of violence. Such pathologization, while projecting an image of the inherent superiority of the colonizers, ultimately served to reinforce vulnerability.

This framing of empire through the lens of the emotions, and particularly through anxiety, has been important for ongoing attempts to undermine an older historiography that presented European empires as rational, orderly, and progressivist forces.[35] Certainly, anxieties cannot be separated from these broader insecurities of empire, including real, imagined, or anticipated threats. As Kalala Ngalamulume's chapter on yellow fever in Saint-Louis-du-Sénégal in this volume shows, in Senegal, the disease environment was perceived to be so dangerous that the very strictest measures were required to prevent disaster. These anxieties, which were tied to the anticipation of an outbreak, were closely linked to concerns about livelihoods, civil liberties, and the legitimacy of segregation based on race. Yet we should remain cautious of focusing too much on the imperial dimensions of such phenomena. The search for common themes and features across imperial contexts risks overinscribing the power of race and racial difference in explaining emotions and can muddy those settings where questions of difference are not so clear cut. It also places more emphasis on defining what united individuals than on understanding differences between them, potentially flattening individual emotional subjectivities. As Ngalamulume and others point out, Africa, in its imagined or "invented" sense, was a place that provoked the most extreme emotions. If, as Robert Peckham has noted, a persistent theme in colonial archives in Asia is "the anxiety induced by Asia's immensity,"[36] then in Africa we might say that such anxiety was also tinged by that of instability, of a "primeval" psychological element in relation to the immensity of its landscape and people.

One provocative line of inquiry is to explore anxieties more fully as constituent parts of African histories and contexts, and particularly in relation to African spaces. By looking at European settler engagement with African performance and dance across three distinct settings in colonial Kenya and Uganda, Cécile Feza Bushidi (this volume) highlights the contingent nature of settler anxieties. Not "merely a trigger for settler anxiety," dance, in certain spaces, could also provoke awe, have the power to soothe, or represent a respectable form of cultural consumption. Whether dance generated anxiety seemed intimately tied to questions of space and context, revealing the need to assess anxiety in relation not only to things but also to "environment" or performance context. Dance observed while on safari, for example, evoked far less anxiety than dance that "invaded" settlers' living spaces. Such landscapes, environments, or distinct spaces might be conceived of as "anxious spaces." Although thinking about them in this way might not necessarily reveal how people felt, it provides ways of thinking about representations and actions within them. King takes up this theme in her examination of the material aspects of anxiety and affect as they relate to people described as thieves, "free-booters," and cattle raiders. The Maloti-Drakensberg Mountains and surrounds, through this lens, constitute an "anxious space" that shaped not only actions but "clothing, material accoutrements," and "how people reacted based on these insensibilities" in ways that acknowledge the agency of both colonizer and colonized. "Raiding movements—part of raiding affects," King notes, "thus confounded authorities in the southern Drakensberg and Natal: try as they might, military operations often failed to understand and respond to raiders' strategies, patterns, or alliances."

Thinking about the ways in which particular social, political, and economic spaces give rise to atmospheres or "moods" that structure the kinds of actions and imaginations that become possible (or not) in the course of everyday life highlights the contingencies of emotions and the emotional communities that might exist in any place at any particular time.[37] Indeed, in looking beyond the colonial, we are invited to consider the wider affective landscape in which anxiety plays a key role, and to move beyond the environment and the physical and emotional landscapes that have received so much attention in the literature on colonial anxieties. Attention to political and social spaces here not only provides a way of decentering empire but can help reveal the complexities of anxieties even when African agency and voices are difficult to discern through written records. Nakanyike Musisi's chapter (this volume) looks at anxieties about gender and masculinity in Buganda within and beyond what was, supposedly, the strictly homosocial space of the *bisakatte* (royal enclosure) within the court compound of Mwanga II (1884–97). These anxieties were coproduced with missionaries, traders, and colonial officials, but were nevertheless deeply situated within Ganda apparatuses of power and sexual politics. "At the core of this anxiety," Musisi contends, "were spirited cultural tensions and contradictions—a struggle over two competing patriarchal cultures (British and missionary on the one hand and Ganda on the other hand) and, more so, their dissimilar assumptions about power, sexual desire, the body and, above all, constructions of masculinity." Anxiety, in this way, has multiple uses, bringing together the personal and the political into one frame. The value of this approach can be seen in other contexts, too. Carina Ray's work on interracial sexual relationships in colonial Ghana, for example, explores such sexual unions not only as a source of colonial anxiety but as both a source and a resource for anticolonial nationalist agitation. Through attention to the personal and political meanings of such unions for the colonized, Ray highlights how such unions were implicated in the ending of empire.[38] Such work cautions us against overattending to anxiety as it plays out in relation to empire or colonial settlers alone.

The themes of power, prestige, and control as highlighted in the literature on colonial anxieties remain key here, but they offer a new way of reading and explaining change, as well as themes such as race and violence. Writing on the Congo Free State, for example, Nancy Rose Hunt draws on the related concepts of anxiety and nervousness to explore violence and the creativity of people living under it. Nervousness—"a kind of energy, taut and excitable"—is not anxiety, she tells us, but instead "suggests being on edge. Its semantics are unsettled, combining vigor, force, and determination with excitation, weakness, timidity."[39] Bringing together the biopolitical and the securitizing, Hunt shows how invasive medical practices and censusing were countered by "therapeutic insurgents" who articulated a different model of healing. This new method of reading the colonial past is made possible "by attending to perceptions, moods, and capacities to wonder and move."[40] It shows that emotional transformation was not unidirectional, something imposed onto colonized "others" while leaving the colonizing unaffected. Similarly, as recent scholarship on emotions and Christian missions has shown, although instilling the "right" kind of Christian emotions into converts was part of a colonial "civilizing" mission, affective relationships across colonial divides could destabilize racialized power structures and support anticolonial activism.[41] In this way, as Claire McLisky and Karen Vallgårda point out, "while emotions in colonial contexts could create lines of division, they could also work to confront or even dissolve such boundaries."[42]

Anxiety, then, can help illuminate the multiplicity of emotions and the ways emotional regimes might shift in nonlinear and potentially contradictory ways.[43] Anxiety does not exist in isolation, but may be experienced in conjunction with and in contrast to other emotions. Taking the 2010 destruction by fire of the Kasubi Tombs—the resting place of Buganda's four preceding kings—as his point of departure, Jonathan Earle (this volume) explores vocabularies of anxiety and calm in Uganda. While anxieties can be read in the writings of intellectuals such as Eridadi Mulira, or in struggles between missionaries and the Baganda over burial practices, it was (and still is) the sense of calm that is more commonly evoked by the Baganda in the envisioning of politics and political spaces. It is precisely anxiety's ambiguity, its shiftiness, in fact, that might make it of particular analytical value. This is what literary theorist Sianne Ngai argues when she considers anxiety as one of the "ugly feelings."[44] Unlike more "noble" feelings such as anger or fear, Ngai argues that "ugly feelings"—not only anxiety but also envy, paranoia, irritation, the racialized affect of "animatedness," and what she terms "stuplimity" (a mixture of shock and boredom)—are more ambiguous and ambient; they are weaker than other emotions and often do not take a direct object. The political effects of these "ugly feelings" are indeterminate—unlike, say, rage or anger, which can spur political action, anxiety or envy do not do so exactly—or, rather, they may or they may not. It is precisely this ambiguous character, however, that "amplifies their power to diagnose situations, and situations marked by blocked or thwarted action in particular."[45] Where there is anxiety, we might say, there is a social, political, and economic context in which individuals have come to feel obstructed, suspended, or blocked. The task of the historian, archaeologist, or social scientist—as opposed to the literary critic, then—is to consider the particular conditions that give rise to this blockage, and how it manifests in lived realities.

Anxiety, Temporality, and Futures

Just as attention to anxiety in relation to African spaces opens up new ways of understanding otherwise dominant narratives, so too does it bring attention to questions of time, temporality, and futures. Colonial anxieties were in part tied to anxieties about the future—the ability for European bodies to survive long-term in tropical climates, as well as concerns about the long-term political viability of the colonial project. Such anxieties coexisted with fears about security and rebellion, and they again underscore the vulnerability and contingency of colonial rule. But the lens of anxiety can do more than this. It can both help us make sense of what happens when imaginations of the future are thrown in doubt by an external force, even if who or what this force might be is ambiguous, and work to permit new questions about the linkages between the past and the present. In pursuing such linkages, it is helpful to ask how anxiety might invite reflections on temporality, particularly the future. Here, work by Ngai, drawing on German Marxist philosopher Ernst Bloch, is instructive. Bloch distinguishes between the "filled emotions" (envy, greed, admiration) and "expectant emotions" (anxiety, fear, hope), arguing that the latter are less object-driven and have an "incomparably greater anticipatory character."[46] Expectant emotions, he writes, "imply a real future; in fact that of the Not-Yet, of what has objectively not yet been there."[47] As many of the contributors in this volume point out, anxiety arises precisely because of the unknowability of the future, and anticipating this Not-Yet can have in many cases physical effects on the body.

Expectation and anticipation are central to understanding the shape and meaning of anxieties in colonial Africa. As a growing body of literature on decolonization is indicating, much of this can be read through what might be regarded as the "afterlives" of colonial anxieties—through the ways such anxieties evolved or were revealed through moments of transition. Indeed, decolonization can be read as a particularly anxious moment, for European settlers and colonial officials, at least, because it was a time when long-standing fears and anxieties seemed to be coming true. As Matthew Stanard has shown for Congo, during colonial rule, anxieties about the weakness of Belgium's hold over the state underpinned colonizers' need to project an image of control—of "Bula Matari," or "breaker of rocks." This projection ultimately made the Congo crisis, with its apparently sudden "eruption of chaos, violence and death," come, to outsiders at least, as a shock.[48] In exploring anxieties felt by white settlers in Kenya on the eve of the country's independence, Will Jackson and Harry Firth-Jones (this volume) similarly trace the shifting contours of anxiety, exposed through searching questions about violence, prestige, and control: "would newly liberated Africans seek revenge on their erstwhile colonizers? Would white life and white-owned land be secure in an independent African state?"

As such new work on anxieties in the context of decolonization shows, approaching decolonization as an emotional moment and a chronological frame allows for connections to be made "that cross the colonial and the postcolonial," to borrow from Jackson and Firth-Jones. In doing so, anxiety provides another way of moving beyond older perspectives that viewed independence and decolonization as moments of rupture. It also provides ways of connecting images of Africa across broader expanses of time and space. Jackson and Firth-Jones, for example, draw links between fears of criminality in Kenya in the 1960s with fears of insecurity, farm seizures, and roadblocks in Zimbabwe in the 2000s. Such an approach links anxiety to attempts to envisage and understand Africa, what Jackson and Firth-Jones call a certain type of scholarly discourse "that attempts to comprehend a postcolonial and characteristically *African* state today." While looking at a much earlier period, Ngalamulume's chapter, too, sees anxieties and fears surrounding African behavior as linking his research on epidemics in Saint-Louis-du-Sénégal with occurrences of influenza across eastern, southern, and western Africa in 1918–19, as well as with panic over HIV/AIDS in the 1980s, Ebola in the 2010s, and COVID-19.

While for Jackson and Firth-Jones the roadblock might be seen as a key expression of anxiety, for Ngalamulume it is quarantine—its use or absence bringing together themes of surveillance and protection, as well as vulnerability. This raises the importance not just of situating anxiety within historical and political contexts but of interrogating the very ways that anxiety relates to the past itself. "Africa's postcolonial era," as Richard Reid has argued, "has been characterized by anxiety about the deeper past."[49] National elites have wanted to "move on" from the past, to carefully manage it, or to eradicate histories that are messy and highlight violence, division, economic instability, and the "superficiality of the nation."[50] Yet while postcolonial leaders might try to "move on" from these deeper histories, they continue to provide important resources for citizens. Indeed, Earle's chapter shows how for the Baganda, the kingdom of Buganda and its kings are understood to provide calm in moments of postcolonial political anxiety in Uganda. This recourse to calm also challenges President Yoweri Museveni's regime, suggesting that there are other ways of governing than the one he and his party, the National Resistance Movement (NRM), have pursued. Here it is calm, not anxiety, that requires analytical attention, and Earle skillfully considers both emotions to provide important insights into the affective political landscape of postcolonial B/Uganda.

Anxiety, then, can be used as a tool through which to explore linkages between the personal and the political, or between the individual and the social. As Musisi shows, at the root of the anxiety found in Mwanga II's court in the late nineteenth century are conflicting patriarchal regimes—one represented by the British and Christian missionaries; the other by the institution of the Buganda kingdom itself—and differing ideas about power, sexual desire, the body, and masculinity. Andrea Mariko Grant (this volume), meanwhile, explores how anxiety arises when "visions" for the postgenocide future of Rwanda come into conflict or are thrown into doubt. Here, anxiety is multidirectional—the affect results when the state intervenes to "thwart" one's plans for the future; but in this very act of thwarting, the state's own anxieties (and fragilities) are revealed. While the state may attempt to inculcate particular kinds of emotional regimes or affective dispositions in its subjects, these attempts are never completely successful. And, indeed, "unseemly" or "unruly" emotions can rather index "mismanagement of the polity and mismanagement of the self," unsettling projects of governance and subject-formation.[51]

What is striking here is that while anxiety is tied up with expectation, anticipation, and conflicting visions, its effects are not always obvious or straightforward. This reinforces the need for close attention to what Kathryn de Luna has described as "the subjective emotional stakes" for individuals in decision-making.[52] Simon Turner (this volume) touches on this in exploring the experiences of Burundians in Kigali, Rwanda, after thousands fled violence in 2015. Faced with protracted stays in Kigali, some of his interlocutors placed their hope in God, believing it was through divine intercession rather than international or regional intervention or rebel movements that a peaceful future would be achieved. Here, while states of uncertainty might have a certain "positive potentiality," anxiety "is concerned with the potential for negative futures." In this way, anxiety cannot be separated from the wider literature on the so-called negative emotions that, ironically, are not necessarily solely negative. As Elizabeth Cooper and David Pratten have argued, uncertainty is productive; it can offer opportunities for individuals to act in the world and create new kinds of social relations, forms of subjectivity, and experiences of time.[53] Marco Di Nunzio elaborates on this insight, arguing that uncertainty can be understood as "a terrain of possibilities."[54] For the young men in Addis Ababa with whom he worked, they in fact "embraced" uncertainty—they moved around, engaged in various kinds of labor and relations, in the hope of getting a "chance" or "stroke of luck" (*idil* in Amharic), which would open up new possibilities for them in the future to escape the conditions of marginality and exclusion in which they lived. Thinking about anxiety and the ways it is tied to possibilities and futures has value because, unlike concepts such as uncertainty, insecurity, or uneasiness, anxiety does not necessarily dissipate once one's material circumstances change. Rather, it may be carried in the body and condition one's subjectivity and intersubjective relations in a present that would seem, at least on the surface, less anxious. Anxiety, then, again has an unsettling role—one that not only helps us understand what it is like to be caught up in a particular moment but provides a lens onto the contradictory, multiple, and potentially nonlinear paths that individuals might take.

Approaching Anxiety

Before we discuss the structure of the book and the individual chapters, it is important to consider the challenges that accompany employing anxiety as an analytical lens. How, after all, can we approach anxiety methodologically? To return to the questions and issues raised at the beginning of the chapter, attention must be paid to what exactly anxiety actually is. What is striking about so much of the scholarly literature that touches on anxiety is that so little of it pays attention to questions of definition or meaning. There is some unevenness here between disciplines. Much of the literature on colonial anxieties, for example, has tended to sidestep the issue, seeing anxiety as a broad and at times vague concept, with historians taking more interest in discovering what anxiety reveals about race, bodies, minds, and sexuality, among other themes, than in the theoretical literature on the emotions. Where there has been attention to questions of definition, this has most often drawn on the distinction made between anxiety and fear, particularly as articulated by Guha and Joanna Bourke: while fear is something that arises in response to an identifiable threat, anxiety is more diffuse and is related to a perceived threat. Anthropologists and sociologists have been somewhat more inclined to question the use and suitability of "anxiety," if only to argue for the use of other terms. Didier Fassin, for example, has suggested substituting "anxiety" with "uneasiness" or *inquiétude*, "which gives it a sense more active than affective."[55] Cooper and Pratten, moreover, in their *Ethnographies of Uncertainty in Africa* (2015), while not focusing specifically on anxiety, instead see it as integral to their understanding of the uncertainty that they argue has come to define everyday life across the continent.[56]

In this volume, we do not attempt to draw clear distinctions between anxiety and related emotions or emotional states, such as fear, uncertainty, and insecurity. This is a deliberate choice. It stems in part from the unease of applying anxiety as an analytical lens in contexts where the term itself has no direct equivalent in language. And it also reflects the desire to avoid dehistoricizing and depoliticizing emotion words in ways that end up limiting their analytical potential. As Bourke has noted, scholars need to be wary of imposing rigid distinctions between such emotional states as fear and anxiety precisely because this distinction "too often rests on a distinction between the rational and the irrational. However, there is no strict division between reason and emotion."[57] Seeking to avoid the vagueness that comes from slippages between anxiety, fear, and uncertainty, among other "negative" emotions, many of the contributors instead reinforce anxiety as a multifaceted and multivocal concept that cannot be fully understood without reference to other emotions, or "fictions," as Earle puts it in his chapter. This is a necessary part of moving anxiety beyond its psychoanalytical and biomedical roots toward a socially, culturally, and historically situated understanding of anxious spaces and lives. Anxiety is not just a psychological state that requires the tools of the psychoanalyst or psychiatrist to uncover, but one that is constituted in many different ways and takes on myriad forms.

A focus on anxiety in African contexts reinforces the need to pay attention to specificity in the logics, mechanisms, and ways that anxiety is constituted. Looking at anxiety across time and space, we cannot necessarily assume an individualized notion of the "self," or that emotions are located in the brain, or even that anxiety has always been a subjective experience of inner life. The somatization of what might be perceived as psychological complaints is a recurrent theme in the literature on psychiatry and mental illness in Africa. Psychiatrists and anthropologists in Uganda in the 1960s, for example, frequently drew attention to the ways that somatic complaints, particularly those affecting the chest, predominated among patients presenting with depression.[58] Broadening the scope, Julie Livingston has similarly pointed out that there is a need for historical specificity, drawing attention to nineteenth-century Bechuanaland, "where individual and dividual personhood (to use McKim Marriott's term) coexist in explicit dynamic tension, and where they are somaticized in the gut, liver, waist, or heart, but rarely the head."[59] In this way, we must take seriously the particular embodied and physical manifestations of anxiety, and the ways in which they are intimately connected to how the body is imagined, and where health and illness might be located. Scholars here must be equally attendant to how particular historical events are locally understood to produce new kinds of affective states. For example, in Rwanda the 1994 genocide against the Tutsi is widely believed to have led to a new form of trauma, known in Kinyarwanda as *ihahamuka*, among genocide survivors. It manifests in the experience of shortness of breath, of feeling that one's heart is constricted, that words cannot leave one's mouth. Distinct from fear (*ubwoba*), "*ihahamuka* is an emotion that blocks your breath and your words."[60]

Scholars interested in anxiety must pay close attention to the ways in which the concept can and cannot be translated across contexts. The meaning of anxiety, after all, is far from self-evident. Moreover, as Rosenwein has noted, emotions are always "delivered secondhand." Individual terms, particularly when mediated through colonial ethnographers, might not only be inscribed with anxiety themselves but also obscure affect and the affective. Giving the example of the Ila practice of *kuweza lubono mung'anda* (lit. "to hunt for wealth at home"), in which husband and wife agree that the wife should take lovers, de Luna highlights how colonial ethnography reduced what was a complicated demonstration—bringing together sensuality, affect, and the material—to prostitution because they could not comprehend this as a sincere sensory experience.[61] More recent work on love in Africa has similarly highlighted the emotional and material aspects of love, suggesting that subsuming such relationships under the notion of Western romantic love might occlude more than it reveals.[62] Bushidi's chapter, moreover, suggests that the Kiswahili term *ngoma*, as used by European settlers, was itself an embodiment of anxiety, encompassing "indigenous forms of bodily musical performance and their presumed essential nature as excessive, disorderly, and noisy." Language, though central to understanding negative emotions such as anxiety, can be difficult to translate. What this suggests is the need for scholars to take a wide-ranging approach to their sources in order to look for the multiple ways in which people might themselves speak of, express, or use emotion words.

In order to unpack rich vernacular vocabularies of the emotions, scholars need to pay close attention to language and terms themselves, a task that might require collaboration between disciplines, particularly anthropology and linguistics. Earle (this volume) highlights how anxieties were interwoven through political and social life in Buganda and can be read through Luganda words. Such "hidden anxieties" were central to missionary-ethnographer John Roscoe's commentary on Luganda greetings, for example, in which he stressed that the "*tya*" in the common greeting "*otyano sebo*" was the verb "to fear," resulting, for him, in a literal meaning of "Have you any cause for fear?" It is important to note that there may be multiple readings of any particular term, and much of the analysis requires a reflexive use of language, as well as a careful unpacking of what in particular the lens of anxiety reveals that other concepts might not. In a study of musicians who play brass instruments in Benin, Lyndsey Copeland notes that her interlocutors use a wide range of words to describe feelings of anxiety, from "worry" or "problem" (*un souci*) to "nervousness" (*nervosité*), but "anxiety" (*anxiété*) is in fact most common.[63] In this context, "anxiety" connotes "a quality of feeling that is subjective, affective and directed inwards," yet it is also "relational, situated and directed outwards." In this way, she writes, anxiety "is at once emotional and expectant, visceral and somatic."[64] Indeed, while for some of the contributors in this volume, "anxiety" as a term has a corollary in local vernaculars (Musisi, Earle), for others, "anxiety" is a term that can be productively employed to characterize the tenor of emotional life encountered on the ground (Bushidi, Grant, Turner).

Considering anxiety in this way requires self-reflection on the part of the researcher. Indeed, scholars across disciplines have long grappled with how to best apprehend and discursively represent emotions in research. As anthropologist Andrew Beatty has asked provocatively, "Where does emotion begin and end? Is it a matter of interpretation, feeling, category, situation, response, expression, or some or all of these?"[65] For his part, Beatty argues for a narrative approach to the emotions—narrating how emotions emerge in the unfolding of social life, insisting on the biographical richness of our interlocutors. This seems to involve relying not only on interviews but also on participant observation over long-term ethnographic fieldwork. Indeed, he is clear on the limits of understanding emotions through interviews. As he writes, "At some abstract level we might learn something about how people think about emotions *in interviews*, but not how they think or feel in practice; much less how emotions occur, are subjectively experienced, how they filter, frame, or direct sequences of action."[66] Perhaps more worrying is the risk that anxiety might emerge as a feeling within the researcher—one that colors the analysis without consideration of whether the focus on anxiety is more reflective of the researcher than of the researched. Here, close attention to the positionality of the researcher is required, along with a sense of caution and an awareness of the limits of anxiety. While we may be able to grasp something of the anxieties, fears, and uncertainties that underpin action, that may be felt subjectively, and that may be expressed through material culture, we cannot necessarily assume that individuals have been conscious of these ways of inhabiting the world. Similarly, researchers must be cautious of over-reading anxiety into past and present lives. Decades ago Susan Reynolds Whyte issued a similar note of warning in reference to the framework of uncertainty. As she noted: "The extreme emphasis that some scholars place on the uncertainties of the present era imply that life was more certain in colonial or precolonial times. In contrast, the classical pragmatists like John Dewey recognised that existential problems always present uncertainties to social actors. But uncertainties themselves change, as do the means available for dealing with them."[67] As the chapters in this book all reinforce, anxiety must be understood in specific social, historical, and political contexts, and as a concept whose contours shift through time and space.

Organization of the Book

This book is organized into three parts that reflect the three entry points to anxiety outlined in this introduction: Part I: "Anxious Spaces"; Part II: "Unsettling Narratives"; and Part III: "Alternative Temporalities." As noted above, there are overlaps between these themes. What we intend by grouping the chapters in this way is to highlight how different approaches (broadly, historical, archaeological, and ethnographic) can bring out what employing anxiety as an analytical lens can do.

The three chapters grouped as Part I: "Anxious Spaces" all emphasize the ways that anxieties might be tied to distinct African spaces or places, but they do so by "reading" anxiety in quite different ways—through material culture, policies, language, and embodied expression.

Archaeologist Rachel King encourages us to consider anxiety not just as inhering in relations between people, but also between people and things. Anxiety in this way, she argues, can be understood as "a material experience." To this effect, she explores the material traces of anxiety as related to "outlaws"—principally thieves, "free-booters," and cattle raiders—in nineteenth-century southern Africa. By examining the construction of jails, fences, and magistracies, King allows us to better conceive of a certain material landscape of anxiety wherein efforts by colonial authorities to curtail "illicit" behavior were often ill-informed, poorly executed, and ultimately unsuccessful. As she asks, can we see one part of African agency in the archaeological past as "the ability to manipulate affect and inspire anxiety?" The very existence of these structures reveals anxiety on the part of colonial power, suggesting a certain material acknowledgment, if you will, that the legitimacy of white rule was precarious indeed.

Cécile Feza Bushidi's chapter explores anxieties around dance in colonial Africa, taking a wide-ranging and explorative approach. She suggests that although dance generated anxiety among colonial officials, settlers, and missionaries—often stimulated by fears about "unruly" African bodies and the political potential they might generate—this is only one side of the story. She argues instead for a multivocal perspective, pointing out that while dance enabled and validated the colonial process, the emotions it conjured in its observers were often much more ambivalent and contingent. In practice this meant that although certain dances were outlawed by colonial authorities and that settlers often expressed alarm when they came into close contact with dancing African bodies, at other moments dance performances fed into romantic and idealized constructions of Africa. Whether dance generated anxiety seemed intimately tied to questions of space and context, revealing the need to see anxiety in relation not only to things but also to "environment" or performance context. Dance observed while on safari, for example, evoked far less anxiety among white settlers than dance that "invaded" their living spaces.

Kalala Ngalamulume's chapter then explores the anxieties that accompanied yellow fever outbreaks in the port city of Saint-Louis-du-Sénégal from the mid-nineteenth century to the early twentieth century. He argues that these outbreaks provoked anxiety in colonial public health officials and had real-world effects: new sanitary measures that disrupted individuals' everyday lives and livelihoods, and new forms of segregation along class and racial lines. If we can read colonial officials' anxieties about "locals" through their material practices, as King suggests, Ngalamulume argues that we can also read them through their quarantine measures: ships arriving from areas suspected of contamination were quarantined or rerouted. Yet these measures were not taken up seamlessly. Rather, colonial officials had to contend with pushback from merchants who put commerce ahead of health. Through careful analysis of archival sources, Ngalamulume reconstructs the anxious debates that took place among colonial officials about how to best contain the disease.

In Part II: "Unsettling Narratives," chapters by Nakanyike Musisi, Will Jackson and Harry Firth-Jones, and Andrea Mariko Grant demonstrate how anxiety as an analytical lens can help destabilize commonsense or normative narratives.

In her chapter, Musisi focuses on a particularly anxious period of Ugandan history: the reign of the Buganda king *Kabaka* Mwanga II (1884–97). She shows how paying close attention to anxiety—on the part not only of Christian missionaries but also of Mwanga himself—reveals the uneasiness that accompanied changes in gender and sex structures. The missionaries sought to dethrone Mwanga in part because of his ambiguous understanding of masculinity—one that did not neatly fit into Christian and European ideas of hegemonic masculinity and heterosexuality. She explores the anxieties that arise when one dominant system is forced, through the colonial encounter, to reckon with another. Here anxiety unsettles narratives about gender and sexuality in Uganda, challenging, for example, postcolonial narratives that see homosexuality as "un-African."

Jackson and Firth-Jones's chapter explores anxieties around decolonization in relation to the evacuation of white settlers from Kenya in 1963–64. Considering letters written by white settlers to the British state requesting evacuation, they show how there was a shift in anxiety around this period: instead of anxiety as related to the natural environment, articulated most clearly through the prevalence of tropical neurasthenia, anxiety was suddenly related to people, to independent Africans whose motivations could not be determined and who were constructed as containing an inherent violence. By tracing these "genealogies of anxiety," the authors argue that we can better trace continuities between colonial and postcolonial representations of Africa and also that anxieties equally shaped other processes of decolonization worldwide. Like Musisi, they draw our attention to the gendered dimensions of anxiety, with white women constructed by white men as being particularly susceptible to anxiety and "nerves." Their chapter highlights shifting understandings of anxiety, calling attention to its multivocal and racialized character. If independence was experienced as a moment of hope for many Kenyans, it was experienced as a moment of profound anxiety for white settlers.

Grant's chapter considers the anxiety that results when a Rwandan pastor's development plans—building a health center with NGO money—are suddenly thwarted by the intervention of the state. At stake, Grant suggests, were conflicting understandings of development: on the one hand, the linear, secular project as envisioned by the state through its "Vision 2020" plan, one wherein only ruling party members should benefit; on the other, the spiritual project of realizing the Kingdom of God on earth, as envisioned by the pastor, one wherein all Rwandan Christians should benefit. What the state's intervention revealed was its own anxieties: fear that its grip on power might not be as tight as it might claim, and that the country's "new" postgenocide Pentecostal churches might pose a threat, especially to its particular developmental "vision."

Part III: "Alternative Temporalities" brings together two chapters that highlight themes of expectation and anticipation and invite reflection on the future.

In his chapter, anthropologist Simon Turner explores the experiences of Burundians in Kigali, Rwanda, after thousands fled the violence in 2015 when President Pierre Nkurunziza controversially decided to run for a third term. Turner argues that although many believed that their stay in Kigali would be temporary, the protracted nature of the conflict meant that many were forced to remain much longer than expected. Turner notes that "as the conflict continued, they had to revise their plans and make the tough choice between returning to an uncertain future in Burundi and remaining in Rwanda without many options of 'making a life.'" For Burundians facing such difficult decisions about whether to return and considering what the future might bring, Turner suggests that anxiety was morphing into despair as they became increasingly convinced that a return home and future in Burundi were no longer possible. While some continued to struggle with their feelings, others were turning—in part—to God "in order to 'live with' despair."

Finally, Jonathon Earle brings both historical and ethnographic analysis to bear on anxiety in relation to the Buganda Kingdom. He argues that although much scholarly attention has been paid to the concept of anxiety as related to both the colonial and the postcolonial state, other competing concepts might be open to our interlocutors. He describes the protests that erupted after the Kasubi Tombs' destruction, with activists convinced that President Yoweri Museveni and his government were behind the fires. Their cogent critiques, which manifested in widely circulated images and pamphlets along with spirit possessions, articulated a particular idea of calm and stability associated with the Buganda monarchy. If Museveni's state is understood as producing anxiety in the country's population, then the kingdom is held up as existing according to another set of principles. Here the message was clear: present-day and present-focused anxiety will give way to the calm and stability of Buganda, which has already endured and outlived the country's postindependence leaders. One placard circulated showing *Kabaka* Muteebi II sitting on a throne, seemingly unperturbed by the protests and disturbances, with the inscription "Buganda is calm." Earle's chapter invites us to consider postcolonial governance while keeping both anxiety and calm in mind.

Taken as a whole, the volume aims to highlight what can be gained from exploring anxiety and anxieties across disciplines. Building on the historical attention to colonial anxieties, this broader perspective shows how the lens of anxiety might also be used to explore contemporary social lives across the continent. The chapters show the multiple ways in which greater attention to colonial histories of anxiety in particular are useful in understanding contemporary conditions. Although anxiety is often associated with the future, as we have seen, it is also a key analytical framework for understanding the colonial past. The point is not to judge whether the colonial period can be considered to be more or less anxious than the postcolonial present—as if time can be so easily bifurcated—but rather to explore the particular ways in which anxieties persist and shape life conditions across the continent. Here, anxiety is not just an internal state—pathological or otherwise—but one that emerges in relation to the outer world, to material objects, circumstances, and social conditions.

Notes

1. Allan Horwitz, *Anxiety: A Short History* (Baltimore: Johns Hopkins University Press, 2013); Roy Porter and Sarah Dunant, *The Age of Anxiety* (London: Virago, 1996); George Rosen, "Emotion and Sensibility in Ages of Anxiety: A Comparative Historical Review," *American Journal of Psychiatry* 124, no. 6 (1967): 771–84.

2. A small selection of this vast literature: W. H. Auden, *The Age of Anxiety* (New York: Random House, 1947); Paul Bramadat, Maryse Guay, Julie A. Bettinger, and Réal Roy, eds., *Public Health in the Age of Anxiety: Religious and Cultural Roots of Vaccine Hesitancy in Canada* (Toronto: University of Toronto Press, 2017); Sian Griffiths and Jennifer Wallace, eds., *Consuming Passions: Food in the Age of Anxiety* (Manchester: Manchester University Press, 1998); Ali Haggett, *Desperate Housewives, Neuroses and the Domestic Environment, 1945–1970* (London: Pickering and Chatto, 2012); Scott Stossel, *My Age of Anxiety: Fear, Hope, Dread and the Search for Peace of Mind* (London: Windmill Books, 2014).

3. Joseph E. LeDoux, *Anxious: The Modern Mind in the Age of Anxiety* (London: Oneworld, 2015).

4. Exceptions include Claire Mercer, "Middle Class Construction: Domestic Architecture, Aesthetics and Anxieties in Tanzania," *Journal of Modern African Studies* 52, no. 2 (2014): 227–50; Matthew G. Stanard, "Revisiting Bula Matari and the Congo Crisis: Successes and Anxieties in Belgium's Late Colonial State," *Journal of Imperial and Commonwealth History* 46, no. 1 (2018): 144–68; and Lyndsey Copeland, "The Anxiety of Blowing: Experiences of Breath and Brass Instruments in Benin," *Africa* 89, no. 2 (2019): 353–77.

5. See, for example, Elizabeth Cooper and David Pratten, eds., *Ethnographies of Uncertainty in Africa* (Basingstoke, UK: Palgrave Macmillan, 2015); Jennifer Cole and Lynn M. Thomas, eds., *Love in Africa* (Chicago: University of Chicago Press, 2009); Hansjörg Dilger, Astrid Bochow, Marian Burchardt, and Matthew Wilhelm-Solomon, eds., *Affective Trajectories: Religion and Emotion in African Cityscapes* (Durham, NC: Duke University Press, 2020); Michael Lambek and Jackie Solway, "Just Anger: Scenarios of Indignation in Botswana and Madagascar," *Ethnos* 66, no. 1 (2001): 49–72; Rebekah Lee and Megan Vaughan, "Death and Dying in the History of Africa since 1800," *Journal of African History* 48, no. 3 (2008): 341–59; and Megan Vaughan, "The History

of Romantic Love in Sub-Saharan Africa: Between Interest and Emotion," *Proceedings of the British Academy* 167 (2010): 1–23.

6. This scholarship includes Nancy Rose Hunt, *A Nervous State: Violence, Remedies, and Reverie in Colonial Congo* (Durham, NC: Duke University Press, 2016); Will Jackson, *Madness and Marginality: The Lives of Kenya's White Insane* (Manchester: Manchester University Press, 2013); Dane Kennedy, *Islands of White: Settler Society and Culture in Kenya and Southern Rhodesia, 1890–1939* (Durham, NC: Duke University Press, 1987); Jock McCulloch, *Black Peril, White Virtue: Sexual Crime in Southern Rhodesia, 1902–1935* (Bloomington: Indiana University Press, 2000); and Kalala Ngalamulume, *Colonial Pathologies, Environment, and Western Medicine in Saint-Louis-du-Senegal, 1867–1920* (New York: Peter Lang, 2012).

7. See, for example, the special issue "The Private Lives of Empire: Emotion, Intimacy, and Colonial Rule" in *Itinerario* 42, no. 1 (2018) as well as the following: Mark Condos, *The Insecurity State: Punjab and the Making of Colonial Power in British India* (Cambridge: Cambridge University Press, 2017); Harald Fischer-Tiné, ed., *Anxieties, Fear and Panic in Colonial Settings: Empires on the Verge of a Nervous Breakdown* (Cham, Switz.: Palgrave Macmillan, 2016); Robert Peckham, ed., *Empires of Panic: Epidemics and Colonial Anxieties* (Hong Kong: Hong Kong University Press, 2015); Ann Laura Stoler, *Carnal Knowledge and Imperial Power: Race and the Intimate in Colonial Rule* (Berkeley: University of California Press, 2002); and Kim Wagner, *Amritsar 1919: An Empire of Fear and the Making of a Massacre* (New Haven, CT: Yale University Press, 2019).

8. Condos, *Insecurity State*, 3.

9. Nicole Eustace et al., "*AHR* Conversation: The Historical Study of Emotion," *American Historical Review* 117, no. 5 (2012): 1487–531; Barbara Rosenwein, *Emotional Communities in the Early Middle Ages* (Ithaca, NY: Cornell University Press, 2006), 1; Joanna Bourke, "Fear and Anxiety: Writing about Emotion in Modern History," *History Workshop Journal* 55, no. 1 (2003): 111–33.

10. Ann L. Stoler, "Affective States," in *A Companion to the Anthropology of Politics*, ed. David Nugent and Joan Vincent (Oxford: Blackwell, 2004), 6.

11. Mateusz Laszczkowski and Madeleine Reeves, "Introduction: Affect and the Anthropology of the State," in *Affective States: Entanglements, Suspensions, Suspicions*, ed. Mateusz Laszczkowski and Madeleine Reeves (New York: Berghahn Books, 2017), 2. See also Begoña Aretxaga, "Maddening States," *Annual Review of Anthropology* 32 (2003): 393–410; Yael Navaro-Yashin, *The Make-Believe Space: Affective Geography in a Postwar Polity* (Durham, NC: Duke University Press, 2012).

12. For a review of this work, see Catherine Lutz and Geoffrey M. White, "The Anthropology of Emotions," *Annual Review of Anthropology* 15 (1986): 405–36. See also Catherine Lutz and Lila Abu-Lughod, eds., *Language and the Politics of Emotion* (Cambridge: Cambridge University Press, 1990).

13. Daniel White, "Affect: An Introduction," *Cultural Anthropology* 32, no. 2 (2017): 177. See also Gilles Deleuze and Félix Guattari, *A Thousand Plateaus*:

Capitalism and Schizophrenia, trans. Brian Massumi (Minneapolis: University of Minnesota Press, 1987); Brian Massumi, "The Autonomy of Affect," *Cultural Critique* 31 (1995): 83–109; Nigel Thrift, *Non-representational Theory: Space, Politics, Affect* (London: Routledge, 2008).

14. Yael Navaro-Yashin, "Affective Spaces, Melancholic Objects: Ruination and the Production of Anthropological Knowledge," *Journal of the Royal Anthropological Institute* 15, no. 1 (2009): 1–18.

15. William Mazzarella, "Affect: What Is It Good For?" in *Enchantments of Modernity: Empire, Nation, Globalization*, ed. Saurabh Dube (London: Routledge, 2010), 291.

16. Elizabeth Cooper and David Pratten, "Ethnographies of Uncertainty in Africa: An Introduction," in Cooper and Pratten, *Ethnographies of Uncertainty in Africa*, 1.

17. Copeland, "Anxiety of Blowing"; Andrea Mariko Grant, "Quiet Insecurity and Quiet Agency in Post-Genocide Rwanda," *Etnofoor* 27, no. 2 (2015): 29–30; Adeline Masquelier, "Teatime: Boredom and the Temporalities of Young Men in Niger," *Africa* 83 (2013): 470–91; Henrik Vigh, "Youth Mobilisation as Social Navigation: Reflections on the Concept of Dubriagem," *Cadernos de estudos africanos* 18/19 (2010): 140–64.

18. Sara Ahmed, *The Cultural Politics of Emotion* (New York: Routledge, 2004), 9.

19. Jeffrey Fleisher and Neil Norman, eds., *The Archaeology of Anxiety: The Materiality of Anxiousness, Worry, and Fear* (New York: Springer, 2015); Sarah Tarlow, "The Archaeology of Emotion and Affect," *Annual Review of Anthropology* 41 (2012): 169–85; Sarah Tarlow, "Emotion in Archaeology," *Current Anthropology* 41, no. 5 (2000): 713–46.

20. See also Rachel King, *Outlaws, Anxiety, and Disorder in Southern Africa: Material Histories of the Maloti-Drakensberg* (Cham, Switz.: Palgrave Macmillan, 2019).

21. Mahone, "Psychology of Rebellion."

22. Chinua Achebe, "Africa and Her Writers," *Massachusetts Review* 14, no. 3 (1973): 617–29; Francis Njubi Nesbitt, "Post-colonial Anxieties: (Re)Presenting African Intellectuals," *African Affairs* 107, no. 427 (2008): 273–82; Tom Odhiambo, "Sexual Anxieties and Rampant Masculinities in Postcolonial Kenyan Literature," *Social Identities* 13, no. 5 (2007): 651–63.

23. Chinua Achebe, *Home and Exile* (Oxford: Oxford University Press, 2000), 18–19.

24. James Ferguson, *Global Shadows: Africa in the Neoliberal World Order* (Durham, NC: Duke University Press, 2006); Achille Mbembe, *On the Postcolony* (Berkeley: University of California Press, 2001); V. Y. Mudimbe, *The Invention of Africa: Gnosis, Philosophy, and the Order of Knowledge* (Bloomington: Indiana University Press, 1988); Sylvia Tamale, ed., *African Sexualities: A Reader* (Oxford: Pambazuka, 2011).

25. Richard Eves, "Unsettling Settler Colonialism: Debates over Climate and Colonization in New Guinea, 1875–1914," *Ethnic and Racial Studies* 28, no.

2 (2005): 304–30; Dane Kennedy, "Climatic Theories and Culture in Colonial Kenya and Rhodesia," *Journal of Imperial and Commonwealth History* 10, no. 1 (1981): 50–66; Dane Kennedy, "The Perils of the Midday Sun: Climatic Anxieties in the Colonial Tropics," in *Imperialism and the Natural World*, ed. John M. MacKenzie (Manchester: Manchester University Press, 1990), 118–40.

26. Philip D. Curtin, *Death by Migration: Europe's Encounter with the Tropical World in the Nineteenth Century* (Cambridge: Cambridge University Press, 1989); Mark Harrison, "'The Tender Frame of Man': Disease, Climate, and Racial Difference in India and the West Indies, 1760–1860," *Bulletin of the History of Medicine* 70, no. 1 (1996): 68–93.

27. Anna Crozier [now Greenwood], "What Was Tropical about Tropical Neurasthenia? The Utility of the Diagnosis in the Management of British East Africa," *Journal of the History of Medicine and Allied Sciences* 64, no. 4 (2009): 518–48; Yolana Pringle, "Neurasthenia at Mengo Hospital, Uganda: A Case Study in Psychiatry and a Diagnosis, 1906–50," *Journal of Imperial and Commonwealth History* 44, no. 2 (2016): 241–62.

28. Warwick Anderson, *Colonial Pathologies: American Tropical Medicine, Race, and Hygiene in the Philippines* (Durham, NC: Duke University Press, 2006); Kennedy, *Islands of White*; Jackson, *Madness and Marginality*.

29. Ryan Johnson, "European Cloth and 'Tropical' Skin: Clothing Material and British Ideas of Health and Hygiene in Tropical Climates," *Bulletin of the History of Medicine* 83, no. 3 (2009): 530–60; Ryan Johnson, "Commodity Culture: Tropical Health and Hygiene in the British Empire," *Endeavour* 32, no. 2 (2008): 70–74.

30. Anna Crozier [now Greenwood], *Practising Colonial Medicine: The Colonial Medical Service in British East Africa* (London: I. B. Tauris, 2007).

31. Crozier, "What Was Tropical about Tropical Neurasthenia."

32. Ranajit Guha, "Not at Home in Empire," *Critical Inquiry* 23, no. 3 (1997): 484.

33. Dane Kennedy, "Diagnosing the Colonial Dilemma: Tropical Neurasthenia and the Alienated Briton," in *Decentring Empire: Britain, India, and the Transcolonial World*, ed. Durba Ghosh and Dane Keith Kennedy (Hyderabad: Orient Longman, 2006).

34. Sloan Mahone and Megan Vaughan, eds., *Psychiatry and Empire* (Basingstoke, UK: Palgrave Macmillan, 2007); Erik Linstrum, *Ruling Minds: Psychology in the British Empire* (Cambridge, MA: Harvard University Press, 2016); Sloan Mahone, "The Psychology of Rebellion: Colonial Medical Responses to Dissent in British East Africa," *Journal of African History* 47, no. 2 (2006): 241–58; David Mills, "British Anthropology at the End of Empire: The Rise and Fall of the Colonial Social Science Research Council, 1944–1962," *Revue d'histoire des sciences humaines* 6, no. 1 (2002): 161–88.

35. Work by Wagner and Condos has been particularly important for this agenda in relation to India.

36. Robert Peckham, "Introduction. Panic: Reading the Signs," in Peckham, *Empires of Panic*, 1.

37. On moods more generally, see C. Jason Throop, "Moral Moods," *Ethos* 42, no. 1 (2014): 65–83.

38. Carina E. Ray, *Crossing the Color Line: Race, Sex, and the Contested Politics of Colonialism in Ghana* (Athens: Ohio University Press, 2015).

39. Hunt, *Nervous State*, 1.

40. Hunt, 1.

41. Claire McLisky and Karen Vallgårda, "Faith through Feeling: An Introduction," in *Emotions and Christian Missions: Historical Perspectives*, ed. Claire McLisky, Daniel Midena, and Karen Vallgårda (Basingstoke, UK: Palgrave Macmillan, 2015). See also Leela Gandhi, *Affective Communities: Anticolonial Thought, Fin-de-Siècle Radicalism, and the Politics of Friendship* (Durham, NC: Duke University Press, 2006).

42. McLisky and Vallgårda, "Faith through Feeling," 10.

43. See Vaughan, "History of Romantic Love" for discussion of this in relation to love.

44. Sianne Ngai, *Ugly Feelings* (Cambridge, MA: Harvard University Press, 2005).

45. Ngai, 27.

46. Ernst Bloch, *The Principle of Hope*, vol. 1 (Cambridge: Cambridge University Press, 1995), 74–75, as cited in Ngai, *Ugly Feelings*, 209–10.

47. Bloch, *Principle of Hope*, as cited in Ngai, *Ugly Feelings*, 389n4.

48. Stanard, "Revisiting Bula Matari," 145–46.

49. Richard Reid, "States of Anxiety: History and Nation in Modern Africa," *Past and Present* 229, no. 1 (2015): 267.

50. Reid, 250.

51. Stoler, "Affective States," 18.

52. Kathryn de Luna, "Affect and Society in Precolonial Africa," *International Journal of African Historical Studies* 46, no. 1 (2013): 123.

53. Cooper and Pratten, "Ethnographies of Uncertainty." See also Julie Archambault, "Cruising through Uncertainty: Cell Phones and the Politics of Display and Disguise in Inhambane, Mozambique," *American Ethnologist* 40, no. 1 (2013); Abdoumaliq Simone, "Rough Towns: Mobilising Uncertainty in Kinshasa," in *African Futures: Essays on Crisis, Emergence, and Possibility*, ed. Brian Goldstone and Juan Obarrio (Chicago: University of Chicago Press, 2016), 139–50.

54. Marco Di Nunzio, "Embracing Uncertainty: Young People on the Move in Addis Ababa's Inner City," in Cooper and Pratten, *Ethnographies of Uncertainty in Africa*, 153.

55. Didier Fassin, *When Bodies Remember: Experiences and Politics of AIDS in South Africa* (Berkeley: University of California Press, 2007), 279.

56. Cooper and Pratten, "Ethnographies of Uncertainty," 1.

57. Bourke, "Fear and Anxiety," 126.

58. See, for example, John Orley, *Culture and Mental Illness: A Study from Uganda* (Nairobi: EAPH, 1970). See also Yolana Pringle, *Psychiatry and Decolonisation in Uganda* (Basingstoke, UK: Palgrave Macmillan, 2019).

59. Livingston, "*AHR* Conversation," 1507.

60. Christopher C. Taylor, "*Ihahamuka*: An Indigenous Medical Condition among Rwandan Genocide Survivors," *Oxford Handbooks Online* (2015). See also Athanase Hasengimana and Devon E. Hinton, "'Ihahamuka,' a Rwandan Syndrome of Response to Genocide: Blocked Flow, Spirit Assault, and Shortness of Breath," in *Culture and Panic Disorder*, ed. Devon E. Hinton and Byron Good (Stanford, CA: Stanford University Press, 2009), 205–9; Grant, "Quiet Insecurity and Quiet Agency," 29–30.

61. Kathryn M. de Luna, "Affect and Society in Precolonial Africa," *International Journal of African Historical Studies* 46, no. 1 (2013): 121–22.

62. Julie Soleil Archambault, *Mobile Secrets: Youth, Intimacy, and the Politics of Pretense in Mozambique* (Chicago: University of Chicago Press, 2017); Jennifer Cole and Lynn M. Thomas, eds., *Love in Africa* (Chicago: University of Chicago Press, 2009); Christian Groes-Green, "'To Put Men in a Bottle': Eroticism, Kinship, Female Power, and Transactional Sex in Maputo, Mozambique," *American Ethnologist* 40, no. 1 (2013): 102–17; Mark Hunter, *Love in the Time of AIDS: Inequality, Gender, and Rights in South Africa* (Bloomington: Indiana University Press, 2010).

63. Copeland, "Anxiety of Blowing," 355.

64. Copeland, 355.

65. Andrew Beatty, "Anthropology and Emotion," *Journal of the Royal Anthropological Institute* 20, no. 3 (2014): 545.

66. Beatty, 553.

67. Susan Reynolds Whyte, "Subjectivity and Subjunctivity: Hoping for Health in Eastern Uganda," in *Postcolonial Subjectivities in Africa*, ed. Richard Werbner (London: Zed Books, 2002), 187.

PART ONE

Anxious Spaces

ONE

Misapprehensions

Outlaws and Anxiety in Southern Africa's Archaeological Past

RACHEL KING

WHAT TRACES DO EMOTIONS LEAVE? THIS IS A LOGICAL STARTing point for discussing archaeologies of anxiety and, more broadly, feelings. Archaeologists have long been comfortable talking about stress, tension, and pressure, often in a survivalist, environmental, or evolutionary sense. Especially since the 1980s and 1990s, many archaeologists have shifted their analytical focus from these sorts of models to consider the lives of people in the past as more contingent, creative, and unpredictable. It does not seem like much of a leap, then, to think of the material past as an emotional place. However, archaeologists interested in discerning emotion urge caution for several reasons. Foremost is concern over potentially "[projecting] western, modern emotions into the past."[1] This point is especially salient for many African contexts, where much archaeological work continues to be carried out by European and North American researchers.[2]

I thank the editors, Andrea Grant and Yolana Pringle, for the invitation to contribute to this volume. Portions of this research were funded by a Clarendon Scholarship from the University of Oxford. This chapter was written during my tenure as Smuts Research Fellow in African Studies and with generous support from the Smuts Memorial Fund. Images are reproduced courtesy of the Southern African Rock Art Digital Archive. I thank Mark McGranaghan for comments on earlier drafts of this chapter.

Writing from the perspective of African archaeology but for a global audience, Jeff Fleisher and Neil Norman have offered a number of analytical points of entry for those wishing to embark on an archaeology of worry, anxiety, and fear: emotional communities, spatial contexts of emotions, the sensuousness of the state and its ensuing legitimacy, among others that I return to shortly. These interventions draw on some particularly archaeological formulations of "affect": the ways in which relations—between humans, animals, things, landscapes—lie "at the heart of how emotions emerge" from the "conjunction of multiple people and things."[3] Put simply, affect allows us to treat anxiety in the past as a material experience. Moreover, we can explore the *relations* underpinning anxiety as much as the physical appearances and actions that anxiety produces.

In this chapter, I consider some material aspects of anxiety and affect, focusing on anxieties related to illicit behaviors and the people with whom they were associated: thieves, "free-booters," cattle raiders. Here, anxiety relates to security and uncertainty, and to practices of "making sense" of people's actions, intents, and identities in order to manage concerns about the future. The material aspects I refer to derive sometimes, but not primarily, from explorations of archaeological sources such as rock art. This is for a host of practical reasons (among them, the archaeological ephemerality of many of the people described here) and because of the relative novelty of this discussion, as anxiety has been minimally explored in southern African history or archaeology. Instead, I draw on archival, historical, ethnological, and newspaper sources, focusing on how illicit figures were stereotyped, mythologized, constructed, and enacted through material culture. Methodologically, this resembles a form of historical ethnography. I submit that it nevertheless remains archaeological in orientation because it retains an emphasis on relationships among people, materials, and time; because its ultimate goal is to recover meaning-making practices that emerged from these relationships; and because it is attuned to where emic perspectives on the past are recoverable from material culture.[4] Therefore, I consider cases in which the aesthetics of certain objects and spaces produced intersubjective responses to anxiety in their wider environments. I examine experiences of anxiety from material remains of encounters between people treated as outlaws and those pursuing them, with the understanding that often the former leave different or more partial traces than the latter do. One goal of my approach is to illustrate where we

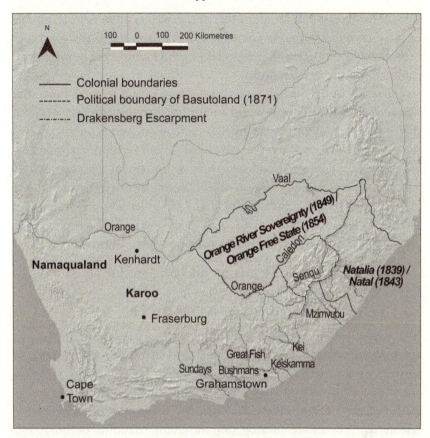

MAP 1. Southern Africa with places mentioned in the text.

can recover a sense of how objects and people behaved through multiple sources, including archival and artifactual ones.

Further, I consider "outlaws" and those involved in cattle raiding as figures produced through anxiety in a particularly social and epistemological sense, rather than simply being defined as people who broke the law.[5] The "misapprehensions" in the chapter's title, then, refer as much to emotions as to the practices used to construe and act on criminality and identity, and the tangible consequences of doing so.

The chapter focuses on two contexts in nineteenth-century southern Africa (map 1), both of which constituted sociopolitically marginal spaces where colonial authority was particularly unstable or uncertain: the Maloti-Drakensberg Mountains and their surrounds (including Natal Colony and the eastern Cape Colony) and the middle Orange River on the Cape's northern boundary.[6] While there are certainly other anxieties and regional variations thereon, as well as other manifestations of these encounters among colonists and Africans across the subcontinent, these two theaters offer especially useful examples of how to think about anxiety in a material way.

Especially in this interdisciplinary volume, I want to drive home the significance of the material world and the challenging intellectual space that it presents. Objects, movements, settlement, and economy all became part of how outlaws were perceived. These perceptions (or, often, misperceptions) in turn produced their own material features such as jails, fences, magistracies, and so on. This array of materials and people did not have infinite creative potential, but rather was constrained by the resources—material, intellectual, perceptual—that people could draw on to conceive of outlaws and manage related anxieties.

Part 1: Anxious Fantasies and Anxious Frontiers

On Affect and Anxiety

In a paper widely seen as a rallying cry for archaeological interest in emotion and affect, Sarah Tarlow challenged archaeologists to reflect on the way we approach "feelings": are we looking for evidence of emotion as a way of explaining people's actions in the past ("people built defenses/made funerary offerings/feasted because they were likely afraid/bereaved/celebratory"), or are we interrogating the emotional power of things and people?[7] The former is a more literal, cause-and-effect way of "reading" the past; the latter is a material culture studies approach, considering the agency of objects and how people and things shape one another. Tarlow directs attention to thinking about emotions in ways that are not purely or primarily psychological: that is, viewing emotions not as located in the mind but rather in the the wider world.[8]

That emotions reside in the interactions between people and the material world leads us to consider affect as one such intersection. For Oliver Harris and Tim Flohr Sørensen, affect (they broaden this to the more ambient "affective field") is a dynamic "network of relations" generated through the actions of human and nonhuman agents.[9] With respect to anxiety, the conceit is that objects are part of how anxiety is experienced not simply because they possess some innately anxiety-inducing quality, but because of a constellation of social relationships, memories, imaginations, and sensations coalescing in them—and manifested in the affect of those objects, just as a similar network of associations composes people's affects.[10] Affect, then, describes the expression of this constellation, and thus becomes recoverable archaeologically. Moreover, some archaeologists (including myself) prefer to discuss affect instead of emotion because the former allows us to focus on the subjective ways in which this constellation was observed in the past, whereas speaking of emotion can suggest that we have an "insider" view of past people's minds.[11] This latter is not always the case: examples discussed later in this chapter draw from historical documents and, to a lesser extent, rock art, which represent different sorts of access to different sorts of emic experiences, some of which we can recover only partially.

Fleisher and Norman offer a range of frameworks for archaeologists to discuss anxiety and affect in the past; their volume represents the first attempt at stimulating specific considerations of anxiety in African archaeology. Of interest here is their suggestion to consider the spatial and sensuous contexts in which anxiety may have emerged, especially within expressions of state power.[12] Susan Kus's long-term work on the politics of the late eighteenth- / early nineteenth-century Merina state in Madagascar exemplifies this particularly well: she draws on a broad repertoire of material culture and architectural layouts, in combination with ethnographic understandings of Malagasy cosmology, to trace how specific symbols and patterns became co-opted into a state "religion" that did not simply appropriate or scale up local knowledges but created new material, aesthetic, and emotional realities.[13] Within colonial southern Africa, Dutch, British, and Afrikaner governments advanced haltingly across the subcontinent over the course of the eighteenth and nineteenth centuries; their apparatuses and agents were unevenly distributed and experienced. This was particularly the case around the Maloti-Drakensberg Mountains (where many of the events discussed in this chapter took place), which constituted a political gray area between the Natal and Cape Colonies and the Orange Free State until the creation of Basutoland in 1871 took in much of the western mountains.[14] This is not to downplay the power of these various states. Rather, it is to suggest that if we take seriously the proposition that affect is "networked" through people and things, then in a settler colonial situation these networks must be as diverse, unwieldy, and contingent as were the material manifestations of state agency.

Put another way, these networks are particularly anxious. Elsewhere, I have suggested that one archaeological approach to anxiety in a settler colony is to treat it as an epistemic practice, related to the ways in which people managed uncertainty.[15] By this, I argue that anxiety "makes sense" of and orders the world, based on often-imperfect information and sensibilities related to past experiences and visions for the future. Affect is part of these sensibilities: the "common sense" perceptions that Ann Laura Stoler has so cogently outlined are largely affective, and therefore material,[16] as colonial actors made decisions about how to control and behave toward native bodies based on their observations and the flawed conclusions that they drew from these. We can witness colonized people engaging in similar epistemic practices, but power inhered in the resources available to manage the anxieties stemming from these practices—and thus favored state apparatuses and officials.[17]

Here, I move to consider the role of affect in processes whereby certain bodies and behaviors were designated as deviant. Particularly in the late nineteenth and early twentieth centuries, colonial states became "ethnographic, taxonomic states, where minute distinctions of race and status were elaborately encoded into forms of rule."[18] These ideas about race and status included observations of criminality, rebelliousness, and other forms of noncompliance with the norms and expectations of colonial authority, and these attributions of disorder often (perhaps always) implicated observations about culture: "Objectifications of culture—the most visible end of a more complex process by which culture and biology were conflated and often deployed as a justification of the natives' civic disability—served to make the 'other' body a natural object for racially discriminatory governance."[19] Perceived dispositions (deviance, obedience, fear, sympathy) were manifested in material practices and behaviors which were often misconstrued, and which colonial agents could acknowledge and act against.[20]

Bandits, Outlaws, and Raiders in Historical Perspective

That certain sorts of criminality were constituted socially rather than legally was at the core of Eric Hobsbawm's formulation of the "social bandit."[21] Hobsbawm's bandits came into existence (or at least into historical view) within political contexts where power was centralized, class systems were entrenched, and access to the forces of production was unevenly distributed. Social bandits sought to undermine the petite bourgeoisie who benefited from the state apparatus, and to redistribute wealth to the lumpenproletariat, who in turn offered support and protection; this of course involved violating a legal system protecting the bourgeoisie. Hobsbawm's argument drew in part on the identification of archetypal "social bandits" in a variety of global and historical contexts, and subsequent critiques of his work have often struggled with whether to take the social bandit as folklore or as empirical observation.[22]

Hobsbawm's "social bandit" linked with his and Terence Ranger's broader discussion of "archaic forms" of dissent;[23] the idea that social crime connected to the rejection of domination and the development of the state resonated with themes in African studies in the 1960s.[24] As the aims and foci of this literature changed alongside African nationalist philosophies of the mid- to late twentieth century, attention fell on how Africans may or may not have been able to confront the (increasingly capitalist) structures of their oppression. Social banditry offered one such explanation and stimulated a lively debate over whether such figures could be located in African history.[25] Despite the ability of Hobsbawm and others to identify individuals who fit the social bandit paradigm, the consensus emerged that the social bandit—as a figure representing a dialectic between moral obligation and self-enrichment—does not apply in Africa, or at least not in studies of Africa's long past.[26]

Two aspects of Hobsbawm's argument are relevant to an archaeological approach to outlaws. First, "banditry" refers to the idea that crime has social meaning, and thus directs us to examine how disorder and attributions thereof are rooted in particular social circumstances. Second, Hobsbawm's "fundamental project" was to understand "criminal deviance" as a form of existence against dominant social values, often drawing on an understanding of historical circumstances.[27] We should therefore consider ontologies of criminality and transgression in particular social and material conditions, in which actors drew on personal experience and historical awareness to make sense of and enact disorderliness. This is not simply another way of discussing "archaic forms," but an acknowledgment of how memory, uncertainty, desire, and aspiration *materialized* at various points in time and contributed to ideas about, for instance, order and disorder.

The idea that criminal deviance was bound up with dissent from moral order is often elided into discussions of resistance. Banditry constitutes a "weapon of the weak" and, as James Scott, Jean Comaroff, and others have argued, whether these outlaws acted out of self-interest or more altruistically was beside the point: they acted against hegemonies that sought domination over consciousness and as such joined a larger moral community.[28] Of the criticisms leveled against this position, most salient here is the metaphysical conceit underpinning these "weapons of the weak": in this schema, what matters are not so much the specific forms that criminality takes as the moral consciousness behind them.[29]

In describing how resistance and dissent more generally can be brought into archaeological thought, Alfredo González-Ruibal suggests that we should look to precisely the forms of criminality that the "weapons of the weak" gloss.[30] This means focusing on where behaviors and bodies in the past were deliberately disruptive and especially where they were misconstrued, as this misconstrual directs attention to how ideas of disruption were constructed and tested. "Outlaw cultures"—pirates, bandits, rustlers, smugglers—lend themselves to a variety of "political interpretations" and "material fantasies" because of the sorts of moral and legal ambiguities to which González-Ruibal alludes.[31] Figures such as the smuggler or the bandit may have been "real," and we may be able to recover historical and archaeological perspectives on what such people did and how. They may also have been produced through the perceptions of those officials charged with controlling colonized bodies.

Affect and anxiety are germane here. If we consider anxiety as a process of making sense in uncertain contexts, drawing on a network of material affects, we then have a framework for interpreting material traces of the past in a way that acknowledges the agency of colonizer and colonized in coping with insecurity and worry about the future.

In what follows, I explore how these sorts of anxieties played out through apprehensions and misapprehensions of the affects of cattle raiders at nineteenth-century southern Africa's colonial margins. I focus on affect in two senses: as physical appearance and material *accoutrements*, and as movement and use of space.

Part 2: Imagining Outlaws

> In stealing cattle, Mercury himself could not have been more expert, or more cunning, than the Bushmen.
> —William John Burchell,
> *Travels in the Interior of Southern Africa*[32]

In his journeys through southeastern Africa in the early 1830s, Captain Allen Gardiner encountered rumors of itinerant "Bushmen"[33] or "Botwas" who procured ivory as part of a supply chain encompassing European traders and African chiefs. When Gardiner eventually met Fodo, the man Nathaniel Isaacs identified as "king of the Botwas," Gardiner sought to correct what he thought was a misapprehension on the

Misapprehensions

part of Isaacs. Fodo, claimed Gardiner, was not in fact a Bushman but a chief and leader of a group (the Nhlangwini) similar to the Bantu-speaking polities that Gardiner and others saw as the region's main form of political leadership. The reason for the confused identifications, said Gardiner, lay in misattributions of material culture: "The erroneous appellation of 'Bushmen,' by which the Inthlangw in [Nhlangwini] are commonly known at Port Natal, has obtained, from the circumstance of their having acquired the method of poisoning the assegais which they use in killing the elephant and other wild animals, from a party of wandering Bushmen with whom they were occasionally associated during their residence on the Umzimvoobo [River]."[34]

Poison and arrows were items particular to Bushmen, it was thought, and the Nhlangwini's uptake of this technology made them liable to be conflated with "wandering Bushmen." Further, Fodo commanded a following of what Gardiner estimated as seven thousand to eight thousand people in twenty-five villages, and claimed that his chiefdom had been dispossessed by the "wars of [Shaka]."[35] Fodo's statement as related by Gardiner implies that this is why the Nhlangwini had become skilled at hunting rather than committed farmers.

The nomenclature of "Bushman" and especially "Botwa" was particularly difficult for ivory traders and missionaries in the area between the Mzimkhulu and Mzimvubu Rivers. In an earlier description of Botwas, Isaacs referenced patterns of movement and settlement more than specific objects: "The 'Botwas' are a people whose sole occupation is elephant hunting; they have no fixed settlement but move as circumstances render it necessary, in search of the elephant. They are separated in four divisions, and take four distinct routes on their hunting excursions. When they have found a herd of these animals, and succeeded in killing some of them, they erect temporary huts, and remain until they have consumed all the flesh and secured the teeth."[36] For Isaacs, Botwas were notable for their occupation, movements, and settlement styles.

While Gardiner's and Isaacs's observations do not stand for all European views of Bushmen, by the mid- to late nineteenth century, visions of "Bushmen" and "Botwas" had become tinged with ideas about itinerancy and social marginality.[37] These associations between race, ethnicity, and disorder—and how these were apprehended in the affects of people perceived as raiders—influenced colonial military activities, settlement policies, and economies in the Cape and Natal Colonies. Moreover, through rock arts we can observe raiders engaging with these constructions, recontextualizing and redeploying some of the material features of the "Bushman raider" for their own purposes. Particularly within Natal (annexed by the British in 1843 and immediately disrupted by raids on settlers), we will see that the stakes of these identifications and misidentifications of Bushman raiders included the security and credibility of the colony, and the autonomy and self-consciousness of raiders themselves.

The figure of the Bushmen or "Bosjesman" gained prominence in historical imagination at the western Cape in the seventeenth and eighteenth centuries, connoting hunter-gatherers who lacked cattle and therefore stole livestock from "Hottentot" pastoralists, although colonists and later historians would struggle to articulate the difference between these categories of person.[38] In his pictorial history of ideas about southern Africa's aboriginal inhabitants in the eighteenth and nineteenth centuries, Pieter Jolly literally illustrates the slippage in racial nomenclature as applied to affective traits like patterns of movement, economy, and material culture:[39] travelers' and explorers' accounts often struggled to articulate why a Bosjesman with cattle was still a Bosjesman. Complicating these taxonomic matters further, the mid- to late eighteenth century saw Indigenous people at the Cape proclaiming themselves as Bosjesmen within movements to resist Dutch settlement by stealing livestock and guns. Despite the confused nomenclature, entangled with notions of "Bosjesman" and its many variations were ideas of primitiveness, lawlessness, and, ultimately, vagrancy.[40]

As Bushmen were observed farther to the east and around the Maloti-Drakensberg Mountains, overtones of criminality remained and were contextualized within settlers' experiences of intercepting bands of mobile cattle-and-horse rustlers based in and around the mountains.[41] John Shepstone, who accompanied a group of Boer farmers on a "reconnaissance" mission for cattle raiders in 1846, described the Bushmen they encountered as small in stature, armed with bows and poison-tipped arrows, and wearing scanty clothing made of skins.[42] Charged with investigating the disruptions of Bushman raiding in the southern Maloti-Drakensberg Mountains in the late 1840s, Henry Francis Fynn and Walter Harding encountered bands of raiders they described as plagued by infighting and tit-for-tat raids; a consequence was that these Bushmen could kill each other with their arrows.[43] Silayi, a Bushman raider interviewed by Sir Walter Stanford in 1884, further described how his cohort defended themselves against a Boer commando (a militia assembled to pursue, and often punish, stock thieves) with bows and arrows.[44] In addition to this equipment, Bushman raiders were frequently observed in possession of firearms, although there are few reports of casualties from their use of these weapons.

Encounters with Bushman raiders in the mid-nineteenth century confirmed to observers such as Shepstone and Fynn that these "mountain Bushmen" were highly mobile and given to dwelling in "caves" (rockshelters, more accurately) in the highlands.[45] The Bushmen that Shepstone met in 1846 allegedly claimed that they would never give up their "roving life" both because they enjoyed it and because it was essential for them to follow migratory game.[46] Fynn's informants described their camps at the headwaters of various rivers in the Drakensberg Escarpment.[47] In a punitive expedition of 1869, Captain Albert Allison tracked a cohort of raiders to a rockshelter on the Senqunyane River in present-day Lesotho stocked with a vast number of horses, cattle, and guns.[48] That such rockshelters could have been inhabited by Bushmen was, for many officials and farmers who became acquainted with the Maloti-Drakensberg during the nineteenth century, confirmed by the presence of rock art within them.[49]

On a broader scale, the emergence in the 1860s and 1870s of a subcontinental intelligentsia interested in the burgeoning fields of anthropology and archaeology meant that racialized and ethnicized scientific categories of Africans were situated amid studies of material cultural history.[50] In their multiyear linguistic and folkloric study of a cohort of |Xam Bushmen, Wilhelm Bleek and Lucy Lloyd solicited descriptions of Bushman material culture and how it was influenced by the arrival of colonial introductions like guns and money.[51] Physical appearance continued to be an important feature of Bushman racial identification, as Bleek and Lloyd's illustrations emphasize.[52] Researchers interested in anthropology and racial history such as George Stow argued for the primacy of Bushmen as the subcontinent's original inhabitants.[53] Archaeology and rock art became significant in these discussions, especially as Stow used his copies of rock art to bolster his claims on behalf of Bushman rights. J. M. Orpen's 1874 report of his "part-Bushman" guide's interpretation of rock art in the Maloti Mountains was connected to the same knowledge networks as Stow and Bleek,[54] and became part of an enduring corpus of information linking Bushmen with knowledge about rock paintings.[55] Thus, when Stanford encountered former members of a Bushman raiding band in the 1880s—speaking a "Bushman" language—who described executing rock paintings, this testimony chimed with what the scientific community held as Bushman culture.[56]

Accoutrements seen as the purview of "savage man"—especially bows and arrows—thus became part of this image of the Bushman raider, along with physical, locative, and behavioral traits such as living in rockshelters that were specific to the Maloti-Drakensberg. This sketch is by no means comprehensive but illustrates how we can see material culture, physical gestures, rumor, and memory—which is to say, affect—contributing to perceptions of Bushman raiders, and thus to anxiety in the process of "making sense" of who these raiders were. While material traits found purchase in the racial taxonomies of late nineteenth-century science and administrative policy, in earlier and more vernacular identifications we can see "Bushman" linking a certain sense of primitiveness with criminality. These racial designations constituted a form of "common sense" about when it was and was not acceptable for Africans to possess horses and cattle, as well as firearms. For settlers and government officials, security was largely contingent on identifying raiders as a threat, ascertaining their behaviors and patterns of movement, and implementing strategies to curtail these. This mandate became increasingly urgent as the nineteenth century wore on and Bushman raiding took a severe financial toll on the Natal Colony, in terms of both the actual cost of raided stock and the indirect costs of mobilizing armed forces and dedicating infrastructure to the cause of pursuing raiders to retrieve stolen animals.[57]

Complicating matters of identifying Bushman raiders was the fact that there were other sorts of outlaws and other sorts of raids on-going in south-eastern Africa, and that settlers and officials were simultaneously attempting to discern and maintain positive associations with chiefs.[58] Ambiguous figures such as Hans Lochenberg—a white farmer described as a "free-booter" who led raids with African chiefs yet held a measure of authority at Buntingville mission station—illustrate where moral and legal boundaries blurred in the political grey space between the Cape and Natal Colonies.[59] Cattle raiding by chiefs and their followers (often against other polities but occasionally against settlers) was ubiquitous throughout the nineteenth century and widely condemned by officials and missionaries alike.[60] Often, these raids appear to have been carried out with Bushman participants, and Shepstone and others commented on how the Bushman raiders they encountered spoke isiXhosa and claimed to have close relations to Mpondo and

Bhaca chiefs.⁶¹ Distinguishing Bushman raiding bands from chiefly raids was a matter of geo-political importance: chiefly raids could be controlled through treaties with colonial government, as well as punitive expeditions and informal commandos;⁶² for Bushman raids, on the other hand, commandos and military expeditions rather than treaties were the norm.

The Maloti-Drakensberg Mountains and surrounds, then, were a difficult space in which to "make sense" of the affects of Bushman raiders, and thus an anxious space. Government officials, armed forces, settlers, and eventually members of the cordon of black farming settlements established as raiding buffers all were engaged in practices of discerning Bushman raiders and formulating responses based on those perceptions or misperceptions. Reiterating a point made above, the security of Natal's settlers, the productivity of their farms, and the credibility of the Natal government were all at stake in the decades-long campaign waged against nineteenth-century montane raiding.

Further, inasmuch as "Bushman raider" was a designation both imagined and bestowed, raiders themselves were actively creating and asserting what it meant to be a Bushman. In Fynn's interviews with raiders, his informants seem to have used the word "Bushman" to refer to themselves (e.g., Qinti's claim, "I am the son of Mdwebo, the Bushman chief") and characterize distinct bands of Bushmen in terms of geographical location and rivalry.⁶³ Moreover, at least one of Fynn's informants apparently took pains to point out that while "Bushmen" may have stolen cattle from one another, not all are guilty of theft from Natal Colony: Mangana's statement reads, "I am sure that neither Nqabayo's Bushmen nor Mdwebo's people have ever stolen cattle from Natal. The Thola Bushmen are the people who steal."⁶⁴

But it would be a mistake to assume that Mangana, Qinti, and others understood and experienced being a Bushman raider in the same way as Fynn, Shepstone, Harding, and their colleagues; rock art can provide some emic perspectives on these experiences. Sam Challis has offered the most detailed description of how one "Bushman" identity emerged, arguing from rock art depicting horses that act as chronological markers, since the horse arrived in the Maloti-Drakensberg about 1835. Following Challis, AmaTola Bushmen were a heterogeneous consortium of raiders who forged a creolized worldview around the act of raiding livestock. This worldview is disclosed through rock art pairing horses (often with riders wearing hats and carrying guns) and baboons (fig. 1):

FIGURE 1. Rock art panel with imagery referencing the relationships between cattle raiding and syncretic identities, as well as brimmed hats and guns. Image courtesy SARADA

baboons were associated in a range of cosmologies with medicines offering protection during cattle raids, and horses were crucial to the technological and social workings of the AmaTola as illuminated through archival testimony.[65] Challis demonstrates how AmaTola identity drew on the particular economic and political contingencies of the frontier and suggests that raiding may have been a form of resistance, given that

AmaTola appear to have had specific raiding targets.[66] Challis's position resonates with that of Geoff Blundell and Lara Mallen, who drew on different traditions of rock art in the same area to suggest that Bushman raiding groups were capable of assimilating difference aided by and in aid of shared raiding practices.[67] In these paintings, we see European (brimmed hats, guns, equestrian equipment) and African (bows, arrows, bandoliers, knobkerries) material culture depicted, articulating raiding identities that recontextualized familiar objects with new ones, alongside practices that carried violent penalties but also promoted social cohesion among cohorts of similarly unruly people. This discussion merits further unpacking than is possible here, but these depictions can be taken as a means whereby certain people could materialize and—more importantly—manipulate raiding affects. In the process, we have a glimpse of raider agency at work in the anxious network of the Maloti-Drakensberg.

Part 3: Policing Affect

While accoutrements such as guns, bows and arrows, and a mélange of objects notionally related to certain cultural groups became part of the "material fantasies" of outlaws, we can also observe where perceptions of movement and use of space intersected with these fantasies and became part of affects considered illicit. Elsewhere, I have argued that we can explore illicit or disorderly movements through and settlement within a landscape, alongside attempts to understand and control those movements, as anxious.[68] Certain raiders utilized particularly inaccessible routes through the Maloti-Drakensberg and established a string of intermittently occupied settlements that permitted strategic flexibility and scrutiny of colonists. Commandos, militia, and government representatives attempted to discern the logic behind these raiding movements and establish institutions to inhibit and regulate them. Again, these networks are anxious in an archaeological sense because they were epistemic practices rooted in observations of material gestures. They were also uncertain, occasionally prescient, and frequently flawed. Here, I want to focus on the establishment of jails and police stations in response to raiding threats (real or perceived) and consider what they can illuminate about how movement and use of space relate to anxiety and affect. I move through three mid- to late nineteenth-century examples: the Maloti-Drakensberg's "Bushman raiders," the chief Moorosi on the eve of his failed rebellion in the southwestern Maloti-Drakensberg, and the Korana Wars of the Cape's northern frontier.

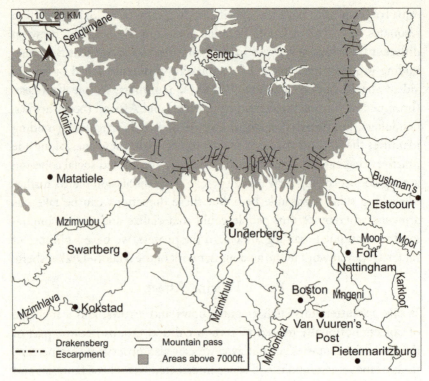

MAP 2. The southeastern Maloti-Drakensberg Mountains, with places mentioned in the text.

One of the earliest pieces of military infrastructure constructed in response to the Maloti-Drakensberg's Bushman raiders was Van Vuuren's Post, established in early 1847 and occupied by a contingent of Cape Mounted Rifles (CMR) to reassure Boer settlers that the newly established British government was indeed protecting them (map 2). Van Vuuren's Post would be effective—it was thought—because of its location in the thick of raiding action, and Boers offered enthusiastic support for this plan. Further, the post's establishment was accompanied by a related strategy of charging Africans, some of whom were assigned to new Locations around farms, with reporting raider activity and serving as buffers between raiders and white settlers.[69]

By the end of 1847, it was apparent that Van Vuuren's Post was poorly suited to its purpose. Despite several deployments by the CMR, during which some stock was recovered but thieves almost always escaped, raids on farms continued unabated. Moreover, by the time the CMR caught up to the stolen livestock, many of these animals were found stabbed or mutilated and could not be returned to their owners. During this period, raiders seemed to be targeting specific farms repeatedly, likely because these afforded the opportunity for a quick and easy getaway via rugged trails along the rivers flowing down from the Escarpment.[70] Additionally, the African Locations (established over the protests of some farmers) appeared to have had minimal effect in deterring or apprehending raiders before they made it through this first line of defense. In one instance in mid-1847, the farmer Andries Pretorius complained that raiders had managed to make their way unchecked through the Location at Swartkop and abscond with cattle and horses, suggesting that Swartkop's residents were somehow in league with the raiders.[71]

Putting aside the accuracy of Pretorius's accusations, Natal authorities had clearly misread the situation around Van Vuuren's Post. The nature of hostilities between African residents and raiders was not what they expected. The post did not deter raiders but constituted a piece of infrastructure that they could simply work around. Raiders' knowledge of the impenetrable nature of the Maloti-Drakensberg landscape thwarted punitive attacks and allowed raiders to escape.

Natal authorities had to change tack. Van Vuuren's Post was abandoned in December 1847 while a new military post was established near present-day Estcourt. The Natal Native Police Corps were recruited from the African communities living in the colony and dispatched to act as a detective squad–cum–enforcement agency, on the basis that they could gather more evidence of raids than could white military forces. When Van Vuuren's Post was reoccupied in July 1848, the new strategy emphasized more thorough reconnaissance and local knowledge: the Native Police Corps were instructed to maintain regular patrols, familiarize themselves with raiders' favorite paths, and on this basis ascertain the best locations for new military posts.[72] The Natal military would be able to act with greater intelligence, and this enhanced military presence at the base of the mountains would surely dissuade raiders from attacking, or at least from doing so with the boldness that they had hitherto.

Again, things did not go to plan. As soon as the Native Police Corps were called away from an area, raiders would strike. Even when the Corps and other troops were present, raiders were able to evade notice, lifting a large number of livestock from a farm very close to another military post at Bushman's River, for instance.[73] Retaliatory expeditions from the 1840s to late 1860s attempted to follow raiders in order to clarify their routes, destinations, and strategies of movement. Some of these were successful, such as Allison's 1869 expedition. More often, raiders confounded their pursuers through a multitude of tactics: covering the animals' spoor, splitting herds among a cohort, choosing paths that were especially rugged. As the nineteenth century progressed and boundaries between Basutoland, the Orange Free State, Griqualand East, and Natal solidified, raiders used political demarcations to their advantage. Moorosi, a subordinate chief of the Sotho paramount Moshoeshoe I who was also an accomplished cattle raider, was known to have taken livestock from Natal across the southern Drakensberg and into Basutoland. Natal authorities could not pursue Moorosi into Moshoeshoe's territory, and British representatives in Basutoland were tepid about confronting Moshoeshoe in order to punish his subordinate.[74]

Raiding movements—part of raiding affects—thus confounded authorities in the southern Drakensberg and Natal: try as they might, military operations often failed to understand and respond to raiders' strategies, patterns, or alliances. As one contemporary commentator lamented: "Britain may beat a Bonaparte, but can't beat a Bushman."[75] Of course, some investigators had more success than others, but the law enforcement infrastructure brought to bear on regulating raiding behavior was inadequate to the task, and thus raids persisted. Further, we can observe incorporated within the figure of the Bushman raider ideas about mobility and subterfuge: striking in the lowlands and retreating to the highlands, keeping stolen stock in rockshelters, transgressing political boundaries.

These last were features not only of so-called Bushman raiders but also of recognized chiefs such as Moorosi, further illustrating how affect related to the conflation of ethnic and criminal designations, and the uncertainty inherent in responding to them. Elsewhere, I have described how during the mid- to late nineteenth century Moorosi's habits of moving through a string of mountaintop settlements offered opportunities to raid cattle and carry out Moshoeshoe's directives while frustrating colonial observation and regulation.[76] Basutoland's borders were codified in 1871 and Moorosi chafed against the major reconfigurations of chiefly powers that the new British administration introduced, reorienting his cattle raids up the Senqu River and into Natal. By 1876 Bastuoland Governor's Agent Charles Griffith had declared that Moorosi and his followers were "about the wildest and most uncivilized of any in this territory,"[77] and it was decided that a new magistracy (including a jail) was necessary to surveil and check Moorosi's activities.

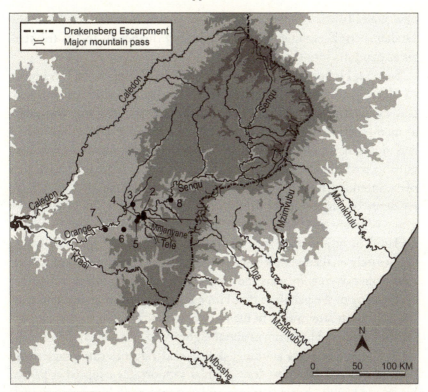

MAP 3. Southwestern Basutoland and places mentioned in the text, including select BaPhuthi settlements used during the late nineteenth century: 1 Bolepeletsa, 2 Quthing magistracy, 3 Maphutšeng, 4 Tulumaneng, 5 Palmietfontein police station, 6 Litapoleng, 7 Lefika la bo Khiba, 8 Mount Moorosi.

In 1877, the district of Quthing was carved out specifically to encompass Moorosi's territories and a magistracy established under the authority of Hamilton Hope (map 3).

Hope, Moorosi, and other Basutoland administrators engaged in a game of "veiled threats and counterfeit claims of friendship" between 1877 and 1878, which Elizabeth Eldredge has detailed and which offers an excellent opportunity for exploring affect and anxiety.[78] First, the magistracy was placed just six kilometers away from Moorosi's settlement at Bolepeletsa, and almost immediately across the Tele River from the Frontier Armed and Mounted Police (FAMP) station at Palmietfontein; while this latter was minimally staffed, Moorosi nevertheless found himself the subject of rapidly intensified scrutiny by law enforcement.[79] He was forced to modify his movements in response to this new surveillance, traveling much less frequently over the Tele River and Drakensberg Escarpment and instead using the Senqu and its tributaries as conduits into the highlands.

Second, Hope was inexperienced, "irascible," "impatient," and given to aggressive posturing.[80] For his part, Moorosi was a skilled showman and excelled at provoking Hope. Put differently, Moorosi was adept at manipulating his affect, conjuring white fears of African unruliness and violence. As Hope attempted to implement Basutoland's new laws gutting traditional chiefly prerogatives, Moorosi responded with displays intended to communicate strength and command over African residents of his territory: after one magisterial ruling, he assembled a group of followers (Hope estimated them to number five hundred) who declared in unison that they obeyed only Moorosi.[81] Moorosi would deliberately challenge new regulations (such as those prohibiting Africans from carrying firearms and chiefs from collecting fines), sometimes acquiescing to the penalties that Hope imposed and sometimes protesting, but often attempting to incite intemperate reactions from Hope.[82] Further, by 1877 Moorosi was about eighty-two years old and had cultivated a reputation as a cunning, skilled, and vigorous cattle raider, and he used this reputation to draw popular support. He adopted as part of his image a white horse that was said to accompany him everywhere,[83] and stories of his battles against chiefs and cannibals alike had been circulating through the Cape and southern Maloti-Drakensberg since at least the early 1870s.[84] Hope's superior Emile Rolland recognized Moorosi's tactics of undermining Hope's authority and enhancing his own, and unsuccessfully begged Hope not to take the bait.[85]

Adding to this already anxious network were British fears of a widespread African uprising stemming from emergent rebellions among Xhosa, Pedi, and Zulu.[86] The (possibly well-founded) concern was that Moorosi would catch the "war spirit" and lead an uprising in Basutoland.[87] Thus, Moorosi's affect was scrutinized both from the perspective of administrators wishing to bring order to a new colonial possession and also to ascertain how much of a threat of rebellion Moorosi actually represented.

Ultimately, Hope was replaced with a magistrate better able to discern these threats: John Austen, previously superintendent of the Wittebergen Native Reserve, where he had become familiar with Moorosi's activities.[88] At Quthing, Austen pursued aggressive tactics and attempted to exploit perceived fault lines within Moorosi's polity. Austen identified potential rebels and acted against their families by confiscating livestock.[89] He used incarceration as a public form of punishment and deterrent, arresting Moorosi's son and others on charges of stealing cattle and horses and imprisoning them in the magistracy's jail.

However, the jail would prove not to be the inviolable apparatus that Austen believed. On New Year's Eve 1878, a rescue party stormed the jail, freed the prisoners, and sent Austen and his family fleeing across the Tele to the Palmietfontein garrison. The jail was no longer sufficient to control or surveil rebels; only a police station would do. Once at Palmietfontein, Austen told the commanding officer of the FAMP to march on Moorosi's BaPhuthi. Moorosi's followers interpreted this as a sign that the British were turning against them and stormed the magistracy.[90] Moorosi's War had been set in motion. It would end in Moorosi's defeat in late November 1880 after an eight-month siege by British and Basotho forces on Moorosi's mountain stronghold.[91]

Anxiety here relates to discerning rebelliousness and the power wielded by government and traditional leadership. Moorosi was adept at manipulating his affect to needle Hope and keep Basutoland's administration preoccupied with assessing his strength. For their part, Basutoland's administrators were responsible for detecting rebelliousness in Moorosi's affect and quelling this. Arguably, both Hope and Austen failed in different ways, as Basutoland's government replaced Hope because they thought Austen was better equipped to manage Moorosi and thereby prevent rebellion. Neither could discern affects or indices of bellicosity, whereas Moorosi was well aware of how to utilize these.

We can observe similar dynamics at work along the Cape's northern border (see map 1). This frontier materialized earlier than its eastern counterpart, owing to the halting expansion of *burgher* settlement during the Dutch period in the seventeenth and eighteenth centuries, which accelerated under British rule as policies governing settler land acquisition were relaxed to encourage growth.[92] The northern frontier became a retreat for *drosters* (runaways) or *skellem* (criminals) of all races who wished to evade public scrutiny. Characters such as Stephanus, a convicted criminal who retreated to the northern Cape and masqueraded as a missionary to obtain followers and "donations," were common.[93]

At the same time, hunter-pastoralist communities in the arid interior Karoo were being excluded from grazing and watering territories by the establishment of settler farms, and often retaliated through raids for livestock. Such communities were many and multifaceted, distinguished by complex linguistic and genealogical differences (eventually including a European component), often subscribing to consensual rather than hereditary leadership; many become historically visible only when they engaged in raids or other transgressive activities.[94] One such group was the Korana, a community of pastoralist stock-raiders against whom the Cape waged campaigns throughout the nineteenth century. During these "Korana Wars," expeditions to discern and control movement hinged on the ability of the Cape's military to read the complex politics at work among various branches of Korana leadership, and to dislodge Korana from their strongholds along the Orange River.

While the Maloti-Drakensberg Mountains were sufficiently rugged to provide a redoubt for Bushman raiders, the Karoo landscape was (and remains), the physical opposite, although equally inhospitable. Despite the Orange being the largest and most fertile waterway in southern Africa, in the center of the subcontinent it is surrounded by over 250 kilometers of arid flatland, with little reliable surface water until one reaches within some 60 kilometers of the Orange itself. Within the middle Orange are dotted a number of reasonably large islands covered with thick bush that one military officer referred to as "a water jungle."[95] Korana used these islands as a base of operations and fallback position from which to launch mounted raiding expeditions against Africans and Europeans alike.

In the early 1830s, a Cape military campaign against the raider *kaptein* Stuurman succeeded in destabilizing much organized raiding along the middle Orange and reorienting raiders' attention toward more profitable targets in southern Namibia. By the early 1860s, however, reconfiguration of local Herero politics, the escalation of commando pursuit of San raiders, and the encroachment of Boer and mixed-race "Bastaard" communities encouraged intensified raiding and the rise of ambitious Korana leaders like Cupido Pofadder.[96] The late 1860s saw reports of robbing and plundering on the borders of Namaqualand and West Griqualand, and burghers complained of losing their cattle and sheep to Korana raids.[97]

The Cape government recognized the imperative to protect settlers on the northern frontier but was unwilling to send a commando of locally recruited Boers and "Bastaards," as such commandos had recently faced trenchant public criticism for the atrocities they committed against San.[98] Thus, in 1868 the Cape established a Special Magistracy with an

FAMP contingent over the northern border at Kenhardt, believing that a more disciplined military force with direct oversight would ensure the moderate but effective control of raiders. Despite this squeamishness, an auxiliary commando was organized to complement Kenhardt's police force.

Part of the challenge the Cape faced in assembling an adequate military on its northern border lay in formulating an appropriate strategy for engaging Korana, or "making sense" of Korana affect: law enforcement had to learn to move like Korana, which is to say quickly, across an immense, arid area, and penetrate the Orange's densely forested islands. Traveling with wagons, for instance, was an encumbrance that slowed both commandos and police forces. The mandate of the newly formed Northern Border Police, then, was to patrol the almost 400-mile frontier, to maintain peace within the border districts, and to dislodge and capture Korana chiefs while acting swiftly from their base at Kenhardt.[99] For a force of only around fifty men, this plan was overly ambitious, to say the least. While the presence of both a magistrate and a police force may have made raiders somewhat more cautious, its most obvious effect on Korana raiding was that Korana incorporated this military infrastructure into their internal politics. Amid Korana kapteins' competition for authority and goods, Cupido Pofadder eliminated one of his rivals, Willem Ruiter, by capturing Ruiter and handing him over to the Special Magistrate.

The imperative to evict Korana from the islands in the middle Orange intensified into the early 1870s, as the FAMP continued to demonstrate its ineffectiveness at patrolling the border. It became increasingly clear to Special Magistrate Jackson and his successors that siege, rather than patrol-and-capture, was a more effective strategy for dealing with Korana based on the islands. At stake was the stability of the Cape's northern frontier: the Cape government came to believe that if colonists could not be persuaded to settle in the country between Namaqualand and Fraserburg, the frontier would effectively be ceded to Korana and other unruly forces in the arid interior. Jackson's solution was rapid settlement of farmers along the Orange, partly to prevent Korana from occupying the area and also to create a community with an interest in helping to halt and punish raids, and thus complement the FAMP's work.[100]

Over time, however, the magistracy at Kenhardt proved to contain the seeds of its own instability. Finding officers capable of successfully assuming command at Kenhardt, and then ensuring that they would stay for an appreciable length of time, was challenging. By 1878, changes in command at Kenhardt resulted in periods of inactivity for the police force, during which time the men became restive and rebellious. Complaints included overdue pay, inadequate equipment, and the fact that, unlike on the Cape's eastern frontier, troops were not allowed to keep a portion of the loot captured during martial maneuvers. A reversal of this policy helped control the situation at Kenhardt somewhat.[101] Recruiting volunteer patrols from communities of newly settled farmers was less effective than planners had hoped, as retaining volunteers was more challenging than attracting them. Kenhardt was simply proving too distant from the Orange to be an efficient base of operations.[102]

Korana for much of the early 1870s continued their internal jockeying for power, often aided by the option of handing captured kapteins over to Kenhardt. Amid drought and political confrontations with "Bastaards" and Griquas, different Korana contingents had moved off onto the fringes of the Kalahari and other aspects of the Karoo, easing away from their reliance on the islands for a time. In 1878, however, possibly encouraged by the geopolitical changes wrought by eastern Cape frontier conflicts and revolt in Griqualand West, Korana reoccupied the islands. There then ensued a massive, final push by law enforcement to penetrate these strongholds. Despite a lack of boats and a relatively unsuccessful attempt at shelling the islands, colonial forces were able to swim, wade, and fight their way ashore. A number of Korana had left the islands and made their way toward auxiliary strongholds in mountains farther along the Orange or to the north and east, but were swept up by contingents of Griqualand Police and military units.

Here, anxiety related to the Cape's "making sense" of Korana movements (affects) and learning to mimic these. Ultimately, what permitted the Cape military to prevail was not that they had "figured out" Korana affects, but that they were able to assemble a critical mass of troops and fragment Korana against the frontier's shifting political landscape. This illustrates an idea that runs through earlier discussions but becomes salient here: inasmuch as British, Boers, Korana, and others were anxiously engaged in practices of "making sense," the resources available to manage those anxieties were not equally available. Power inhered in the ability to access and deploy these resources. Korana were much more successful than Cape and Boer militaries at being able to discern their opponents' movements and weaknesses and turn these to their advantage. That knowledge, however, did not prevail in the face of the larger, decades-long weakening of the Korana's environmental and sociopolitical networks on the frontier, as well as the Cape's access to (often imperfect) military manpower.

Part 4: The Past Is an Anxious Country

In archaeological terms, we can think of anxiety as an affective and epistemic practice. In both senses, anxiety relates to the ways in which perceptions of people, things, space, sensuousness, memory, and desire are bundled together. Inasmuch as affect can be deliberately performed, it can also be misconstrued. Anxiety, then, refers to the ways in which affective traits such as clothing, material accoutrements, physiognomy, occupying certain spaces, and moving in certain ways worked in practices of "making sense," and then in how people reacted based on these sensibilities. Apprehending and misapprehending outlaws and cattle raiders refer not only to the imposition of colonial law but to practices through which race, criminality, and ethnicity were constructed, conflated, and acted on, often with devastating consequences.

Approaching aspects of the southern African past with this anxious, affective orientation permits us to ask some new questions of many of the violent encounters that characterize the region's history. Is it useful to think of cattle raiding as deviant or transgressive, and if so, can we nuance our conceptions of how laws and colonial sensibilities were being transgressed? If not—and evidence from certain southern African contexts suggests that raiding could constitute a complex sociopolitical institution rather than outright theft[103]—can we set aside considerations of raiding as illicit to achieve a better understanding of how warfare or conflict operated among African polities?[104] Can we probe the intersection between raids that *appeared* as illicit, bellicose, or disorderly and raids that *actually were* these things for the people involved, and thereby gain insight into how African agency included the ability to manipulate affect and inspire anxiety? These questions can be asked of multiple contexts in precolonial and colonial southern Africa: the fusions and fissions of Highveld chiefdoms over the last five hundred years, competitions among nineteenth-century African leaders like Mzilikazi, Moletsane, Sekonyela, and Moshoeshoe on the southern Highveld, Griqua and Oorlam kapteincies along the Orange and in the Karoo. They could also be applied to a broader range of contexts on the continent, especially where interpretations of violence in the past hinged on categories of thought that included lawlessness, disruption, unrest, and uprising. Framing anxiety as I have done here enables critical revision of related concepts like disorder, and prompts the question of where our interpretations of these experiences could focus more on the aesthetic, emotive encounters and imaginations surrounding reports of civil or military disquietude.

Paying attention to "outlaw cultures" thus directs us to examine how—and, specifically, with what materials—deviance and disorder were constructed in the past, and how these perceptions made the settler colonial past a particularly anxious place.

Notes

1. Jeffrey Fleisher and Neil Norman, "Archaeologies of Anxiety: The Materiality of Anxiousness, Worry, and Fear," in *The Archaeology of Anxiety: The Materiality of Anxiousness, Worry, and Fear*, ed. Jeffrey Fleisher and Neil Norman (New York: Springer, 2016), 2.

2. John Giblin, Rachel King, and Benjamin Smith, "Introduction: De-centring Ethical Assumptions by Re-centring Ethical Debate in African Archaeology," *Azania: Archaeological Research in Africa* 49, no. 2 (June 2014): 131–35.

3. Fleisher and Norman, "Archaeologies of Anxiety," 12.

4. For more detail about this sort of approach, see Rachel King, *Outlaws, Anxiety, and Disorder in Southern Africa: Material Histories of the Maloti-Drakensberg* (London: Palgrave Macmillan, 2019).

5. Rachel King, "Living on Edge: New Perspectives on Anxiety, Refuge, and Colonialism in Southern Africa," *Cambridge Archaeological Journal* 27, no. 3 (August 2017): 533–51.

6. For constructions of these spaces as "frontiers," see Martin Legassick, "The Frontier Tradition in South African Historiography," in *Economy and Society in Pre-industrial South Africa*, ed. Shula Marks and Anthony Atmore (London: Longman, 1980), 44–79; Denver A. Webb, "Further beyond the Pale: Decolonisation, Historians and Military Discourse in the 18th and 19th Centuries on the Eastern Cape 'Frontier,'" *Journal of Southern African Studies* 43, no. 4 (June 2017): 681–97. For a more recent "interior world" framework, see Rachel King and Sam Challis, "The 'Interior World' of the Nineteenth-Century Maloti-Drakensberg Mountains," *Journal of African History* 58, no. 2 (July 2017): 213–37.

7. Sarah Tarlow, "The Archaeology of Emotion and Affect," *Annual Review of Anthropology* 41 (2012): 169–85.

8. Tarlow, 175.

9. Oliver J. T. Harris and Tim Flohr Sørensen, "Rethinking Emotion and Material Culture," *Archaeological Dialogues* 17, no. 2 (December 2010): 150–51.

10. Alfred Gell, *Art and Agency: An Anthropological Theory* (Oxford: Clarendon Press, 1998), 15.

11. Cf. Stephen D. Houston, "Decorous Bodies and Disordered Passions: Representations of Emotion among the Classic Maya," *World Archaeology* 33, no. 2 (November 2001): 206–19.

12. Fleisher and Norman, "Archaeologies of Anxiety," 12.

13. Susan Kus and Victor Raharijaona, "House to Palace, Village to State: Scaling up Architecture and Ideology," *American Anthropologist* 102, no. 1 (March 2000): 98–113; Kus, "Matters of Belief: Middle-Range Theory, Religion, and the 'State,'" *Archaeological Papers of the American Anthropological Association* 21, no. 1 (March 2011): 11–22.

14. King and Challis, "Interior World."

15. King, "Living on Edge."

16. Ann Laura Stoler, "Epistemic Politics: Ontologies of Colonial Common Sense," *Philosophical Forum* 39, no. 3 (August 2008): 349–61.

17. Joanna Bourke, "Fear and Anxiety: Writing about Emotion in Modern History," *History Workshop Journal* 55, no. 1 (April 2003): 127.

18. Anupama Rao and Steven Pierce, "Discipline and the Other Body: Humanitarianism, Violence, and the Colonial Exception," in *Discipline and the Other Body: Correction, Corporeality, Colonialism*, ed. Anupama Rao and Steven Pierce (Durham, NC: Duke University Press, 2006), 4.

19. Rao and Pierce, 4.

20. Barbara Voss, "Sexual Effects: Postcolonial and Queer Perspectives on the Archaeology of Sexuality and Empire," in *The Archaeology of Colonialism: Intimate Encounters and Sexual Effects*, ed. Barbara Voss and Eleanor Conlin Casella (Cambridge: Cambridge University Press, 2011), 17.

21. Eric Hobsbawm, *Bandits* (New York: New Press, 2000).

22. E.g., Graham Seal, "The Robin Hood Principle: Folklore, History, and the Social Bandit," *Journal of Folklore Research* 46, no. 1 (January–April 2009): 67–89.

23. Eric Hobsbawm, *Primitive Rebels: Studies in Archaic Forms of Social Movement in the 19th and 20th Centuries* (Manchester: Manchester University Press, 1959); Terence Ranger, "The Invention of Tradition in Colonial Africa," in *The Invention of Tradition*, ed. Eric Hobsbawm and Terence Ranger (Cambridge: Cambridge University Press, 2012 [1983]), 211–62.

24. Donald Crummey, "Introduction: The Great Beast," in *Banditry, Rebellion, and Social Protest in Africa*, ed. Donald Crummey (London: James Currey, 1986), 1–29.

25. E.g., Allen Isaacman, "Social Banditry in Zimbabwe (Rhodesia) and Mozambique, 1894–1907: An Expression of Early Peasant Protest," *Journal of Southern African Studies* 4, no. 1 (1977): 1–30; David A. Maughan Brown, "Social Banditry: Hobsbawm's Model and 'Mau Mau,'" *African Studies* 39, no. 1 (1980): 77–99; Frederick Cooper, "Peasants, Capitalists, and Historians: A Review Article," *Journal of Southern African Studies* 7, no. 2 (1981): 284–314; Nigel Penn, "Estienne Barbier: An Eighteenth Century Cape Social Bandit?," *Social Dynamics* 14, no. 1 (1988): 1–19; Jonathon Glassman, *Feasts and Riot: Revelry, Rebellion, and Popular Consciousness on the Swahili Coast, 1856–1888* (London: James Currey, 1995), 13–14.

26. Ralph Austen, "Social Bandits and Other Heroic Criminals: Western Models of Resistance and Their Relevance for Africa," in Crummey, *Banditry, Rebellion, and Social Protest*, 89–109; Klaas van Walraven and Jon Abbink, "Rethinking Resistance in African History: An Introduction," in *Rethinking Resistance: Revolt and Violence in African History*, ed. Jon Abbink, Mirjam de Bruijn, and Klaas van Walraven (Leiden: Brill, 2003), 7–8.

27. Austen, "Social Bandits," 102.

28. Jean Comaroff, *Body of Power, Spirit of Resistance: The Culture and History of a South African People* (Chicago: University of Chicago Press, 1985); James Scott, *Weapons of the Weak: Everyday Forms of Peasant Resistance* (New Haven, CT: Yale University Press, 1985).

29. Timothy Mitchell, "Everyday Metaphors of Power," *Theory and Society* 19, no. 5 (October 1990): 559–62.

30. Alfredo González-Ruibal, *An Archaeology of Resistance: Materiality and Time in an African Borderland* (Lanham, MD: Rowman and Littlefield, 2014).

31. Shannon Lee Dawdy and Joe Bonni, "Toward a General Theory of Piracy," *Anthropological Quarterly* 85, no. 3 (Summer 2012): 676.

32. William John Burchell, *Travels in the Interior of Southern Africa*, vol. 2 (London: Longman, Hurst, Rees, Orme, Brown, and Green, 1824), 71.

33. For aesthetic purposes, I place the words Bushman or Bushmen in quotation marks only where I discuss the construction of the term or archetype directly, or as part of a quotation. Otherwise, while the terms remain without quotation marks, readers should note that I continue to treat these as subjectively constructed identifications.

34. Allen Gardiner, *Narrative of a Journey to the Zoolu Country in South Africa* (London: William Crofts, 1836), 313–14.

35. Gardiner, 312.

36. Nathaniel Isaacs, *Travels and Adventures in Eastern Africa*, vol. 2 (London: Edward Churton, 1836), 43–44.

37. Cf. Rachel King, "In Praise of Outlaws," *Archaeological Dialogues* 25, no. 2 (December 2018): 116–21.

38. Shula Marks's constructivist understanding of Bushman identifications focuses on the creation of these categories (largely by Europeans) to describe economic distinctions between hunter-gatherers and pastoralists, which then took on an array of criminal and labor-related meanings. Positivist analyses have focused more on the sociocultural and linguistic features of those people included under the heading of Bushman and follow these attributes to better understand how related communities of Khoe pastoralists and San hunter-gatherers became designated as criminal. The two positions can be seen as complementary. See Shula Marks, "Khoisan Resistance to the Dutch in the Seventeenth and Eighteenth Centuries," *Journal of African History* 13, no. 1 (1972): 55–80; Pippa Skotnes, ed., *Miscast: Negotiating the Presence of the Bushmen* (Cape Town: University of Cape Town Press, 1996); John Wright, "Sonqua, Bosjesmans, Bushmen, abaThwa: Comments and Queries on Pre-Modern Identifications," *South African Historical Journal* 35, no. 1 (November

1996): 16–29; Susan Newton-King, *Masters and Servants on the Cape Eastern Frontier, 1760–1803* (Cambridge: Cambridge University Press, 1999).

39. Pieter Jolly, *Sonqua: Southern San History and Art after Contact, An Illustrated Synthesis* (Cape Town: Pieter Jolly, 2014).

40. Elizabeth Elbourne, *Blood Ground: Colonialism, Missions, and the Contest for Christianity in the Cape Colony and Britain, 1799–1853* (Montreal: McGill-Queen's University Press, 2002), 237.

41. John Wright and others have traced the "provenance of received ideas" about Bushmen at the Cape from the seventeenth century until the Kalahari Debate over the "intactness" of modern hunter-gatherer identities in the 1990s. For those identified as Bushmen in the southeast of the subcontinent, however, the debate could be nuanced to take in the experiences of Africans and settlers alike as the boundaries between the Orange Free State, Basutoland, and the Natal and Cape Colonies closed from the late 1840s to the 1890s. Cf. Wright, "Sonqua, Bosjesmans, Bushmen."

42. Patricia Vinnicombe, *People of the Eland: Rock Paintings of the Drakensberg Bushmen as a Reflection of Their Life and Thought* (Johannesburg: Wits University Press, 2009 [1976]), 30. These notes are from Shepstone's memoirs that he wrote in later life, so it is worth considering how much his memories were colored by further conclusions he had come to about "Bushmen."

43. E.g., Vinnicombe, *People of the Eland*, 60.

44. Vinnicombe, 62–63.

45. John Wright, *Bushman Raiders of the Drakensberg, 1840–1870* (Pietermaritzburg: University of Natal Press, 1971), 126.

46. Vinnicombe, *People of the Eland*, 30.

47. Vinnicombe, 55.

48. Cape Archives (henceforth, CA), Secretary for Native Affairs 1/3/19, Albert Allison, "Statement of Dinilape a Basuto Resident near Silesa's Kraal," 1869.

49. E.g., Joseph Millerd Orpen, "A Glimpse into the Mythology of the Maluti Bushmen," *Cape Monthly Magazine*, n.s., 9 (July 1874): 1–13; George McCall Theal, *Basutoland Records*, vol. 5 (Rome: Institute for Southern African Studies, 2002), 127.

50. Saul Dubow, "Earth History, Natural History, and Prehistory at the Cape, 1860–1875," *Comparative Studies in Society and History* 46, no. 1 (January 2004): 107–33.

51. Andrew Bank, *Bushmen in a Victorian World: The Remarkable Story of the Bleek-Lloyd Collection of Bushman Folklore* (Cape Town: Double Storey, 2006), 213.

52. See papers in Skotnes, *Miscast* and *Claim to the Country: The Archive of Lucy Lloyd and Wilhelm Bleek* (Athens: Ohio University Press, 2007).

53. George Stow, *The Native Races of South Africa* (London: Swan Sonnenschein, 1905); Pippa Skotnes, *Unconquerable Spirit: George Stow's History Paintings of the San* (Athens: Ohio University Press, 2008).

54. Orpen, "Glimpse into the Mythology"; Mark McGranaghan, Sam Challis, and J. David Lewis-Williams, "Joseph Millerd Orpen's 'A Glimpse

into the Mythology of the Maluti Bushmen': A Contextual Introduction and Republished Text," *Southern African Humanities* 25, no. 1 (November 2013): 137–66; Rachel King, "'A Loyal Liking for Fair Play': Joseph Millerd Orpen and Knowledge Production in the Cape Colony," *South African Historical Journal* 67, no. 4 (October 2015): 410–32.

55. E.g., Victor Ellenberger, *La fin tragique des Bushmen: Les derniers hommes vivants de l'Age de la Pierre* (Paris: Amiot Dumont, 1953); Marion Walsham How, *The Mountain Bushmen of Basutoland* (Pretoria: J. L. Van Schaik, 1962).

56. J. W. Macquarrie, ed., *The Reminiscences of Sir Walter Stanford*, vol. 1, *1850–1885* (Cape Town: Van Riebeeck Society, 1958), 29.

57. Wright, *Bushman Raiders*, 138.

58. King and Challis, "Interior World."

59. John Wright, "Bushman Raiders Revisited," in Skotnes, *Claim to the Country*, 124. This point deserves further consideration elsewhere, but it is worth noting Robert Ross and Nigel Penn's observations about status in Cape society: that we should distinguish between behaviors regarded as criminally deviant and those seen as dishonorable, as the two are not necessarily synonymous and implicate different sorts of power relations. These ideas have been explored at the Cape but not, to my knowledge, in later frontier society. See Robert Ross, *Status and Respectability in the Cape Colony, 1750–1870: A Tragedy of Manners* (Cambridge: Cambridge University Press, 1999); Nigel Penn, *Murderers, Miscreants and Mutineers: Early Colonial Cape Lives* (Cape Town: Jacana, 2015), viii.

60. Much historical literature treats cattle raiding as analogous to warfare or as a sign of social distress; see Rachel King, "Cattle, Raiding and Disorder in Southern African History," *Africa* 87, no. 3 (August 2017): 607–30.

61. Wright, *Bushman Raiders*, 126; Vinnicombe, *People of the Eland*, 30, 58–62.

62. E.g., Timothy J. Stapleton, "Faku, the Mpondo and Colonial Advance in the Eastern Cape, 1834–53," in *Agency and Action in Colonial Africa: Essays for John E. Flint*, ed. Chris Youé and Tim Stapleton (Basingstoke, UK: Palgrave Macmillan, 2001), 12–33.

63. Vinnicombe, *People of the Eland*, 70n26.

64. Vinnicombe, 70n26.

65. Sam Challis, "Creolisation on the Nineteenth-Century Frontiers of Southern Africa: A Case Study of the AmaTola 'Bushmen' in the Maloti-Drakensberg," *Journal of Southern African Studies* 38, no. 2 (June 2012): 265–80.

66. Sam Challis, "Re-tribe and Resist: The Ethnogenesis of a Creolised Raiding Band in Response to Colonisation," in *Tribing and Un-tribing the Archive: Critical Enquiry into the Traces of the Thukela-Mzimvubu Region from the Early Iron Age until c. 1910*, ed. Caroline Hamilton and Nessa Leibhammer (Pietermaritzburg: University of KwaZulu-Natal Press, 2016), 282–99.

67. Geoffrey Blundell, *Nqabayo's Nomansland: San Rock Art and the Somatic Past* (Uppsala: Uppsala University, 2004); Lara Mallen, "Rock Art and Identity in the North Eastern Cape Province" (MA thesis, University of the Witwatersrand, 2008).

68. King, "Living on Edge." See also Rachel King, "Among the Headless Hordes: Missionaries, Outlaws, and Logics of Landscape in the Wittebergen Native Reserve, c. 1850–1879," *Journal of Southern African Studies* 44, no. 4 (August 2018): 659–80.

69. Vinnicombe, *People of the Eland*, 38.

70. Challis has suggested that leaving the slaughtered remains of livestock and focusing on a handful of farms constituted a program of resistance deployed by the raiders: Challis, "Re-tribe and Resist."

71. Vinnicombe, *People of the Eland*, 37–38.

72. Vinnicombe, 38.

73. E.g., Wright, *Bushman Raiders*, 78–83.

74. Theal, *Basutoland Records*, vol. 5, 126, 381–82.

75. Vinnicombe, *People of the Eland*, 40.

76. King, "Living on Edge"; King and Challis, "Interior World."

77. CA, Native Affairs (henceforth, NA) 273, C. Griffith to C. Brownlee, 9 September 1876.

78. Elizabeth Eldredge, *Power in Colonial Africa: Conflict and Discourse in Lesotho, 1870–1960* (Madison: University of Wisconsin Press, 2007), 46.

79. Peter Sanders, *"Throw Down White Man": Cape Rule and Misrule in Colonial Lesotho, 1871–1884* (Morija: Morija Museum and Archives, 2011), 35.

80. David-Frédéric Ellenberger, "History ea Basotho," *Leselinyana la Lesotho*, 25 June 1915.

81. CA, A.49-'79, Hamilton Hope to Charles Griffith, 23 June 1877.

82. Eldredge, *Power in Colonial Africa*, 46–47.

83. CA, A.49-'79, "Statement of Mapara" in John Austen to Charles Griffith, 24 January 1879.

84. E.g., CA, Accession 302, Joseph Orpen Papers, vol. 1, Joseph Orpen to Undersecretary for Native Affairs, 30 May 1907.

85. CA, A.49-'79, Emile Rolland to Hamilton Hope, 28 November 1877.

86. Eldredge, *Power in Colonial Africa*, 48–49.

87. CA, NA 277, "Statement of Mofetudi, 23 February" in John Austen to Charles Griffith, 3 March 1880.

88. King, "Among the Headless Hordes."

89. CA, A.49-'79, John Austen to Emile Rolland, 28 September 1878; NA 275, John Austen to Charles Griffith, 23 November 1878, enclosed in Charles Griffith to James Ayliff, 9 December 1878.

90. CA, NA 276, Charles Griffith to James Ayliff, 26 February 1879.

91. Anthony Atmore, "The Moorosi Rebellion: Lesotho, 1879," in *Protest and Power in Black Africa*, ed. Robert Rotberg and Ali Al'Amin Mazrui (New York: Oxford University Press, 1970), 2–35.

92. Nigel Penn, *The Forgotten Frontier: Colonist and Khoisan on the Cape's Northern Frontier in the 18th Century* (Cape Town: Double Storey Books, 2005), 41.

93. Penn, 166.

94. Robert Ross, "The !Kora Wars on the Orange River, 1830–1880," *Journal of African History* 16, no. 4 (October 1975): 562.

95. Ross, 563.

96. Ross, 568.

97. Unlike with Bushman raiders of the Drakensberg, we have little information as to the specific components of affect that led observers to designate a raider as "Korana" versus "Bushman" or any other of a number of active raiding affiliations. Ross suggests that one component of distinguishing between Korana and Bushman was the possession or lack of horses, respectively; see Ross, "!Kora Wars," 571. For a discussion of Karoo rock arts relating to communities of stock thieves and farm laborers and drawing on a range of material culture imagery, see Mark McGranaghan, "The Death of the Agama Lizard: The Historical Significances of a Multi-authored Rock-Art Site in the Northern Cape (South Africa)," *Cambridge Archaeological Journal* 26, no. 1 (February 2016): 157–79.

98. By the late nineteenth century, humanitarian interests in London and Cape Town had lobbied successfully to extend a measure of protection and consideration to those aboriginal San perceived as victimized by commandos (including white and Coloured members). Particularly on the northern frontier, San were still viewed to some extent as criminals but deserving of sympathy as victims of more ferocious "Bastaard" and Korana raiders. See especially José Manuel de Prada-Samper, "The Forgotten Killing Fields: 'San' Genocide and Louis Anthing's Mission to Bushmanland, 1862–1863," *Historia* 57, no. 1 (May 2012): 172–87.

99. Teresa Strauss, *War along the Orange: The Korana and the Northern Border Wars of 1868–9 and 1878–9* (Cape Town: Centre for African Studies, University of Cape Town, 1979), 45.

100. Strauss, 56.

101. Strauss, 85–86.

102. Strauss, 98.

103. Cf. Fred Morton, *When Rustling Became an Art: Pilane's Kgatla and the Transvaal Frontier, 1820–1902* (Cape Town: David Philip, 2009); King, "Cattle, Raiding, and Disorder."

104. Richard Reid, "Past and Presentism: The 'Precolonial' and the Foreshortening of African History," *Journal of African History* 52, no. 2 (July 2011): 150–52.

TWO

Between the Anxiogenic and the Soothing

Settlers' Engagements with Africans in Dance in Colonial Africa, 1920s–30s

CÉCILE FEZA BUSHIDI

THE HISTORIES OF DANCE ARE BOUND BY ANXIETY. THE somatic has long been suppressed in Western thought: Platonic hierarchies valued the reasoning mind over the undisciplined body, while Cartesian dualism divided matters of the flesh from rational consciousness. Euro-American histories of dance have organically absorbed two millennia

---

I wish to thank Andrea Grant and Yolana Pringle for inviting me to join this edited volume. At the National Museums of Kenya, I am grateful for the help and friendship of senior archivist Immelda Muoti. At the Kenya National Archives, I thank Richard Ambani and Peterson Kithuka for their assistance. I extend my thanks to Adam Branch for some book recommendations. I feel so lucky to share the classroom with Angie Epifano, Alison Kibble, and Alexandra Thomas, who are changing my way of thinking about performance and the politics of dance scholarship. To Mhoze Chikowero, Thomas DeFrantz, Cécile Fromont, Brett Shadle, Aniko Szucs, and Seth Steward Williams, all of whom have read or commented on this work-in-progress, I extend my most sincere appreciation. Various versions of this chapter have been presented at the Centre of African Studies Seminar Series and the Newnham College History Group at the University of Cambridge, and as part of the African Humanity Workshop at Yale University. I wish to extend my warmest gratitude to my Spring 2019 Fellows colleagues at the Center for Ballet and the Arts at NYU. An exceptional group of dance artists, scholars, and writers, they inspire me every day. No one but myself bears full responsibility for any errors herein of fact, interpretation, or judgment.

of mind-body tensions. Bodies in contact and in motion have been steeped in sentiments of malaise, thus enfeebling the body in aesthetic movements and the mind-body holistic balance.[1] Dance historians have also drawn attention to Christianity's discomfort with dance. Early European Classical and Christian texts condemned public dances—their denunciations based on the perception of bodily movements as prurient in nature. Christianity's espousal of Cartesian dualism further nurtured the Christian church's antipathy toward the fully fleshed public body in jouissance.[2] From the fifteenth century, the expansion of the missionary movement into Africa, the Americas, and beyond has infused moral anxieties about dance with starkly condemnatory discourses about pagan cultures that were regarded as "primitives."

In sub-Saharan colonial Africa, Catholic and Protestant mission bodies were ardent dissectors of indigenous expressive cultures that constructed systems of knowledge about local bodily and musical habits. Missionaries collected wooden masks and produced photographs and gouache paintings of ecstatic adorned bodies and religious processions. Dance and art historians have brilliantly mined these unique visual and material cultures to reimagine indigenous creative espousals of Christianity.[3] More often than not, however, missionaries tended to misunderstand indigenous body cultures, reacting with horror to a myriad of "ungodly" performed ceremonies and processions.[4] That colonial officials, missionaries, and Africans themselves felt uneasy about African gatherings through dance has received renewed attention in recent colonial historiography. African performances have instigated mayhem and fueled anxieties about political order and the perceived corrosive effects of modernity on African societies and cultures.[5] As dance writers and artists are well aware, anxieties about dance have given voice to a whole host of interrelated concerns.[6]

This chapter begins from the premise that if histories of dance have been bound by anxiety, such histories have been more contingent rather than innate. There is no truth in the claim that dance has only generated anxiety among its most fervent critic groups. Indeed, as Alessandro Arcangeli tells us, rather than sustained moral condemnation, both the Catholic and Protestant Churches tended to oscillate between a strict moral stance and an explicit tolerance of dance, with dance being decried as sinful under circumstances contingent upon "time, place, person, manner, intention."[7] Despite the moral panic surrounding close-couple dance genres, African adaptations of these ballroom-style dances have been praised for their so-called ability to enhance African sophistication.[8] Drawing on such ambivalent attitudes toward dance, this chapter constructs a framework through which to make sense of European settlers' anxieties about African performance as contingent. That is, as contingent upon the spatial context of dance itself; contingent upon individual and collective experiences of dance and energized bodies; and contingent upon the real, imagined, and projected ideas about the materiality of performance aesthetics.

I meditate on three scenes of settlers' lived experiences of Africans dancing in colonial Kenya and Uganda in the 1920s and 1930s—specifically, in the Kiambu district of Kenya's Central Province, the North Kavirondo district of the Nyanza Province, and Acholiland in northern Uganda. Settlers' transcultural contacts with African bodies in states of excess in performance fomented a complex of anxieties and quotidian angst.[9] Such negative emotions have been the staple of a recent body of literature on settler colonialism in Africa, particularly in regard to the entwined anxieties about disease, racial segregation, and white prestige.[10] European populations established in colonial cities incessantly complained about noisy local drums that grated on their nerves and affected their sleep.[11] But a narrow focus on dance as merely a trigger for settler anxiety fails to account for the contingency of such discomforts, frustrating any attempt to provide a holistic picture of settlers' diverse engagements with indigenous performance. Accordingly, this chapter also explores a scenario in which "African dance" soothed settlers' bodies and minds: the scenic safari environment created a space wherein the settler gaze turned African performance into a performing art worthy of aesthetic interest.

I examine three case studies that stage what Ann Laura Stoler has identified as the "unique cultural configurations" in which European middle-class morality and cultures "were given new political meaning in specific social orders":[12] the Limuru Settler's Association in Kiambu, settler responses to the trespass of Luhya mourners on a white woman's property in North Kavirondo, and the colonial gaze and interpolation of Africans performing during a safari in Acholiland. First, after 1920, Kenyan colonial authorities seized increasing amounts of land for the benefit of former British soldiers. The next two decades proved critical in the evolution of settler power and land politics in the colony. In the Rift Valley and Central Province, land grievances among the Kikuyu peoples reached new heights in the early 1930s, particularly in the southern district of Kiambu, which had long witnessed very brutal land appropriation policies. The Kenya Land Commission was appointed in April 1932 to address such land issues. As this case study explores, the Limuru Settlers' Association became increasingly concerned about settler land and security in Tigoni, a settled area located in the southern district of Kiambu. Centering on Kikuyu dances and performed festivities, the association's anxieties reflected settler fears regarding their forced cohabitation with Africans, as well as cattle disease, crime, land ownership, and Kikuyu politicization.

Second, the 1931 discovery of gold in the district of North Kavirondo was followed by an influx of European settlers and international prospectors and traders in Kakamega. These settlers reinvented their homes within the reserves of the Luhya peoples, but remained intolerant of physical proximity to Africans. This second case study examines the loud and panicked response of Mrs. Ingles to Luhya funeral processions, and the perception of this incident in the broader settler community. Although a short-lived and isolated episode, both Mrs. Ingles's response and those of her mining neighbors—who had renamed their quarter Piccadilly Circus—reveal the dynamics of Europeans' adaptive behavior and excessive worrying about race relations.

The third case study examines the musings of a colonial wife on safari, revolving around her interwar memories in an unnamed location of Acholiland. The Protectorate of Uganda did not have as many European settlers as Kenya. By the early 1920s, the prospect of white settlement had failed, partly due to an unclear policy, a limited availability of "unclaimed" land, and the 1920–21 slump of cotton prices.[13] The northern Ugandan territory of Acholiland remained on the margins of colonial developmen. Mavis Stone's recollection of safari experiences in this region promised European readers a sensory escape. I wish to suggest that her memories of the Acholi peoples dancing seem to have soothed her mind in Africa while staging a peculiar Otherness dancing.

Aware that space affects our experience and readings of reality and bodies, the use of written and visual sources in this chapter draws on the cognizance that "bodies are frequently marked as in place or out of place."[14] The oral testimony that the Kenya Land Commission collected from the Limuru Settlers' Association exposes settlers' unease about the official recognition of a Kikuyu vicinity in the heart of Tigoni. When confronted with local debates about the prohibition of Kikuyu dances on European farms, it becomes apparent that such evidence is entwined with antecedent and concomitant settler anxiety about specific performance genres that staged Kikuyu protest between the late 1920s and the mid-1930s. An unpublished official report on the perceived excesses of African leisure, Mrs. Ingles's stressful encounter with ecstatic African bodies yields considerable emotional weight when woven into settler women's writings on the topography of Kakamega. Finally, Mavis Stone's memories of Acholiland are extracted from *Tales from the Dark Continent*—a volume largely inspired by the 1979 BBC Radio 4 recordings of some fifty British men and women who lived and worked in colonial Africa.[15] I sense that Mrs. Stone's snapshots of her experience of "Acholi dance" in safari settings resonated with the visual aesthetics of ballet. My interpretation centers on how the visuality invested in such recollections may have operated to comfort Mrs. Stone. Colonial-era and contemporary ethnographies provide valuable details regarding the aesthetics and sociology of performance. In addition to enhancing our understanding of why certain styles have generated so much tension, these ethnographies shed light on the complexity of performance that settlers and colonial records often failed to register. I hope that the overall readings of sources offer insight into how settlers' emotional responses to dance have been shaped by cultural and social expectations within specific spaces.

By putting a spotlight on settlers' wavering anxieties about African corporealities, this discussion gives center stage to "African dance" as a settler matter. From contested working and living spaces to those of recreation and wonder, I seek to expand the analysis of the range of the behavioral, linguistic, and epistemic tools that colonists have used when constructing a racial and cultural alterity for themselves.[16] Doing so prompts the question of how their anxieties elucidate the material and affective effects of colonial-era representations of performance and bodies in/from Africa. Indeed, how stories of settlers in contact with performing Africans converse with those regarding their adaptations to African cultures, peoples, and environments needs to be considered, in large part because these stories exhibited "the quotidian assertion of European dominance in the colonies."[17]

In making sense of the origins of such antipodal sentiments toward African performance, it is important to remember that since the late 1860s, European spectatorship had been castigating visual tropes of "African dancers" as worrisome and wonderful. Much has been said about the European and North American spectacles that constructed an anxiogenic dance archive from Africa wherein tableaux, performers, and drums depicted visual cultures as emotional sites of wariness. These shows evoked wavering emotions of admiration, wonder, and disgust among metropolitan viewers, while celebrating the imperial and colonial projects.[18] Early twentieth-century image-making practices similarly projected pictures of an overwrought Africa on Euro–North American screens. By the 1930s, American and British adventure films like *Trader Horn* (1931) and *Sanders of the River* (1937), as well as safari documentaries such as *Dark Rapture* (1938), featured images of frenzied prewar "blood dances" and colorful "welcoming" dances in threatening and enchanting sceneries of Africa.[19]

These interlaced histories reveal the significance of dance in the visual and sensory histories of Africa. I wish to situate settlers' contingent anxieties about dance within these broader visual materials that disseminated images of "Africa as a dream/nightmare," and as an emotional territory in which threat, nuisance, beauty, and pleasure co-existed.[20] Such a conception of African spaces may explain why settlers could experience both anxiety and, in certain instances and spaces, awe when witnessing or engaging with African performance.

The Calamity of Ngoma, Animals, and People in Tigoni

In 1932, the Kenya Land Commission was appointed to consider the practicalities of increasing land for African occupation and to address the unequal distribution of land between settlers and Africans and the inadequacies of the African reserves. Europeans had settled in some of the colony's most lush and arable lands: from Nairobi and Kiambu in the south to Fort Hall in the north, and from Nakuru in the west to Nyeri and Kerugoya in the east. Their presence put tremendous pressure on many Kikuyu communities, forcefully altering their ancestral ties to land. By 1933, about 109.5 square miles of Kikuyu arable land had been seized for colonial settlement, most of it in the Kiambu and Limuru areas.[21] While some Kikuyu families and individuals lived—"squatted"—on settler-owned farms under various forms of tenancy agreements, many of them were pushed into reserves, with the most able-bodied men providing a workforce for European holdings. By the early 1930s, the land necessary for Kikuyu sociocultural life had become scarce, and the reserves were inadequate and unhealthy.[22] As part of the commission's objective of collecting oral and written evidence from both settlers and Africans, colonial officials began touring Kenya's rural regions toward the end of 1932.

In the district of Kiambu, the proceedings emerged as a platform whereby the Limuru Settlers' Association voiced settler concerns about the prospective recognition of a Kikuyu-owned island in the middle of Tigoni. Neighboring the town of Limuru, Tigoni was a small highlands area located at an altitude of roughly 7,000 feet. Blessed with a temperate climate ideal for tea plantations, Tigoni was promoted as an location suitable for white settlement from the early 1920s. A farmhouse had been converted into a hotel, the Diocesan Limuru Girls High School for settlers' daughters had been founded, and the whites-only Kentmere Club offered settlers a space of exclusive sociability for shooting parties, dinners, dancing soirées, and retreat. By the early 1930s, construction plans were under way for the erection of rest houses for colonial officials who had the misfortune of being sent to unhealthy districts. During their leave, these men, their wives, and their children would reside and regain their health in Tigoni. A space where metropolitan cultures were recreated, Tigoni was envisioned as essential to the existential and territorial expansion of European populations in Kiambu and the rest of the colony. With several stretches of the district already relinquished to the Kikuyu reserves, the Limuru settlers were steadfast in their desire to protect Tigoni from any African physical and cultural influences, which were conceived as unsuitable. While a few Kikuyu had already been "squatting on the land without sanction," they had been allowed to stay because they provided labor for colonists, particularly on dairy farms.[23]

The Limuru Settlers' Association's testimony on behalf of the settler community makes clear that their reluctance to concede more land to Africans was entwined with the projected disastrous consequences of "ngomas [dances] and native gatherings."[24] The emergence of the threat that Kikuyu dancing cultures represented throughout the district of Kiambu had coincided with colonists' territorial claims to Tigoni from the mid-1920s. It transpires that the Kiambu settlers' anxieties about Kikuyu dances were entangled with moral concerns about Africans' so-called primitiveness and the physical health of farmers' cattle stock, as well as spatial segregation and crime. In addition, farmers' negative attitudes toward Kikuyu dances unveil some of the premises on which they based their demands for more power at a time of increased Kikuyu protest.

There is little doubt that most Kiambu settlers sensed Kikuyu performance traditions as a cacophony of loud shouts and incessant drumbeats.

Indeed, the Kiswahili term *"ngoma"* as used by this European group subsumed any indigenous forms of bodily musical performance and their presumed essential nature as excessive, disorderly, and noisy. By March 1928, a few landowners had complained to the district commissioner (DC) about the dance-music style *ndarama* being held on their *shamba* (farm or plantation). Irritated and angry, they experienced ndarama's drumbeats and vocals as mere deafening noise produced through "a competition between persons cowing as to who will make the most noise." They construed ndarama as crude and having a "bad moral effect on natives," characterizing the revelers' enthusiastic screaming as half beast, half human.[25] Having developed as a postwar rhythmic freestyle during which the dancers freely shook their heads and bodies to rhythmic beats, ndarama music-dance—as well as new couple dances performed to accordion and guitar music and drums—brought together men and women living between their Kiambu homes and Nairobi. By the early 1930s, this crowd had turned Limuru's outdoor spaces into joyful hubs of youthful sociability. It is hardly surprising that the Limuru Settlers' Association anxiously anticipated that a Kikuyu-reserved island would become a hotbed of "savage" behavior and youthful debauchery. Settler apprehensions about ngoma close to their shamba conveyed their concerns less for the so-called moral progress of Africans than for the proximity of uncouth modes of leisure that were antithetical to their perceptions of themselves as sophisticated and restrained.

A Kikuyu-owned space enveloped by a European community was one of projected afflictions, particularly the spread of disease. Such anxieties were inevitably bound with Kikuyu performed festivities. Fears that "native" beasts—which were deemed impure—on settled areas would contaminate European dairy farmers' purebred cattle were genuine. Although "native-owned cattle" had "been kept out of the area," the grim prospect of having to bear ngoma affairs involving cattle certainly filled dairy farmers with dread.[26] It is true that such ngoma events still occurred in Kiambu in the early 1930s. For instance, the record of *nguru* dancing events in Kiambu attests to the continued presence of one of the oldest forms of Kikuyu sociability—a feast celebrating the *anake* (warriors). With their waists adorned with belts made of leather, their heads encircled by a crown of feathers, and their chests decorated with bead chains, nguru glorified Kikuyu warriors in choreographed drill movements. Nguru had long served as preparation for raiding and military defense by bringing together warriors from different territorial units across southern central Kenya. Come raiding time, the Kikuyu elders organized meat feasts in honor of the warriors.[27] The colonial administration had suppressed Kikuyu raids by the mid-1910s. But in the late 1920s, some young Kikuyu men were still celebrating traditions of warriorhood in their full warrior array and dance. Nguru festivities had remained closely associated with meat consumption. Such cattle requirement was a settler and administrative problem based on the argument that it incited cattle theft. In 1928, the DC even considered prohibiting nguru on European farms on the grounds that it was at the source of such crimes.[28]

Thus, dairy farmers' anxieties over dancing events compounded fears about stock health, crime, and the breakdown of law and order, amplifying moral rationales for total segregation. In Tigoni, spaces for Africans were to be physically distinct from white settled lands. Arguing for the removal of "illegally" settled "natives," a counter to the official recognition of a Kikuyu-owned vicinity in Tigoni claimed that police would struggle to control crime (induced by ngoma) because they had little jurisdiction over African reserves.[29] In settlers' minds, the Tigoni land arrangement seemed a nightmare scenario for the preservation of law and order because of its unclear status. If the space were to be converted into a reserve—albeit one physically detached from the reserve proper—they could not fathom how the police would safeguard order in this African domain. Settler wariness was not entirely unfounded. Legally speaking, a Kikuyu-owned space turned reserve would make it difficult for the police to control African performed events—such as funeral processions—that remained sanctioned within the reserves. Moreover, jurisdiction over ngoma dancing within the Kiambu reserves had been handed over to the Kikuyu chiefs and headmen in the mid-1920s.[30] As far as Tigoni's settlers were concerned, the absence of border and police control would leave their economic and existential interests vulnerable to "native" encroachment.

In addition to this, their anxieties about Kikuyu dances on Europeans' estates possibly attested to broader public unease about Kikuyu challenges to settler hegemony in the White Highlands. In 1929–30, central colonial Kenya went through an unprecedented sociopolitical crisis when colonial authorities attempted to ban the clitoridectomy of girls, a central tenet of Kikuyu culture. This crisis polarized the Kikuyu community—some supporting the prohibition of the practice, while others called for its continuance. During this period of turmoil, thousands of Kikuyu peoples performed the *muthirigu* dance-song in front of missions and on settler farms in protesting against colonial interference. The political organization Kikuyu Central Association (KCA) largely supported such protests. Despite being banned by the colonial government in 1929, muthirigu kept on being performed well into the mid-1930s throughout the Central Province and the Rift Valley. The popularity of the genre triggered the anxiety of colonial officials and settlers about the political nature of dances such as ndarama and nguru, which were being performed on European farms at that time.[31] Although a government notice prohibited muthirigu and ndarama in Thika, located near Limuru, officials struggled to uniformly enforce the notices in all the Kikuyu districts.[32] The region-wide proliferation of Kikuyu protest dances during the first half of the 1930s could only threaten settler hegemony. The Limuru settlers' apprehensions of Kikuyu ngoma and gatherings have given indirect voice to genuine concerns about the political undercurrents of such dancing events, as well as the direct challenge to settlers' status and legitimacy that such genres symbolized.

Further west, in the North Kavirondo district of Nyanza Province, the 1931 discovery of gold in Kakamega precipitated European and international settlement on the Luhya reserves. Mrs. Ingles's reaction to ngoma illuminates settlers' thorny adaptive behavior and provides a lens into old and new scenes of social discord among settler communities, between settlers and the colonial administration, as well as between settlers and Africans.

Disorder in Piccadilly Circus

On a stormy day in March 1934, Mrs. Ingles, settled a few miles south of Kakamega town, got very irritated when she found a "crowd of natives" seeking shelter on her veranda. The horde, she soon found, were mourners engaging in a funeral ceremony. To her dismay, they "even pressed into her house" twice, prompting her to call the Kakemega police to remove the "invaders." Twice in the course of the mourning rituals the police swiftly sent *askari*—Africans responsible for maintaining order—to sweep the ngoma mob off her patio.[33]

Most of the grievers were from the Isukha and Idakho communities. Belonging to the wider Luhya ethnic group, these populations had long inhabited the Kakamega region, where rich soil and water sources were favorable to agriculture.[34] On that day, the mourners were lamenting the passing and celebrating the life of Mlango Mulama. No doubt the crowd made for a colorful spectacle: some were topless, their bodies adorned with red ochre and sisal fibre aprons; some held sticks and spears; others wore cotton shirts, trousers, and skirts. All wailed, sang, and danced. While he was living in North Kavirondo, German colonial anthropologist Günter Wagner hardly recorded any Isukha and Idakho funerals. He nonetheless noted how Luhya mourners could often display a highly energetic and cheerful behavior.[35] By 1934, the Isukha and Idakho celebrants may have been involved in performance genres akin to the *isukuti* processional dances, the social substance of which drew on long-established local funeral arts. Unfolding across several days, weeks, or months after a burial, the fast-paced and energetic isukuti processions, which derived their name from the deep sounds of the isukuti drum, brought together wailing and singing families, clans, and neighbors in rites of passage such as funerals and initiation ceremonies.[36]

Mrs. Ingles's sudden physical proximity with the Isukha and Idakho mourners reflects the tension between colonial and colonized bodies, and particularly between colonial women and indigenous men. She was the first to lodge a complaint against these celebrants in the Sigalagala location, which settlers had renamed Piccadilly Circus by the early 1930s.[37] Her isolated reaction and response to such a festival of noise and ecstatic bodies invading her living space are nonetheless worth further consideration. The brief episode not only points to an individual case of a settler's perplexing adaptations to African lives, but also is enmeshed in the salient male-dominated discursive features of gendered histories of colonialism. Moreover, Mrs. Ingles's short-lived stress provides a lens through which to think about the fragility of a temporary settler community whose gold-mining ventures in North Kavirondo did not go unchallenged by the Luhya communities.

In her fascinating historical account of the Kakamega gold rush, Priscilla Shilaro writes that the 1931 discovery of goldfields in the Luhya reserves provoked a rapid increase in white settlement. Driven by the sensational outpourings of gold findings, Kenya's settlers, whose farming activities had been hit by the Great Depression and locust invasion, rushed to Kakamega with saucepans and sieves. They were soon followed by foreign private individuals, wealthy prospectors, and large companies. With the support of the Colonial Office in London and the Kenya Land Commission, gold seekers from all walks of life were granted short-term renewable mining licenses. By 1931, the Mining Ordinance granted settlers unrestricted rights to exploit the colony's mineral wealth. The alienation of land from the Luhya reserves violated the 1930 Native Land Trust Ordinance, which legally protected such areas from non-African intrusion. In 1932, the Kakamega gold rush precipitated a controversial amendment to this ordinance, so that the demands for land from gold miners and mining companies were met. While the colony and London hoped to reap the benefits of this temporary measure, they wrongly assumed that it would promote Luhya prosperity. Although the Crown enjoyed unlimited access to the gold underneath the Kakamega reserves, surface land rights still belonged to the Luhya peoples.[38]

The changing topography of Kakamega and its proximate surroundings offers a rather more complex picture, since Mrs. Ingles's frustration with the ngoma funeral processions unfolded in a reimagined London. Until the discovery of minefields, Kakamega township had been a quiet station with a few Indian shops and an African-owned market. By 1934, when large mining companies were engaged in reef mining, Kakamega township became crowded, boasting luxury camps, hotels, bars, European shops, and commercial enterprises.[39] Piccadilly Circus became the center of mining activity. As settler Eve Bache recalls, "There [was] a strangely homely feeling and air about this African Klondyke."[40] Indeed, on the road to Piccadilly, one would walk past Seven Dials (Covent Garden's road junction in London). Northwest of Piccadilly, Golders Green was colored by British gardens, and so was Palmers Green further west. Further south, a wealthy American speculator had "opened the district" by building the Hampstead Heath Aerodrome.[41] Mrs. Ingles's discomfort unfolded in a place where gold miners reimagined home while being much aware that Kakamega's London was not truly theirs. Such cognitive dissonance inevitably caused anxiety.

When a furious Mrs. Ingles asked Kakamega's mining warden how he intended to deal with "native ngomas in future," both the warden and the DC of North Kavirondo were aware of the "good deal of prominence [that had been] given to this incident in certain circles." As the DC noted, a woman living alone on a business plot who had Africans invading her living space could very well be "alarming."[42] There is no doubt that Piccadilly's settlers were inclined to the chronic feelings of isolation pervasive among rural Kenyan settler communities. Maybe they were filled with fictional dreads about "black peril"—the exaggerated and mostly imagined fear that black men intended to rape white women.[43] In the peculiar quotidian of male domination and cross-cultural contacts that shaped the lives of European populations, white women—vastly outnumbered by men—were assumed (by white men) to lack the knowledge required to "handle" black men appropriately. As such, white women's presence in colonial spaces seemed to necessitate a more stringent policing of race relations. It was they who enforced the color line in order to maintain both their own reputation and the colonial racial hierarchy.[44] For these reasons, it is hardly surprising that the mining warden recommended that if "such a complaint is received by the Police from a European lady within half a mile, a European Officer should proceed at once personally to the spot."[45] This suggests that African forces were deemed insufficient and undependable when it came to defending the bodies of white women like Mrs. Ingles from the threat posed by dancing African bodies, a threat connected to the perceived states of excess activated by performance.

The most salient feelings of insecurity that Piccadilly gold seekers experienced lay in plausible fears of menaces from Africans, the latter of whom were considerably anxious about the rapid alienation of their lands. As early as 1931, Luhya resistance to foreign prospectors and miners was commonplace. In response to Europeans and North Americans freely pitching their tents without showing any respect to Luhya landowners, some Luhya individuals and groups assaulted foreigners or confiscated their mining materials. By 1932, race relations in Kakamega were tense: the prosecution and imprisonment of a Luhya man for obstruction bred widespread anti-mining and anti-European sentiments.[46] Although the number of foreign miners had declined by March 1934, organized resistance to the mining industry took shape through the efforts of the North Kavirondo Central Association (NKCA). United in their grief for the loss of land, the NKCA and Kikuyu Central Association established a working relationship.[47] It may be that this confluence of events explains why Piccadilly's European circles felt directly concerned by Mrs. Ingles's plight. Indeed, the incident symbolized a case of racial confrontation instigated by one of their members: considering that the Luhya peoples had surface rights to the land on which she lived, Mrs. Ingles had been wrong to complain that the mourners were trespassing or invading her land.

While the mining warden and the DC assured Mrs. Ingles that they would protect her, the ngoma incident soon became a matter of her moral decline, and provided an outlet for anxieties about the vulnerability of the colonial body politic in Kakamega's London. The DC wished he had the "power to prevent such a European woman from living alone in the Reserve, or for that matter, alone on a business plot in the Township."[48] Mrs. Ingles was scorned for acting recklessly in seemingly choosing to live alone, thus inviting the threat of assault. In essence, she was cast in male projections onto the white female body in the colonial space. Police assurances turned into chastisement.[49] Besides, her social status was deemed dangerous in the familial space of Piccadilly society. Husbands, wives, and their children had settled on the minefields. Families even organized a Christmas party for the ninety white children.[50] Needless to say, Mrs. Ingles "fell outside the colonial space to which European women were assigned: custodians of family welfare and respectability and dedicated and willing subordinates to and supporters of men."[51] Compounded by her behavior and unreasonable reaction to ngoma, Mrs. Ingles's idiosyncratic status represented a threat to white hegemony and respectability in Kakamega's London. None of her entrepreneurial spirit and professional competence was considered in the incident. In light of the dominance of large companies from 1933 onward, she may have been working for or have owned a company operating in the area. Kakamega's minefields have been home to determined women settlers and colonial wives who became prospectors and entrepreneurs in their own rights.

The mourning-performing crowd was exculpated by colonial officials. As the DC noted, "there was no criminal intention from the crowd nor even a desire to annoy, merely to seek shelter as any native will," and the rain could not have been foreseen. Such large-scale funeral performances were so rare by that time that the mining warden found "it a mistake on [their] part to prohibit native ceremonials of this kind but [they] would endeavour to control them better though [they] seldom had notice of them." Mrs. Ingles simply had to cope with "inconveniences of this kind [which] were unfortunately unavoidable sometimes in a native Reserve."[52] Straddling London and Africa, Mrs. Ingles inhabited an uncanny space that conditioned her cultural expectations of life in Piccadilly while creating potential for discomfort when such expectations were disturbed. She was unable to adapt to cultural environments that she had chosen to inhabit in order to strike it rich.

As a whole, the excessive nature of settlers' demands, their economic ambitions, and the character of their settlements restricted Africans' performance space. Reflecting a perverse insight into the consequences of the Kakamega's gold rush on the Luhya peoples, the DC objected to "shepherding ngoma" on the grounds that Africans would think that the reserve was no longer theirs.⁵³ By the time the Kenya Land Commission was launched, land expropriation had already pushed Luhya and Kikuyu modes of celebration, mourning, and worship into restricted ngoma spaces. By the mid-1930s, land set aside for Luhya ceremonies was shrinking as the reserves became crowded.⁵⁴ By the time the Limuru Settlers' Association testified before the Kenya Land Commission, spaces dedicated to Kikuyu ceremonies were gradually being erased from Kikuyuland. In the southern areas of the Nyeri district, the Kikuyu elders testifying before the Commission deplored the loss of sacred lands for worship and ceremonies.⁵⁵ No space had been set aside for Kikuyu cultural traditions in areas like Kiambu. In fact, as the Commission Report explicitly acknowledged, no arrangements had been made "for the creation of public dancing grounds and for markets" in the entire colony.⁵⁶ While the problem of securing land for sociocultural purposes was particularly pressing in the Kikuyu districts, the Commission failed to listen to Luhya concerns and protect Luhya land rights, thus affecting their cultural rights.

In both the Limuru and Kakamega scenes, settler attempts to recreate exclusive European worlds fomented real, exaggerated, and projected negative contacts with ngoma, bodies, and animals. In Tigoni, the anxiogenic language that merged the issue of ngoma with those related to cattle health, the district's health, and white security was integral in the shaping of a domineering but contested and threatened settler-farmer identity. Such unnuanced emotive language about ngoma provided the gist of segregationist reasoning and allowed settler-farmers to make their demands for land more heard, thus further expropriating the Kikuyu communities in the economic fiefdom of Kiambu. The Piccadilly episode implied that settler communities in Kakamega's London were by no means unified and homogeneous in their reactions to ngoma. There, concerns about ngoma operated less as a powerful claim to legitimacy than as a reminder of the fragile and temporary status of the white minority. Ngoma as a settler matter encapsulates a mosaic of individual and communal exposures to colonial situations both internal and external to settler communities.

A third scenario in nonsettled space offered colonists a markedly different experience and contrasting expectations of Africa's performing cultures. I shall now consider settler engagements with Africans dancing in the safari space. In this regard, I seek to close the circle of the original idea that settlers' anxieties about African dancing cultures have been contingent upon the spatial context of dance and ideas about the aesthetics of performance. Colonial Africa was construed as an emotional realm in which displeasure and pleasure coexisted. In stark contrast to ngoma in Kenya's settled areas, isolated pictures of dance in the seemingly "uncolonized" landscapes of northern Uganda soothed settlers in a way that spawned other means of European self-reinvention in Africa.

Ngoma Safari: Imperial Images of Enchanted Africa

No theme in settlers' bodily encounters with ngoma offers starker contrast to Mrs. Ingles's stress than that of the hearing and observation of ngoma in the safari context. Despite their wariness towards ngoma in European settlements, colonists' sensory experiences of African dancing cultures in the escapist, exotic, and romanticized safari space soothed their embodied selves. Safari as a recreational Western practice has been captured in twentieth-century adventure films, which were embedded in the history of Western visual and literary imaginings of Africa. Adventure safari films shot in East Africa gained prominence in the 1950s, particularly with Hollywood films like *Mogambo* (1953) and *Safari* (1956). Yet prior to this period, the emergence of new forms of mobility and film technology in the late 1930s enabled Western filmmakers to capture African worlds in stylized motion.[57] Symbolizing Western transcultural contacts with African peoples, these films featured villagers eager to perform "welcome" dances for the traveling camera, disseminating images of the spectacular dances, colorful costumes, animals, and nature encountered on safari.

Mavis Stone looked back on a safari trip that took place in the northern Acholi district of Uganda. Acholiland, notably, had remained on the margins of colonial development in Uganda. Taxes and the monetization of the economy were of course introduced. While the region provided labor for the southern parts of the Protectorate, the system of touring officers facilitated the collection of taxes.[58] Strong and resistant to disease, Mrs. Stone considered herself fortunate to be capable of withstanding the rigor of outdoor life in Central East Africa. It was such resilience that enabled her to travel with her husband, a colonial executive, on a safari tour intended to collect taxes and create bonds with the northern populations.[59]

It was on safari that she appears to have experienced typical touristic modes of safari encounters that speak to contrasting settler sensitivities to African corporeal and musical cultures. It was on safari that she recalls being enraptured by ngoma combining people, drums, and nature. Her memories conjured images of peace and tranquility that reflected imperial visual tropes of Africa: people were musicking and moving in their so-called natural environment, in the exotic realm of the timeless and the unchanging. Flanked by a "tribal" storyteller who entertained them on their tour, Mrs. Stone recalls her pleasure at camping in a region with "magnificent scenery, long khaki-coloured plains with the flat-topped thorn trees and scrub bushes—with a lot of game near the game reserves, particularly buffalo, waterbuck and elephant." She recalls her delight at hearing the sounds of drumbeats from nearby villages. At night, seated by the campfire and gazing at the stars, she recalls feeling that she could cope with ngoma because she and her husband felt emotionally closer to "the heart of Africa" and Africans themselves. Indeed, she said, "they [Africans] were at their best then."[60] Mrs. Stone's recollections of her safari trip seem to imply that Africans behaved better in an environment eliding colonial impositions, ideas of modernity, and settler demands.

She could have been a supporting actress in the interwar safari documentary *Dark Rapture* (1938). Helmed by Belgian-born documentary filmmaker Armand Denis and his American-born producer wife, Leila Roosevelt (second cousin of Eleanor Roosevelt), *Dark Rapture* documents the couple's expedition from Belgium to the Congo. The film captures their risky and scenic journey through the snowy peaks of Morocco's Atlas Mountains, the lush scenery of Central and East Africa, and Congo's "flagellation rituals."[61] Projecting performing cultures in Africa as moments of joyful transcultural contacts and African "hospitality," *Dark Rapture* constitutes a watershed moment in the visual history of Africa. As Amy Staples notes, this is particularly true of the film's immersive images of spectacular dances, headdresses, and clothes. Shot with the highly mobile Akeley camera mounted on a car, the safari documentary engaged metropolitan viewers with shots of dancing Africans and quick-moving wildlife. Performed for the camera, the colorful customs of the Mangbetu and Tutsi peoples dancing unfold as immersive touristic attractions in which expedition members—along with the film audiences—could experience the village space. Homemade sound technologies recorded "sounds from Africa," magnifying the audience's sense of embodied and aesthetic realism of faraway realities.[62] Where the "blood dances" of *Trader Horn* (1931) and *Sanders of the River* (1937) projected nightmarish images of Africa, scenes of *Dark*

Rapture's "African dances" portrayed a magical and sentimental Africa "in the heart of Africa," to borrow Mrs. Stone's take on the stock phrase.

Her memories of observing, hearing, and feeling the "welcoming" dancing Africans in stunning landscapes produced romanticized moments of human warmth and pleasure rather than dread, fear, and irritation. Of the fragments of dance movements, scenes, craft, and clothing she remembers seeing, Mrs. Stone said: "Wherever we went there was nearly always a dance laid on. In Acholi, particularly, they did the most beautiful dancing with little drums and leopard skins and those magnificent headdresses that they wore made out of sisal, almost like long blond hair. They did this leaping and dancing and it was almost like a ballet."[63] Mrs. Stone's snapshots of her experience of "Acholi dance" in a visually striking scenery elevated ngoma to a performing art valued in Western canons: classical ballet, the highest form of European dance canon at that time. Here, dancers' leaps resonated with ballet's aesthetic ideals of ethereal elevation and graceful athleticism. The comparison of the sisal headdresses to blonde hair conjured romantic imageries of beauty, delicacy, and litheness.[64] By investing such visual power in memories of ngoma enmeshed in sceneries that evoked romantic feelings, Mrs. Stone conveys the harmonious vision of idealized bodies in dance as calming; the effects and vitality of such memories seem to have offered a tranquil escape from the perils of her colonial quotidian.[65]

Her recollection of ngoma by viewing it through the lens of ballet reflects Andrew Apter's discussion of the imperial spectacles that negotiated relations between colonized and colonizers in Nigeria and on metropolitan stages.[66] Drawing on a dynamic approach to imperial productions of visuality, Apter examines these relationships through the lens of photography, sports, performances of durbar and celebrations of empire. It is unclear whether the ballet that Mrs. Stone remembers observing in Acholiland was a serendipitous encounter or whether it formed the mise-en-scène of a cultural "welcome" spectacle staged for and adapted to the gaze of traveling officers. This dance, however, as recalled and sensed through the prism of balletic aesthetics, morphed into a metropolitan form of spectacle (ballet). Through this process, Mrs Stone recast *ngoma* into what Apter calls "culture as theatre, an idiom adroitly 'recognized' as worthy of elevation" to a western stage.[67] Mrs. Stone's act of ratifying unfamiliar dances through ballet transformed the recalled "Acholi dance" into an aesthetically suitable and legible spectacle for both herself and an audience eager to consume vivid stories of embodied exotic encounters. An antithesis to the perceived excess of ngoma and bodies treated with anxiety in settled colonial areas, Africans dancing in safari settings gained a sense of respectability that almost allowed it to fall into a canonical category of performing art to be consumed.

Mrs. Stone's amalgamation of romanticized exotic Otherness and familiarity in depicting "Acholi dance" fails to consider Acholi dancing cultures as an integral part of dance history. Indeed, she fails to note that the Acholi clans possess some of the richest oral performance customs of Central East Africa, a variety of dance (*myel*) forms incarnating Acholi cosmologies and customs. From the royal dance (*bwola*) to the courtship dance (*laraka-raka*), performance has been central to Acholi clans' sociability and religious practices.[68] Her account lacks any interest in these Acholi performance idioms in the historical, social, political, and aesthetic contexts of their display.[69] This is important to note because she was traveling with her colonial official husband as part of taxation enforcement, which means that the observed communities were not free of colonial coercion and thus fully immersed in history. Indeed, the Acholi clans' early encounter with British colonial rule has been marked by violent colonial pacification, enforced mass displacement, and punitive collective violence.[70] In societies within which power, influence, and status had long been widely distributed, the colonial impositions frustrated Acholi compromise with the colonial authorities.[71] This raises questions about some of the ways in which dance may have translated the Acholi clans' traumatic history with colonial power.

Scenes of settler lives and memories in colonial Kenya and Uganda offer a contrasting mosaic of emotional reactions to and understanding of ngoma. The Kenyan district of Kiambu was plagued with struggles over land, as settler farmers were obsessed with maintaining economic, territorial, and racial hegemony. In this context, the concerns of the Limuru Settlers' Association about settlers' proximity to ngoma were entwined with fears of cattle disease. Anxieties over ngoma heightened calls for greater rural segregation and exacerbated local concerns about crime and the breakdown of law and order. Dance generated political anxiety as Kikuyu protest in performance challenged settlers' status and legitimacy. In North Kavirondo's Eldorado of Piccadilly, Mrs. Ingles's dismay at the invasive bodies of mourning "natives" in her business space constructed ngoma as a threat to the hegemony of a temporary settler body politic. "Native" performances evoked prejudice, mistrust, and aversion between settlers and African communities, as well as between settlers themselves. Both scenarios portrayed ngoma as an existential threat to settlers' ability to create new worlds that were distinctively their own, which Africans were not expected to inhabit. In the context of environments reflecting an obsession with the spatialization of social order, Africans' bodies in states of excess in dance were felt as disruptive elements. But the ngoma problem as a settler problem has to be cast in terms of the issue of European settlements disrupting lands that had long been sacred domains of indigenous performance and worship. As part of this, the settler matter with ngoma ought not to be isolated from the fragilities of colonial governance, notably the administration's inability to command space in central colonial Kenya.

Drawing on the visual history of representations of Africa as a continent of emotional paradox—a land of beauty and menace—settler sentiments toward Africans dancing demonstrate how the reductionist belief that ngoma were merely off-putting to settlers should be reconsidered. Indeed, a deeper reading of settler anxieties about "native" dance yields insights into how such negative and condemnatory reactions varied from one spatial context to another, and from one person to another. Such readings reveal that "African dance" as experienced by Europeans generated both horror and delight. One can argue that in environments that seemingly elided the perverse nature of colonial structures, ngoma against the backdrop of scenic natural landscapes—an image far removed from that of the African reserves, as well as spaces of settler economic domination—transformed from a threat to settlers' interests and well-being into a soothing spectacle. Settlers' reaction to and engagement with ngoma thus depended on their unique experiences of Africa's colonized spaces.

Aware of the limitations of the case studies examined in this chapter, I have no intention to make generalizations. Yet it is very likely that in the living, mining, and escapist-safari spaces of settler colonies of Southern and East Africa, settlers' emotive language about ngoma emerged as original documents of space-related claim-making integral to the settler project. By navigating between fear and wonder through the language of impending catastrophe or familiar dance epistemology, settlers' lived experiences of dance in Africa offer a window into the limitations of teleological narratives of their encounters with African performing cultures. Evidently, settler engagements with dance in

Africa were more often a matter of reframing peoples, cultures, and environments in ways that facilitated the multiple ways in which they strove to reinvent themselves in colonial settings. It is also through the settler gaze and somatic encounters with African dancing cultures that hierarchies of performing genres from Africa have emerged.

Notes

1. Roy Porter, "History of the Body Reconsidered," in *New Perspectives on Historical Writing*, ed. Peter Burke, 2nd ed. (Cambridge: Polity, 2005), 233–60, 233–34; Christophe Apprill, *Sociologie des danses de couple: Une pratique entre résurgence et folklorisation* (Paris: L'Harmattan, 2005), 46. For insightful criticisms of this mind-body dualism that is still alive despite its disavowal by philosophers, health practitioners, sociologists, and anthropologists, see, for instance, Marie-Claude Defores, *Du Védanta à la psychanalyse ou le chemin de connaissance* (Gretz: Centre Védantique Ramakrishna, 2005) and Marie-Claude Defores and Yvan Piedimonte, *La constitution de l'être* (Paris: Bréal, 2009).

2. Alessandro Arcangeli, "Dance under Trial: The Moral Debate 1200–1600," *Dance Research: The Journal of the Society for Dance Research* 12, no. 2 (1994): 127–55, 127–28.

3. Paul A. Scolieri, *Dancing the New World: Aztecs, Spaniards, and the Choreography of Conquest* (Austin: University of Texas Press, 2013); Cécile Fromont, *The Art of Conversion: Christian Visual Culture in the Kingdom of Kongo* (Chapel Hill: University of North Carolina Press, 2014).

4. Judith Lynne Hanna, "African Dance: The Continuity of Change," *Yearbook of the International Folk Music Council* 5 (1973): 165–74, 166; Mhoze Chikowero, *African Music, Power, and Being in Colonial Zimbabwe* (Bloomington: Indiana University Press, 2015), 19–111.

5. See, for example, Peter Muhoro Mwangi, "Silencing Musical Expression in Colonial and Post-colonial Kenya," in *Popular Music Censorship in Africa*, ed. Michael Drewett and Martin Cloonan (Aldershot, UK: Ashgate, 2006); Marissa J. Moorman, *Intonations: A Social History of Music and Nation in Luanda, Angola, from 1945 to Recent Times* (Athens: Ohio University Press, 2008); Emily Callaci, "Dancehall Politics: Mobility, Sexuality, and Spectacles of Racial Respectability in Late Colonial Tanganyika, 1930s–1961," *Journal of African History* 52, no. 3 (2011): 365–84; Marc Matera, Misty L. Bastian, and Susan Kingsley Kent, eds., *The Women's War of 1929: Gender and Violence in Colonial Nigeria* (New York: Palgrave Macmillan, 2013); Chikowero, *African Music*; Cécile Feza Bushidi, "Dance, Socio-cultural Change and Politics among the Gikuyu People of Kenya, 1880s–1963" (PhD diss., School of Oriental and African Studies, University of London, 2016).

6. From anxieties about economic hardship, youth intimacy, and delinquency to fears about changing sexual mores and angst-ridden debates about national dance cultures and national identity, anxieties about dance have led to a wide range of concerns; see, for instance, Margaret D. Jacobs, "Making

Savages of Us All: White Women, Pueblo Indians, and the Controversy over Indian Dances in the 1920s," *Frontiers* 17, no. 3 (1996): 178–209; Sophie Jacotot, *Danser à Paris dans l'entre-deux-guerres: Lieux, pratiques et imaginaires des danses de société des Amériques (1919–1939)* (Paris: Nouveau Monde, 2013); Inger Damsholt, "Rock around the North," in *Nordic Spaces: Practicing and Imagining a Region*, ed. Karen Vedel and Petri Hoppu (Farnham, UK: Ashgate, 2014), 19–48; James Nott, *Going to the Palais: A Social and Cultural History of Dancing and Dance Halls in Britain, 1918–1960* (Oxford: Oxford University Press, 2015).

7. Arcangeli, "Dance under Trial," 130.

8. See, for instance, Terence Ranger, *Dance and Society in Eastern Africa 1890–1970: The Beni Ngoma* (London: Heinemann, 1975); Callaci, "Dancehall Politics"; Bushidi, "Dance, Socio-cultural Change and Politics."

9. The bodies of peoples of African descent have been (and continue to be) coded and read as essentially inferior, "primitive," and threatening by many individuals (often but not systematically Caucasian): see, for instance, Thomas F. DeFrantz, "Simmering Passivity: The Black Male Body in Concert Dance," in *Moving History/Dancing Cultures: A Dance History Reader*, ed. Ann Dils and Ann Cooper Albright (Middletown, CT: Wesleyan University Press, 2001), 342–49; P. Sterling Stuckey, "Christian Conversion and the Challenge of Dance," in *Dancing Many Drums: Excavations in African American Dance*, ed. Thomas F. DeFrantz (Madison: University of Wisconsin Press, 2002), 39–58; Ruth Holliday and John Hassard, "Contested Bodies: An Introduction," in *Contested Bodies*, ed. Ruth Holliday and John Hassard (London: Routledge, 2001), 1–18. In the colonial settler context, the admixture of bodies energized, adorned, at times scantily clad, and experienced as threatening creates expressive bodies which can decidedly be viewed as *in excess* in colonized settings. Thanks to Thomas DeFrantz, I am also inspired by Saidiya Hartman's incisive and poetic *Wayward Lives, Beautiful Experiments: Intimate Histories of Social Upheaval* (New York: W. W. Norton, 2019). The African American women (and men) who migrated into the streets of New York and Philadelphia at the turn of the twentieth century disrupted a white-dominated public space, generating profound discomfort and a multitude of real, imagined, and exaggerated fears and anxieties. Whether standing still, at home, in the streets, in the clubs, or at parties dancing or singing, such Black presence was experienced by public authorities, law enforcers, social reformists, and various individuals as too much, too visible, and indeed, often out of place.

10. This chapter is at the heart of three entwined growing fields of research: the "affective turn" in the history of Africa; studies of white settlers in colonial and imperial settings (and more globally, of whiteness); and studies on the daily negative emotions that have affected colonizers. For a literature on colonial anxieties about the corporeal, the afflictions of the mind, Africans committing "crime," spatial segregation, and white prestige in Kenya, see, for instance, Dane Kennedy, *Islands of White: Settler Society and Culture in Kenya and Southern Rhodesia, 1890–1939* (Durham, NC: Duke University Press, 1987); Will Jackson, *Madness and Marginality: The Lives of Kenya's White Insane* (Manchester:

Manchester University Press, 2013); Dominique Connan, "La décolonisation des clubs Kényans: Sociabilité exclusive et constitution morale des élites africaines dans le Kenya contemporain" (PhD diss., University of Paris, 2014); Brett L. Shadle, *The Souls of White Folk: White Settlers in Kenya, 1900s–1920s* (Manchester: Manchester University Press, 2015); Joël Michel, *Colonies de peuplements: Afrique XIXe–XXe siècles* (Paris: CNRS Editions, 2018); Dane Kennedy, "Minds in Crisis: Medico-moral Theories of Disorder in the Late Colonial World," in *Anxieties, Fear and Panic in Colonial Settings: Empires on the Verge of a Nervous Breakdown*, ed. Harald Fischer-Tiné (Houndmills, UK: Palgrave Macmillan, 2016), 27–47. As Shadle notes, this field is sometimes criticized for "obsessing over whites," therefore pushing Africans to the margins of history (*Souls of White Folk*, 11). My view is that the focus on African performance does not veil any commitment to an Africa-centered approach to colonial history. Here, Africans remain at the heart of the reconstruction of the colonial past, for I transpose African expressive performing cultures (that ostensibly featured in the lives of many African societies) to the nexus of colonial engagements with them. Performance creates a fertile domain to evaluate various kinds of localized histories of connection between individuals. To include Africans' own anxieties about dance would be to write a whole different chapter. I am aware that the theme of "anxieties about dance" in colonial Africa can (and will) live several lives that illuminate the porosity of categories between Europeans and Africans. As part of my research on dance in colonial Africa, understanding European settlers' own responses to "native" bodies in motion is essential to understanding the construction of dance in the history of Africa.

11. Ranger, *Beni Ngoma*, 88; Didier Gondola, "'*Bisengo ya la joie*': Fête, sociabilité et politique dans les capitales congolaises," in *Fêtes urbaines en Afrique: Espaces, identités et pouvoirs*, ed. Odile Goerg (Paris: Karthala, 1999), 88–89.

12. Ann Laura Stoler, *Carnal Knowledge and Imperial Power: Race and the Intimate in Colonial Rule* (Berkeley: University of California Press, 2002), 24.

13. Roger M. A. van Zwanenberg with Anne King, *An Economic History of Kenya and Uganda, 1800–1970* (London: Macmillan, 1975), 57–64; Phares Mukasa Mutibwa, *A History of Uganda: The First 100 Years, 1894–1995* (Kampala: Fountain Publishers, 2016), 104–18.

14. Holliday and Hassard, "Contested Bodies: An Introduction," 12. As part of the introduction to the second part of their book (a section entitled "Bodies in Space"), Holliday and Hassard remind us of the ways in which places and localities are central in the readings, experiences, constructions, and consumptions of contested bodies. The various bodies considered—the "respectable" and "non-respectable" body, the pregnant body, the butch body—in the private/public spaces of the streets, the public toilets, and offices constitute potent sites of negative and positive emotions, as well as criminalization and surveillance; see Holliday and Hassard, "Contested Bodies: An Introduction," 12–14.

15. Charles Allen, *Tales from the Dark Continent* (London: Andre Deutsch British Broadcasting Corporation, 1979).

16. Edward Said, *Orientalism* (New York: Vintage, 1979).

17. Stoler, *Carnal Knowledge*, 41. Here, Stoler particularly refers to the gendered, class, and racial dynamics of the performance of European power in the colonies. As usual, her intellectual generosity allows us to enlarge on her thought.

18. See, for instance, Paul Greenhalgh, *Ephemeral Vistas: The Expositions Universelles, Great Exhibitions and World's Fairs, 1851–1939* (Manchester: Manchester University Press, 1988); Raymond Corbey, "Ethnographic Showcases, 1870–1930," *Cultural Anthropology* 8, no. 3 (1993): 338–69; Sylvie Chalaye, *Du noir au nègre: L'image du noir au théâtre (1550–1960)* (Paris: L'Harmattan, 1998); Bernth Lindfors, *Africans on Stage: Studies in Ethnological Show Business* (Bloomington: Indiana University Press, 1999); Sylvie Chalaye, "L'imaginaire colonial et la scène: Corps et décors d'une Afrique fantasme," *Africultures*, no. 52 (November 2002): 7–15.

19. *Trader Horn* (1931), United States, director: Woodbridge Strong Van Dyke; *Sanders of the River* (1935), Britain, director: Zoltan Korda; *Dark Rapture* (1938), United States, director: Armand Denis; Kevin Dunn, "Lights . . . Camera . . . Africa: Images of Africa and Africans in Western Popular Films of the 1930s," *African Studies Review* 39, no. 1 (1996): 149–75, 162. Robert Gordon argues that since the turn of the twentieth century, indigenous dancing has attracted the attention of cinematographers in Africa; Robert J. Gordon, "'Captured on Film': Bushmen and the Claptrap of Performative Primitives," in *Images and Empires: Visuality in Colonial and Postcolonial Africa*, ed. Paul S. Landau and Deborah D. Kaspin (Berkeley: University of California Press, 2002), 212–32.

20. Dunn, "Images of Africa and Africans," 162.

21. Tabitha Kanogo, *Squatters and the Roots of Mau Mau, 1905–63* (Athens: Ohio University Press, 1987), 9–11, 80.

22. Bruce Berman and John Lonsdale, "Crises of Accumulation, Coercion and the Colonial State: The Development of the Labour Control System, 1919–1929," in Bruce Berman and John Lonsdale, *Unhappy Valley: Conflict in Kenya and Africa, Book One: State and Class* (Athens: Ohio University Press, 1992), 109.

23. Kenya National Archives [hereafter KNA] GP 333.2 KEN vol. 1, Kenya Land Commission Evidence, 618.

24. KNA GP 333.2 KEN vol. 1, Kenya Land Commission Evidence, 619.

25. KNA VQI/28/32, Minutes from the Kiambu LNC held at Kiambu on 5 March 1928, "Prohibition of certain Native Dances on European farms."

26. KNA GP 333.2 KEN vol. 1, Kenya Land Commission, 619.

27. Louis S. B. Leakey, *The Southern Kikuyu before 1903* (London: Academic Press, 1977), 424–29.

28. KNA VQI/28/32, Minutes from the Kiambu LNC held at Kiambu on 5 March 1928.

29. KNA GP 333.2 KEN vol. 1, Kenya Land Commission, 619.

30. KNA VQI/28/32, Minutes from the Kiambu LNC held at Kiambu on 5 March 1928.

31. David P. Sandgren, *Christianity and the Kikuyu: Religious Divisions and Social Conflict* (New York: Peter Lang, 1989), 90; Yvan Droz, "La morale de

l'interdiction de la clitoridectomie en pays kikuyu," *Anthropologie et Sociétés* 33, no 3 (2009): 118–37, 133; Mwangi, "Silencing Musical Expression," 158; David Anderson, *Histories of the Hanged: The Dirty War in Kenya and the End of Empire* (New York: W. W. Norton, 2005), 18–23.

32. KNA XA1/1/2 Unauthorized meetings and Mithirigo Songs 1930–1949, DC Fort Hall to DC Thika, "Native Dances," 5 December 1930; DC Thika to DC Fort Hall, "Native Dances," 15 July 1931.

33. KNA PC NZA/2/1/68 ST.C. Tisdall, Warden of Mines, to the District Commissioner, Kakamega, 20 March 1934.

34. Günter Wagner, *The Bantu of North Kavirondo*, vol. 1 (London: International African Institute and Oxford University Press, 1949), 4–6.

35. Wagner, 460.

36. George Senoga-Zake, *Folk Music of Kenya: For Teachers and Students of Music and for the Music-Loving Public* (Nairobi: Uzima Press, 1988), 31; Florence Ngale Miya, "Educational Content in the Performing Arts: Tradition and Christianity in Kenya" (PhD diss., University of Cape Town, 2004), 55–60.

37. Priscilla M. Shilaro, *A Failed Eldorado: Colonial Capitalism, Rural Industrialization, African Land Rights in Kenya, and the Kakamega Gold Rush, 1930–1952* (Lanham, MD: University Press of America, 2008), 71.

38. Shilaro, *Failed Eldorado*, 23–45, 61–76. In 1933, on one of her returns to Kenya, author Elspeth Huxley stopped by Kakamega with the prospect of writing two articles (for the *Times*) about the controversial goldfields that had been discovered in Kenya and further south across the border, in the Tarime district of Tanganyika's Mara region: see Elspeth Huxley, *Out in the Midday Sun: My Kenya* (London: Chatto and Windus, 1985), 10–11, 18–22; Christine S. Nicholls, *Red Strangers: The White Tribe of Kenya* (London: Timewell Press, 2005), 203–5. Owing to World War II and the high costs of production, the gold-mining business was over by 1952, having barely provided long-term benefits to settlers; see Shilaro, *Failed Eldorado*, 82–90. As Shilaro further points out, the Luhya peoples did not benefit from Kakamega's gold-mining industry: the mining agreements stifled Luhya entrepreneurship; many households lost land and saw their agricultural production reduced; deadly incidents in the mines were of course frequent (*Failed Eldorado*, 18–22, 144–63, 166–69, 174–79).

39. Huxley, *Out in the Midday Sun,* 20; Eve Bache, *The Youngest Lion: Early Farming Days in Kenya* (London: Hutchinson, 1934), 234; Shilaro, *Failed Eldorado*, 179–80.

40. Bache, *Youngest Lion,* 236.

41. Bache, *Youngest Lion,* 236–37; Nicholls, *Red Strangers*, 204. I thank Dr. Christine Nicholls for our fruitful email conversation.

42. KNA PC NZA/2/1/68 Office of the District Commissioner of North Kavirondo, Kakamega, to the Provincial Commissioner of Nyanza, "Funeral Procession near Piccadilly Circus: Case of Mrs Ingles," 21 March 1934 (hereafter cited as "Case of Mrs Ingles").

43. As Shadle writes, although some African men did commit sexual violence against white women and children, one should not exaggerate their

numbers compared to white-on-black assaults. Black perils were extremely rare: see Shadle, *Souls of White Folk,* 92–96. On the Black peril scare in Kenya, see also Kennedy, *Islands of White*, 117, 110–47; David Anderson, "Sexual Threat and Settler Society: 'Black Perils' in Kenya, c. 1907–30," *Journal of Imperial and Commonwealth History*, 38, no. 1 (2010): 47–74; Connan, "La décolonisation des clubs kényans," 64; and in colonial settings more broadly, see Stoler, *Carnal Knowledge*, 58–60.

44. Shadle, *Souls of White Folk,* 85–92. Stoler offers an insightful discussion and comprehensive literature about the complexity of colonial discourses about white women in the colonies; Stoler, *Carnal Knowledge*, 55–65.

45. KNA PC NZA/2/1/68 ST.C. Tisdall, Warden of Mines, to the District Commissioner, Kakamega, 20 March 1934.

46. Shilaro, *Failed Eldorado,* 99.

47. Shilaro, 104–9.

48. "Case of Mrs Ingles."

49. Feminist scholarship has challenged the negative stereotypes of women in colonial settings. Margaret Strobel has notably argued that settler women were not detrimental to colonial relations, but essential to bolster a fragile empire and to maintain race relations, see Margaret Strobel, "Gender and Race in the Nineteenth- and Twentieth-Century British Empire," in *Becoming Visible: Women in European History*, ed. Renate Bridenthal, Claudia Koonz, and Susan Stuard, 2nd ed. (Boston: Houghton Mifflin, 1987), 375–98.

50. Huxley, *Out in the Midday Sun*, 20; Nicholls, *Red Strangers*, 203; Bache, *Youngest Lion*, 239.

51. Stoler, *Carnal Knowledge*, 61.

52. "Case of Mrs Ingles."

53. "Case of Mrs Ingles."

54. Shilaro, *Failed Eldorado,* 6.

55. KNA GP 333.2 KEN vol. 1, Kenya Land Commission, 82–83.

56. KNA GP 333.2 KEN Report of the Land Commission September 1933 presented by the Secretary of State for the Colonies to Parliament by Command of His Majesty in May 1934, 130.

57. Amy J. Staples, "Safari Adventure: Forgotten Cinematic Journeys in Africa," *Film History: An International Journal* 18, no. 4 (2006): 392–411, 392–94. During the late nineteenth and early twentieth centuries, the Swahili word *safari* (referring to a trip or journey) was appropriated by European and American travelers in Africa and popularized as a mode of hunting and recreation.

58. Mutibwa, *History of Uganda*, 70–72.

59. Charles Allen, *Tales from the Dark Continent* (London: Andre Deutsch British Broadcasting Corporation, 1979), 120, 79–94.

60. Allen, 119–20.

61. *Dark Rapture* (1938); Staples, "Safari Adventure," 402–4.

62. Staples, "Safari Adventure," 403–4. As Staples notes, these performances would become emblematic of local cultures that were recycled in tourist photographs and Hollywood safari films such as *King Solomon's Mines* (1950),

Mogambo (1953), *Safari* (1956), and *Hatari!* (1962); see Staples, "Safari Adventure," 394.

63. Allen, *Tales from the Dark Continent*, 120–21.

64. David Freedberg, *The Power of Images: Studies in the History and Theory of Response* (Chicago: University of Chicago Press, 1989), xxi. Freedberg's introduction and first chapter have helped me think about how to frame a holistic picture of settlers' engagements with Africa performance. Indeed, in this book, Freedberg calls for consideration of the wide range of human responses to images of art, from the most embarrassing, rude, or "uncultured" impulses to the most "refined" reactions to the images of art considered and experienced as highly refined.

65. Here, I draw on Helen Thomas's succinct history of the power of the visuality in ballet; see Helen Thomas, *The Body, Dance and Cultural Theory* (New York: Palgrave Macmillan, 2003), 95–102.

66. Andrew Apter, "On Imperial Spectacle: The Dialectics of Seeing in Colonial Nigeria," *Comparative Studies in Society and History* 44, no. 3 (2002): 564–96.

67. Apter, "On Imperial Spectacle," 588.

68. In the mid-1930s, colonial official Armine Charles Almroth Wright, who showed more interest in studying African cultures than conducting road projects in Uganda, traveled to Gulu district, where he recorded various kinds of performed religious and spiritual ceremonies; see Armine Charles Almroth Wright, "Some Notes on Acholi Religious Ceremonies," *Uganda Journal*, no. 3 (1936): 175–202. By comparing Acholi and Lango orature and written literature, Okot p'Bitek's 1963 doctoral thesis in sociology is a monumental study on performance that illuminates the association between dance, proverbs, tales, songs, philosophy, and social and spiritual education in the history of Acholi and Lango cultural practices; see Okot p'Bitek, "Oral Literature and Its Social Background among the Acholi and Lango" (PhD diss., University of Oxford, 1963). See also Okot p'Bitek, *Song of Lawino* (Nairobi: East African Publishing House, 1966); and Okumu pa' Lukobo, "Acholi Dance and Dance Songs," *Uganda Journal* 35, no. 1 (1971): 55–61.

69. That Western observers have historically showed little interest in, misunderstood, or dismissed the aesthetics, sociology, and politics of African-derived dance has been (and continues to be) pointed out in dance scholarship; see, for instance, Thomas F. DeFrantz, *Dancing Revelations: Alvin Ailey's Embodiment of African American Culture* (New York: Oxford University Press, 2004); Kariamu Welsh Asante, "Commonalities in African Dance: An Aesthetic Foundation," in Dils and Albright, *Moving History/Dancing Cultures*, 144–51.

70. Adam Branch, *Displacing Human Rights: War and Intervention in Northern Uganda* (New York: Oxford University Press, 2011), 47.

71. T. V. Sathyamurthy, *The Political Development of Uganda: 1900–1986* (Aldershot, UK: Gower, 1986), 341–42.

THREE

Epidemics and Anxiety in Saint-Louis-du-Sénégal, from the Mid-Nineteenth to the Early Twentieth Century

KALALA NGALAMULUME

ANXIETY IS AN EMOTIONAL RESPONSE TO A PROBLEM OR A danger. In its various expressions—including doubt, worry, fear, panic, and hysteria—anxiety has played and continues to play an essential role in individual and collective destinies. It takes little effort to identify its presence in every aspect of daily life as well as in collective behaviors. Yet, for a long time, the topic has been the *chasse gardée* of cognitive psychologists and psychiatrists who have focused on the internal mechanisms of emotions' production and the subjective experience of their patients, and have made anxiety a legitimate mental illness, referring to it as anxiety disorder and anxiety sensitivity. As such, individual emotions belong to the "private-affective sphere" of activity. Historians of emotions, by contrast, have concerned themselves with collective anxiety, which belongs to the "public-instrumental" sphere of activity.[1] Collective anxiety is triggered by stressful circumstances and situations

---

I would like to thank Yolana Pringle and Andrea Grant, organizers, and the participants in the conference "Anxiety in and about Africa" held at the University of Cambridge, England, for their comments on the earlier draft of this chapter. I am grateful to copyeditor Nancy Basmajian for correcting my omissions and lapses. All shortcomings are mine.

caused by broad forces and factors that are perceived as a threat to the community. In some cases, it can become unbearable, excessive, and almost pathological to the point of provoking mental blocks and the inability to assess the reality, thus resulting in aberrant, irrational, and even suicidal behaviors.

The history of the emotions in Africa is still in its infancy compared to its development in Europe or in North America.[2] Yet, the historical record and contemporary news reports contain evidence of how people experienced and tried to address various manifestations of anxiety. A few examples will suffice as illustration. The outbreak of bubonic plague in South Africa in 1900 led to the use by the medical and colonial authorities of the imagery of infectious disease as a societal metaphor, which, combined with their racial attitudes, was instrumental in the development of urban residential segregation.[3] The discovery made by Ronald Ross of the Indian Medical Service that the *Anopheles* mosquito was the vector for malaria influenced the implementation of the same policy in Sierra Leone with the construction of the Hill Station.[4] However, the policy was not fully implemented because of the resistance from the British merchants in Freetown. The spread of bubonic plague in West Africa provoked a major health crisis in Dakar in 1914, in Saint-Louis in 1917,[5] and in Lagos and Kumasi in 1924[6] as a result of the implementation of unpopular and racialized antiplague measures. Toward the end of World War I, a virulent strain of the 1918–19 influenza epidemic spread through East Africa, Gold Coast,[7] and Southern Rhodesia,[8] killing hundreds of thousands of people. Fear-related behaviors were also observed during the expansion of the 1980s HIV/AIDS pandemic, with an epicenter in South Africa and an added burden of tuberculosis.[9] More recently, fear-related behaviors spread across the globe during the 2013–16 West Africa Ebola virus disease outbreak, which saw nearly 300,000 cases and more than 10,000 deaths. It led to an epidemic of fear and anxiety, especially in the United States and in Europe, and required a worldwide mobilization of resources.[10] The latest anxiety epidemic is linked to the COVID-19 pandemic that has resulted in over 15.3 million confirmed cases and over 629,700 deaths globally by mid-July 2020. It has overwhelmed the capacity of healthcare systems and has forced governments to close down schools and businesses, and to enforce travel restrictions, quarantine, and social distancing. These measures have resulted in high unemployment and provoked fears of an economic crisis.

This chapter examines the link between the responses to the outbreaks of yellow fever epidemic diseases in Saint-Louis (Senegal) and the production of anxiety, the words and gestures contemporaries used, the functions anxiety has played as a tool with which people have managed their lives, and the outcomes. It argues that high mortality from epidemic diseases provoked high anxiety that took different forms, ranging from worry to an epidemic of fear and suspicion, panic, and hysteria. Anxiety inspired sanitary measures (hygiene and quarantines) that threatened people's livelihoods and civil liberties, disrupted commerce, and introduced racial/class residential segregation. In taking this action, French public health officials were instrumental in the creation of an "emotional community," to borrow Barbara Rosenwein's expression,[11] by making available to the public emotional words and their meanings, emotional gestures, practices, expectations, and perceptions. The growth of Saint-Louis-du-Sénégal from a trading post to a port city/capital of Senegal is an excellent case study for the discussion of the role and importance of anxiety, which could be discerned at three levels: the framing of disease; the responses to the immediate disease threat; and long-term preventive measures.

Framing Disease

Both British and French physicians in West Africa shared the same perception about the dangers of the tropical disease environments, the differential susceptibility of whites, blacks, and mixed races to different diseases, and the possibility of "acclimatization" through limited "seasoning," appropriate lifestyles, and medicine.[12] The French version of the "White Man's Grave" was what localists called *hivernage*, a word that inspired fear and terror. It referred to the hot, rainy, and humid season, from June to November in Senegambia. The main characteristics of the season were its constant variations in temperature and its association with the outbreaks of yellow fever and dengue fever and the high incidence of malaria, which were perceived as detrimental to the health of the Europeans. Hivernage also witnessed the multiplication of mosquitoes and fleas, which made it the most depressing season for the Europeans.[13] One of the negative effects of the climate of Senegal was a condition known as the "tropical anaemia."

Besides hivernage, another emotional vocabulary used by French physicians in Senegal was the "miasma" or the "pernicious emanations," that is to say, the highly poisonous vapors resulting from the decomposition of all types of organic matters in the stagnant water present everywhere in the surroundings of Saint-Louis (swamps, bogs, and moat) or resulting from floods and torrential rainwater.[14] There were three additional sources of the pestilential emanations (miasmas): the cemeteries, the petrified matters in soil, and the frequent and terrible "winds from the south" (*harmattan*). These emanations were associated with the outbreak and spreading of yellow fever epidemics. The "evil" time, when the prevailing "evil" wind was in motion and the chance for contamination high, was the evening. In addition, physicians described unsanitary housing and overcrowding as "one imminent and fatal cause" of the reemergence of the 1881 yellow fever epidemic.

In contrast, contagionists believed that yellow fever was not locally produced; instead, it was allegedly imported to Saint-Louis from Sierra Leone, Gambia, Portuguese Guinea, or Grand-Bassam via Gorée and Dakar,[15] but it found in the local "natural insalubrities of the climate" a fertile ground for its spread and lethality.[16] Thus, the epidemiological theory of disease contained the emotion-laden terms, such as hivernage, insalubrity, pernicious emanations, infectious emanations or miasmas, cemeteries as a "permanent danger" to a city's health, and the hospital as "focus of infection" during the outbreaks of epidemics, which inspired fear and terror. Medical knowledge underlined the geography of emotion, for fear upholds boundaries; and it contributed to the formation of "emotional communities" focused on disease and the body.

Yellow Fever Mortality and Anxiety

The evidence suggests that the recorded high mortality observed among the Europeans as well as the social status of the victims provoked fear and panic. The 1867 yellow fever epidemic killed 320 Frenchmen in Saint-Louis—half of the European population. The cholera epidemic ravaged the city in November 1868 and within a month had killed 1,112 *indigènes* (the urban poor)—5,000 according to missionary sources—and 92 Europeans, including Governor Pinet-Laprade, out of a population of 20,000.[17] Ten years passed without another epidemic, and then came the 1878 yellow fever epidemic that killed 652 Europeans out of a European population of 1,300, including 14 Sisters of the Congregation of Saint-Joseph de Cluny who had cared for the sick, and an undetermined number of middle-class members and indigènes.[18] When it reemerged in 1880 and 1881, yellow fever killed 80 and 503, respectively, among the European residents, including the newly arrived Governor De Lanneau.[19] The perception that yellow fever was the "white man's disease" and that it was then endemic to Senegal worried everyone. During the outbreak of 1900, the third victim of yellow fever was Bishop Buléon, Bishop of Cariopolis, apostolic vicaire of Senegambia. Governor General Chaudié stated that "it was the social status of the deceased that provoked high emotion not only in Senegal but also in France; it also helps explain the exaggeration accorded to the news about the recrudescence of the epidemic"; however, he cautioned that "the rains of the soon-approaching *hivernage* will reveal the true character of the malignancy of the affliction and will help appreciate the degree of contamination of the colony."[20]

Rumors, Panic and Flight

Responses to the outbreaks of yellow fever ranged from rumors, worry, fear, panic, and flight to accusations and protests. Given the anxiety surrounding yellow fever, rumors of confirmed or unconfirmed outbreak reports in Gorée or Dakar provoked panic in Saint-Louis. Often panic led to flight. In 1867, missionaries reported that "a general panic spread among the inhabitants; families were in consternation; physicians themselves were afraid. The hospital was sealed: only the [Catholic] Brothers and [hospital] employees could get in."[21] The panic provoked by the sound of the clarion was such that the governor ordered on request from the elite that the official funeral ceremonies for the military officers proceed "as taciturn as possible."[22]

In 1878, infected individuals fled the city in panic, incubating the disease and spreading it into the countryside. The return of the yellow fever epidemic generated new waves of fear. The subsequent high mortality generated more fear-related behaviors, as illustrated by a heated debate that took place on 14 May 1879 during a key meeting of the Sanitary Commission, presided over by Pierre Carpot, Ordonnateur, who represented the colonial administration. The objective of the meeting was to discuss the offensive smells from rotting fish coming from Guet N'dar slum that was viewed as the "focus of infection." The administration blamed Mayor Gaspard Devès, from one of the leading métis families, for not implementing recent sanitary measures. Describing himself as the "defender of the material interests of the indigènes and those of the city," Devès argued that the indigènes had the right to dry fish and to earn a living. But the Sanitary Commission voted to ban the fishing activities every year on 1 May.[23] Such a radical measure was clearly dictated by fear-inspired anxiety, as the rainy season, associated with yellow fever epidemics, was quickly approaching. Consequently, it destroyed the livelihood of the fishermen. Although the archival materials are silent about the responses of the urban poor to anti–yellow fever measures, their opinions are reflected in the statements of the mayor, their main defender.

A couple of years later, Father Deplanches noted on 23 July 1881, "Today, when we least expect it, the city is quarantined; several cases of yellow fever are reported. This sanitary measure causes a great emotion."[24] For over one hundred passengers who were preparing to leave for France via Dakar aboard the *Castor*, the declaration of an epidemic and the imposition of a quarantine eliminated the last opportunity for escape and condemned them to a certain death, which explains the intensity of the emotion. Indeed, the perception of Africa as "a mysterious land full of dangers" greatly contributed to the hysteria.[25]

Some years later, city residents first learned about the 1900 yellow fever epidemic through rumors: "there is a rumor in the city that Rufisque and Gorée are contaminated. After verification, it is true, indeed!"[26] The confirmation of the outbreak gave way to an epidemic of fear: "we have nothing to envy to Dakar, we are caught. An infantry soldier came down this evening with all the symptoms of the terrible disaster."[27] The epidemic of fear led to suspicion, and accusations and counteraccusations.

On 18 January 1882, Mayor A. de Bourmeister issued a new ordinance on sanitation and hygiene that went beyond concerns for cleanliness to pathologize the urban poor's survival economic activities that would now require the mayor's authorization. These activities included drying fish and animal skins within the city's limits, slaughtering animals outside of slaughterhouses (article 2), and raising pork in the city (article 4).[28] Women were not allowed to pound millet at night between 10 p.m. and 4 a.m. (article 10). The ordinance also prohibited all the noise associated with cloth making between 8 p.m. and 4 a.m. (article 15). Thus, medical and government responses to yellow fever reflected the sanitation syndrome, described by Maynard Swanson in South Africa, which dealt with urban race relations in the imagery of infection and epidemic disease.[29] In Saint-Louis the yellow fever epidemics gave way to the epidemic of fear and suspicion and to an epidemic of stigmatization of indigènes.[30] Guet N'dar, the most populous faubourg, was now seen as the focus of infection and, to borrow from Michael Taussig, the "space of death."[31]

Automatic Quarantine: Key Expression of Anxiety

The limits of biomedicine in face of a disease about which physicians were tentative concerning the epidemiology and appropriate therapies heightened anxieties that the French felt about Senegal. Control measures combined both sanitationist and quarantinist approaches. The localists, or sanitarians, favored strategies aimed at improving sanitation and hygiene, while the contagionists relied mainly on the disinfection of suspected and contaminated houses and objects, the isolation of European troops, and a surveillance program, including sanitary cordons and quarantines of ships arriving from contaminated or suspected regions.[32] The high mortality provoked by the 1878–81 great yellow fever epidemics led to the pathologizing not only of Senegal but also of the coastal region south of Pointe Sangomar. Indeed, contagionists had identified Freetown (Sierra Leone) and Sainte-Marie-de-Bathurst (Gambia), both British colonial port-cities, as the "foci of infection," and such determination led to the imposition of an automatic annual quarantine of ships arriving from regions suspected of contamination.

Despite the imposition of a quarantine in July,[33] the outbreak of an epidemic of yellow fever in Dakar in November 1882 convinced medical officers to adopt a sweeping twenty-one-day quarantine on ships arriving from Dakar and its hinterland.[34] By mid-December, the epidemic had subsided. Yet the danger of infection was again heightened in early 1883 by confirmed reports that some ship captains arriving from the south with clean bills of health were not in compliance with the regulations prohibiting contacts with secondary ports where public health officials were not present. The fear of another yellow fever epidemic pushed the authorities to enforce control measures at the quarantine station of Gandiole aimed at protecting Saint-Louis. New legislation also imposed a five-day observation quarantine between 1 June and 15 December on all ships arriving from areas located between Pointe Sangomar and Gabon. The evidence suggests that the possession of a clean bill of health and the absence of disease aboard were no longer a sufficient condition, even in emergency, for a free navigation.[35]

Fearing another major yellow fever epidemic, the contagionists recommended, on 19 June 1884, the imposition of a strict quarantine of 23 days on ships arriving directly from Sierra Leone, and a quarantine of observation of variable duration on ships arriving from "countries in free communication with Sierra Leone."[36] Then, medical officers turned their attention to the other perceived dangerous region. The automatic observation quarantine was also imposed at Bakel on all ships arriving from Upper Senegal without clean bills of health; if not, ships were required to stop at the posts of Podor, Dagana, and Richard-Toll, or if needed, at Bop N'Kior. One exception concerned ships arriving directly from Gabon with clean bills of health issued by the French authorities if they had "no compromising communication" with other ships or on land since departure.[37] The rationale behind this radical measure was that past epidemics that struck Senegal originated from localities on the West African coast (mouth of Niger, Sierra Leone, and Côte d'Ivoire).[38] The multiplication of the quarantine measures aimed at protecting Saint-Louis, the capital of colonial Senegal, from yellow fever was a good indicator of the panic that seized the medical authorities.

Not all city residents shared the same perception of the efficiency of the quarantine, however. French, British, and Portuguese merchants were worried about the disruption of commercial activities and communication between the port cities that the new measures created. So, they began to protest the inefficiency that characterized the implementation of the quarantine measures for commercial and practical reasons. The delays were due to a certain number of factors. There were not enough buildings in the lazarettos and sanitary stations to accommodate different cohorts of passengers who arrived at different dates, or to store merchandise. There was a shortage of medical personnel who could undertake the medical examination of the passengers, deliver free health care to the sick, and disinfect merchandise; and there was a shortage of sanitary guards who could police lazarettos and sanitary stations. In addition, delays were also due to either the incompetence or the unwillingness of the bureaucrats and ship crews to fulfill their duties.

By early 1890, there was a consensus among the colonial officials and the business community that automatic quarantine was inefficient and ruinous for the colony and commerce because of long delays in ports and reported cases of fraud. The urgent question concerned the ways in which to conciliate the interests of commerce and those of public health. There were reports that the British colonial officials and business leaders in Sierra Leone and Gambia placed their commercial interests above health security considerations. They issued fraudulent clean bills of health where cases of yellow fever bore fantasist names, such as "the ordinary African fever," that helped them avoid quarantines.[39] Ship captains often disembarked their passengers before entering the ports of Rufisque and Dakar to avoid medical inspections.

French merchants offered suggestions that could make the quarantines work smoothly, including the suppression of the more restrictive provisions of the quarantine legislation, the appointment of a Navy physician at the British port city of Bathurst (Gambia) to supervise the issuance of bills of health, and more involvement from the French Consuls in Sierra Leone and Gambia.[40] However, none of these suggestions for regional cooperation seemed workable as far as the British colonial authorities were concerned, in part because of the impression that the French policy makers were trying to interfere with their internal affairs. The authorities in Saint-Louis continued to keep a watchful eye on the ships arriving from Sierra Leone and Gambia.[41]

Soon, the Chamber of Commerce in Saint-Louis began to express doubts about the very scientific knowledge that inspired those "radical measures" and "irrational practices." Public opinion had shifted as newspapers were featuring advertisements about new disinfection machines "capable of destroying the microbes of yellow fever in a few minutes at a temperature of more than 100 degrees." Merchants mobilized to purchase the disinfection machine "no matter the sacrifice."[42] Navy officers too contended that the quarantine was detrimental to the conduct of war in Sudan because it affected supplies for the troops.[43]

Bowing to the pressure from various chambers of commerce in Senegal, Governor de Lamothe recommended either the abrogation or, at least, the modification of articles 113 and 114 of the decree of 29 August 1884, which targeted ships arriving from the region between Pointe Sangomar and French Congo. Even the outbreak of cholera in Saint-Louis in 1893, which revealed the deep social and economic disparities between sanitary citizens and unsanitary subjects as well as the inadequacies of public health policies, did not weigh on his mind. Physicians, attributing the absence of epidemics in Senegal since 1884 to the effectiveness of the automatic yearly quarantine, despite the outbreaks reported in coastal trading posts, recommended the status quo, however. In the end, all the parties reached a consensus and agreed on a compromise solution. The decree of 29 October 1893 modified the articles in question by making provisions for the delivery of clean bills of health after the boarding of those ships, unless there were suspected cases on board the ships and the information concerning the sanitary situation of the region seemed insufficient and insincere, in which case observation quarantine would be in place. The authorities had hoped that the modification of the sanitary legislation would allow French merchants to compete effectively again with British and Portuguese merchants operating on the West African coast, while protecting the colony against epidemics.[44]

However, the situation changed in March 1897 when, in compliance with the resolutions of the 1893 Dresden International Sanitary Convention (15 April) promulgated in France in 1894 (decree of 22 May), another decree unified and consolidated different pieces of legislation applied until then in French colonies. It required passengers to obtain sanitary passports and imposed an observation quarantine of seven days for cholera and nine days for yellow fever or plague at the lazaretto for passengers without sanitary passports, the unloading and disinfection of merchandise, and the disinfection and quarantine of ships.[45]

The success of the new decree depended on renovations in sanitary services in terms of sufficient personnel and equipment. Nevertheless, in practice, the implementation of the decree faced enormous challenges. The medical personnel were insufficient, and the medical infrastructure was inappropriate and, in many coastal trading posts in Côte d'Ivoire, French Guinea, Dahomey, and French Congo, very embryonic. In addition, the decree rested on the questionable assumptions that sanitary agents would implement all the provisions of the decrees and merchants would not protest. However, the majority of merchants voiced their opposition to the new quarantine measures they described as "inefficient and absurd," in part because of the deficient organization or the underdevelopment of health services. The Chamber of Commerce and the Sanitation Commission even recommended the acquisition of disinfection machines as a solution to "the costly and unpopular quarantine."[46] The evidence shows that all the measures adopted since 1893 represented a compromise between the interests of public health and those of commerce.

Following reports of the outbreaks of yellow fever epidemics in Côte d'Ivoire and Gambia on 2 May 1899, the Sanitary Commission imposed quarantine on suspect or contaminated ships arriving from Côte d'Ivoire. The decision provoked more discussion concerning the merit of the quarantine system per se.[47] What increased the anxiety was the fact that the news spread only after the *Stamboul*, which had arrived from Côte d'Ivoire, had departed with a clean bill of health after spending a few hours of transit in the port of Dakar. Thus, fear of infection greatly contributed to the malaise. However, the minister of colonies in Paris, increasingly under pressure from merchants who pushed for rational sanitary measures, on 29 May requested that the Sanitary Commission examine the possibility of allowing the African Steamship Company to enter the ports of Côte d'Ivoire not contaminated by yellow fever, given that the disease outbreak concerned only Grand-Bassam. Nevertheless, the Sanitary Commission rejected his proposal based on the argument made by the chief medical officer that the absence of a regular medical service in these localities made it difficult to determine the presence or absence of yellow fever.

Governor General Chaudié feared the "incalculable economic and social consequences of an eventual epidemic." He warned the minister that "in Senegal, yellow fever epidemics were always so serious that it was necessary not to neglect one single precaution to prevent the disaster from entering the colony," thus expressing the anxiety the colonial administration officials and physicians felt about Senegal's disease environment.[48] However, noting that the authorities in Dahomey had applied precautionary measures and given clean bills of health to ships from ports of Côte d'Ivoire other than Grand-Bassam, the minister urged in a cable the same day that the authorities in Senegal follow the example of Dahomey. This time, the Sanitary Commission not only stood its ground but also overwhelmingly endorsed physician Lafage's proposition to revive article 113 of the decree of 29 August 1884 and to ignore the modifications made in 1893. In other words, the Sanitary Commission suggested a reimposition of the five-day automatic annual observation quarantine to ships arriving in ports of Gorée, Dakar, Rufisque, and Saint-Louis from regions located between Pointe Sangomar and Gabon between 1 June and 15 December, even if they held clean bills of health. Physician Lafage attributed the reemergence of yellow fever to the compromise solutions adopted since 1893 under pressure from the business community. He argued that the surveillance system of automatic annual quarantines inaugurated in 1884 had succeeded in protecting Senegal against yellow fever attacks, that its suppression had increased the colony's vulnerability, and that "the return of epidemics would be a calamity and ruin of the colony."[49]

During another debate of the Sanitary Commission of 6 June 1899 in Saint-Louis, presided over by Th. Bergès, secretary general of the government, the discussion centered on finding the best solution to protect Saint-Louis and the colony against the outbreak of yellow fever striking Grand-Bassam without penalizing the other ports in Côte d'Ivoire where there were no yellow fever cases. The participants were faced with two contradictory demands. One came from the authorities in Paris, who reiterated a proposal already rejected by the Sanitary Commission about providing a clean bill of health to ships arriving from ports of Côte d'Ivoire other than Grand-Bassam after taking the necessary precautions, as was the case in Dahomey. The other demand came from Chief Medical Officer Lafage, who opposed such laxity. In a report to Bergès, he had argued in favor of the reinstatement, until further notice, of article 113 of the decree of 29 August 1884. Lafage's rationale was that the lack of sanitary surveillance outside Grand-Bassam as well as the absence of sanitary agents on the coast of Liberia did not allow a close monitoring of the spread and prevalence of the "disaster" along the West African coast. He warned, "We will suddenly learn that it just broke in Sierra Leone, in Guinea, in Casamance, in Bathurst. We will then be close to being caught and it will probably be very late to take measures the efficiency of which we can rely on."[50]

Lafage's fear of another epidemic was justified not only by the presence in the Dakar/Gorée area of two thousand European soldiers who were living in insanitary conditions at the approach of rainy season, but also by the evidence of unreliability of the statements made by ships' captains arriving from the south. Lafage's theory was that "the [yellow fever] epidemic will continue its ascendant march toward the north and it is when it will appear extinguished, in places where it is now ravaging, that it will break in other places." He presented the evidence from the 1881 yellow fever epidemic, which started in Gorée in a store where clothes were stored for three years, to make his point. He strongly believed that the outbreak of an epidemic in Senegal would be the ruin of the colony. Although Lafage's argument was based on contagionist assumptions, his observations about the general pattern of the march of yellow fever epidemics were correct: there was an initial attack that subsided, only for the yellow fever to later reemerge in a more virulent and deadly form.

Bergès approached the question in legal terms. From his perspective, the sanitary authorities could not impose quarantine on ships arriving from colonies without reported sources of infection and which were "distant by several days of navigation from places where the epidemic is declared." The ports of Côte d'Ivoire other than Grand-Bassam fell under that category. Most participants expressed concern over the provision related to a careful disinfection of passengers, luggage, and merchandise; they found that such a measure could negatively affect economic activities and result in the payment of damages to merchants. In the face of such resistance, Chief Medical Officer Lafage proposed to limit the operation of disinfection to the objects and clothes used by the passengers, a proposal the participants adopted.[51] In the meantime, as his first cable remained unanswered, the minister of colonies in Paris cabled the governor general again on 7 June; the latter had just received a telegram from Governor Cousturier of Guinea informing him that the last reported yellow fever case was dated twelve days earlier.

In a comprehensive response to Paris, Governor General Chaudié hastily held, on 8 June, a special meeting of the Conseil Privé[52] that was extended to the mayors of the four main cities of Senegal and to the representatives of the army (Colonel Pujol), the Saint-Louis Chamber of Commerce (Fr. Rabaud), and General Council (G. d'Erneville). His objective was to evaluate the sanitary situation of the colony. The participants were asked to examine two crucial questions: (1) the continuation of the quarantine measures dictated by the decree of 31 March 1897 that were applied to ships arriving from Côte d'Ivoire, and (2) the examination of Chief Medical Officer Lafage's proposed reinstatement of article 113 of the decree of 29 August 1884. In his opening statement, Governor General Chaudié invited "any person well knowledgeable about the needs and desiderata of the population to interpret [for the audience] the *public sentiment* concerning the quarantine measures adopted so far or to be adopted in case of an epidemic" (emphasis added). In response, Raymond Martin, *conseiller privé* and representative of Buhan and Tesseire Company in Saint-Louis and Dakar, affirmed that the population's response to the suppression of (traditional) preventive measures was negative and that people perceived current measures as insufficient in light of the physicians' inability "to quickly declare the existence of the affliction." Referring to the 1878 yellow fever epidemic, he explained that physician Massola and his colleagues' inability to agree on the result of the autopsy performed on attorney Batut left them powerless in face of a growing danger that required immediate preventive actions, since it took a month and a half for yellow fever to incubate. A closer look at the details of Martin's account suggests that he had read the epidemiological theory developed by Bérenger-Féraud in his *Traité théorique et clinique de la fièvre jaune* (1891), even if he did not mention him explicitly.

Chief Medical Officer Lafage, who used the data from the 1881 great yellow fever epidemic, corroborated Martin's account of the epidemiology of yellow fever. According to his theory, yellow fever broke out after physician Jullien ordered the cleaning of the office next to his, which contained a suitcase belonging to a *tirailleur* (rifleman) who had succumbed to yellow fever three years earlier. By opening the suitcase, physician Jullien was "struck by the terrible affliction to which he soon succumbed." Chief Medical Officer Carpentier also died from the disease, which reemerged in Gorée. Martin added that the 1881 epidemic broke out "with an extraordinary intensity" after Governor de Lanneau ordered the cleaning of some storage rooms located on the first floor of the Hôtel du Gouvernement. The governor, all officers, and almost all civil servants working in the building succumbed to the disease shortly after. Martin concluded, given that the beginnings of the disease were difficult to diagnose while contagion through objects was "tenacious and durable," that it was indispensable to take "severe measures to prevent the disaster from entering Senegal." Thus, both Martin and Lafage repeated the dominant theory of the mode of transmission of yellow fever that stressed contact with infected objects that were untouched since the last epidemic.

Responding to Martin and Lafage, Governor General Chaudié argued that in recent years "science has made progress and [that], in fact, the decree of 31 March 1897 had provisions that the highest medical authorities find efficient enough to prevent and stop contagion." However, he also recognized that the key to the success of preventive measures depended on the ability of the Sanitary Service "to assure their total implementation either at the point of departure in the contaminated country, or on the way, or and mostly at the point of arrival." Bergès, secretary general of the government of Senegal, underlined the fact that the embryonic state of the Sanitary Service in Côte d'Ivoire rendered the clean bills of health delivered by the medical authorities there untrustworthy. Nevertheless, Governor General Chaudié insisted that, given that the *rainy season* was favorable for the spread of yellow fever, "now is the time for us to be stricter." Following this exchange, the participants unanimously voted to uphold the quarantine measures imposed on ships arriving from Côte d'Ivoire despite the absence of new yellow fever cases in the past twelve days. They also approved the content of the cable directed to the minister of colonies in Paris, as follows: "The Sanitary Commission, the Conseil Privé and all the Mayors of the Colony, despite the news brought to our attention by your cablegram dated 1 June, are of the opinion that, because of the season specially favorable to the spread of yellow fever, it is absolutely impossible to issue clean bills of health to any ship that has communicated with Côte d'Ivoire. In any case, the public sentiment unanimously acquiesces with this opinion."[53]

If the participants easily agreed on quarantine measures against Côte d'Ivoire, they sharply disagreed concerning the decision reached by the

Sanitary Commission to revive the provisions of article 113 of the decree of 29 August 1884, which imposed the much-hated automatic annual quarantine on ships arriving from the region between Pointe Sangomar and French Congo. Two camps opposed each other but in a way that was not easy to predict. The opposition to the reenactment of article 113 was led by Fr. Marsat, mayor of Dakar, who disliked the "draconian decree" and recalled the long struggle led by the Chambers of Commerce and municipalities to convince Chief Medical Officer Ayme to abolish the quarantine measures that constituted a tremendous handicap for the freedom of commerce. The opposition camp did not see the need to impose the five-day observation quarantine on uncontaminated regions and to deny clean bills of health to ships arriving from Dahomey and Côte d'Ivoire. Instead, they were in favor of the strict implementation of the decree of 31 March 1897, approved by the Sanitary Commissions and the chief medical officer, which took into account the incubation period for yellow fever and had provisions for the disinfection of passengers and merchandise (article 55).

The support for the imposition of an automatic quarantine came from unexpected places, however. R. Martin was the most outspoken member of the group that favored the reenactment of article 113 of the decree of 29 August 1884. In his capacity as a representative of a major company that had big business interests in the Dakar region, he contended that sanitary measures imposed on ships arriving from the south were not harmful to commerce in the Dakar region. He rejected the quarantine measures outlined by the decree of 31 March 1897 as insufficient. He called on the participants to be "more rigorous toward the bizarre manifestations of yellow fever which, as we have seen, often take a very long time before manifesting themselves," and he insisted that in special circumstances like this one, "*commerce must sacrifice its interests*" (emphasis added). Fearing the increasing tension, Chief Medical Officer Lafage suggested that the reenactment of article 113 be limited to the current rainy season. At the end of the debate, the majority of participants voted by nine voices in favor and three against the reenactment of the article concerned. Governor General Chaudié emphasized the temporary character of the measure and read the second part of the cable prepared for the minister to the participants, as follows: "These authorities asked me, in contrary, to revive, temporarily and for the current rainy season, the provisions of the decree of 29 August 1884 which imposed five-day observation quarantine to any ships arriving from the South. I request your instructions."[54]

The participants unanimously adopted the content of the cablegram. By emphasizing the temporary character of the new quarantine measures and by dissociating himself from the just adopted text ("these authorities asked me"), Governor General Chaudié expressed his displeasure with the attitude of the radical members of the Conseil Privé. Raymond Martin seized the nuance, and, after the adoption of the cablegram, he requested that a sentence be added to the text:"The Head of the Colony associates himself with the request formulated by the majority of the Assembly." Governor General Chaudié was not enthusiastic about the addendum. His response was straightforward. He explained that he had the duty to keep his opinion to himself concerning going back to the more severe provisions of an act whose abrogation was approved only after mature examination and on request from the most competent and most qualified authorities for the preservation of the public health in the colonies as well as in France. Nobody requesting the floor, the session that had started at 4 p.m. ended at 5:30 p.m.

The minister of colonies, more sympathetic to the merchants' interests, reversed the decision made by the Conseil Privé, however, and instructed the governor general to impose the quarantine only on ships arriving from Côte d'Ivoire, while urging the *médecin sanitaire* of Dakar to be more vigilant with the medical examination of the arriving passengers and the disinfection of merchandise. Governor General Chaudié remained convinced that the decision to reimpose article 113 of the decree of 29 August 1884, even for one rainy season, was "inspired by the fear, even by the terror, that people in Senegal have of the possibility of the reemergence here of a yellow fever epidemic." In a letter to the minister of colonies, dated 15 June 1899, Chaudié explained that

> no measure seems severe enough or draconian enough to them (the people of Senegal) to the point that Mr. Raymond Martin, *conseiller privé* for fifteen years and certainly one of the most enlightened minds in Senegal, did not hesitate, along with the large majority of participants, 9 versus 3, to insist on the return to the implementation of the provisions of the decree of August 29, 1884.[55]

Despite the setback they experienced, the supporters of radical measures continued to put pressure on the administration officials in both Saint-Louis and Paris to rethink their public health policies aimed at protecting the colony from yellow fever that broke out in Grand-Bassam. They still had sympathizers within the General Inspection of

Health Service in the Ministry of Colonies in Paris who believed that as long as French colonies south of Senegal did not implement sanitary measures prescribed by the 1897 decree, the medical authorities in Senegal were entitled to declare all ships arriving from their ports suspect. From their point of view, the central administration in Paris was equally responsible for any future disasters if they did not put more pressure on the local colonial authorities still behind in the implementation of the provisions of the 1897 decree.[56]

The evidence presented here illustrates the complexity of the decision-making process, the interests at stake, the differences in the perception of disease threats, and how the final vote very often represented a compromise between the interests of commerce and those of public health but in an unpredictable way. One can understand the debate about the quarantines in the framework of a larger debate that was going on in France animated by the members of the Colonial Party, who were pushing for a policy of *mise en valeur* or development of the colonies. However, opposition to anti–yellow fever measures and anxiety increased when yellow fever returned to Senegal during the 1900 rainy season.

The evidence from the second half of the nineteenth century in Senegal indicates that the stress provoked by the threat of epidemic diseases and high mortality from yellow fever, in particular, generated the epidemic of fear and collective anxiety over the disease environment and the viability of Saint-Louis as a colonial port city / capital and of Senegal as a colony. French physicians played an important role in the construction of Senegal as an "unhealthy" colony and in the constant reformulation of the fears of the tropics that centered on the concepts of climatic determinism of disease, racial susceptibility, levels of seasoning, and repatriation policy. Furthermore, physicians contributed to the construction of the urban poor as "carriers" of infectious agents. The colonial authorities used the available resources to combat an enemy that remained elusive and reemerged when unexpected. Physicians also contributed to the cultivation of racial difference through the construction of yellow fever as the "White Man's Disease" in opposition to cholera, which was framed as the "Black Man's Disease." Heightened anxiety led to the adoption of policies of urban residential segregation based on class and to the imposition in 1884 of the automatic quarantine that lasted almost a decade before being seriously challenged by commercial interests.

During the postcolonial period, the evidence suggests a continuity in the discourse on anxiety in relation to urban Senegal. It focused on the presence in the public spaces in Dakar and Saint-Louis of lepers, beggars, Koranic school students (*talibés*) seeking food, and other physically challenged individuals. The authorities used anxiety-ridden expressions, such as "human wastes" (*déchets humains*) or "human obstructions" (*encombrements humains*), to refer to this segment of the urban poor who could be seen standing at major crossroads and near red lights, and almost "blocking" the passage in front of office buildings, banks, and even hospitals.[57] The news media were referring to those people whose lives were destroyed by the broad processes of neoliberalism, the migrant labor system, urbanization, and westernization. The new bureaucratic and military bourgeoisie feared that the urban poor would spread disease and become a threat to city life through their activities, including begging aggressively, obstructing sidewalks, and even littering in the very heart of the business and administration districts.

Notes

1. Benno Gammerl, "Emotional Styles—Concepts and Challenges," *Rethinking History: The Journal of Theory and Practice* 16, no. 2 (2012): 164.

2. Jean Delumeau, *La peur en Occent* (Paris: Hachette, 1978), 13–14; Barbara H. Rosenwein, "Review Essay: Worrying about Emotions in History," *American Historical Review* 107, no. 3 (2002): 842.

3. Maynard W. Swanson, "The Sanitation Syndrome: Bubonic Plague and Urban Native Policy in the Cape Colony, 1900–1909," *Journal of African History* 18, no. 3 (1977): 387–410.

4. Leo Spitzer, "The Mosquito and Segregation in Sierra Leone," *Canadian Journal of African Studies / Revue canadienne des études africaines* 2, no. 1 (1968): 49–61; Stephen Frenkel and John Western, "Pretext or Prophylaxis? Racial Segregation and Malarial Mosquitos in a British Tropical Colony: Sierra Leone," *Annals of the Association of American Geographers* 78, no. 2 (June 1988): 211–28; Odile Goerg, "From Hill Station (Freetown) to Downtown Conakry (First Ward): Comparing French and British Approaches to Segregation in Colonial Cities at the Beginning of the Twentieth Century," *Canadian Journal of African Studies / Revue canadienne des études africaines* 32, no. 1 (1998): 1–31.

5. Kalala Ngalamulume, "Plague and Violence in Saint-Louis-du-Sénégal, 1917–1920," *Cahiers d'études africaines* 183 (2006): 539–65.

6. See Raymond F. Betts, "The Establishment of the Medina in Dakar, Senegal, 1914," *Africa* 41, no. 2 (April 1971): 143–53; Elikia M'Bokolo, "Peste et société urbaine à Dakar: L'épidémie de 1914," *Cahiers d'études africaines* 22, nos. 85/86 (1982): 13–46; Myron Echenberg, *Black Death, White Medicine: Bubonic Plague and the Politics of Public Health in Colonial Senegal, 1914–1945*

(Portsmouth, NH: Heinemann, 2001); Liora Bigon, "Bubonic Plague, Colonial Ideologies, and Urban Planning Politics: Dakar, Lagos, and Kumasi," *Planning Perspectives* 31, no. 2 (2016): 205–26.

7. K. D. Patterson and G. F. Pyle, "The Diffusion of Influenza in Sub-Saharan Africa during the 1918–1919 Pandemic," *Social Science and Medicine* 17, no. 17 (1983): 1299–307; K. D. Patterson, "The Influenza Epidemic of 1918–19 in the Gold Coast," *Journal of African History* 24, no. 4 (1983): 485–502.

8. Terence Ranger, "The Influenza Pandemic in Southern Rhodesia: A Crisis of Comprehension," in *Imperial Medicine and Indigenous Societies*, ed. David Arnold (Manchester: Manchester University Press, 1988), 172–88.

9. S. S. Abdool Karim and Q. Abdool Karim, eds., *HIV/AIDS in South Africa* (Cambridge: Cambridge University Press, 2005, 2008); Didier Fassin, *When Bodies Remember: Experiences and Politics of AIDS in South Africa*, trans. Amy Jacobs and Gabrielle Varro (Berkeley: University of California Press, 2007).

10. J. M. Shultz et al., "The Role of Fear-Related Behaviors in the 2013–2016 West Africa Ebola Virus Disease Outbreak," *Current Psychiatry Reports* 18, no. 11 (November 2016): 104; Ann O'Leary, Mohammed F. Jalloh, and Yuval Neria, "Fear and Culture: Contextualising Mental Health Impact of the 2014–2016 Ebola Epidemic in West Africa," *British Medical Journal Global Health* 3, no. 3 (2018): e000924.

11. Rosenwein, "Review Essay," 842.

12. Portions of the materials on yellow fever appeared in *Colonial Pathologies, Environment, and Western Medicine in Saint-Louis-du-Senegal, 1867–1920*. I wish to thank Peter Lang Publishing, Inc., for allowing their inclusion here.

13. Bérenger-Féraud, *Traité clinique des maladies des Européens au Sénégal*, vol. 1 (Paris: Adrien Delahaye, 1875), viii.

14. All quotations in this paragraph are from Archives Nationales du Sénégal [hereafter ANS] H20/Senegal, records of the Hygiene and Public Sanitation Council meeting, 10–11 January 1868.

15. ANS/H20/Senegal, records of the Hygiene and Public Sanitation Council meeting, 10–11 January 1868; for more on contagion and infection, see Peter Baldwin, *Contagion and the State in Europe, 1830–1930* (Cambridge: Cambridge University Press, 1999), 3–5.

16. A. du Mazet, "Note sur l'assainissement du Sénégal," *Moniteur du Sénégal*, 21 February 1882, 31–33.

17. Archives of the Congrégation du Saint-Esprit, Chevilly-la-Rue [hereafter ACSE], *Bulletin général*, t. 6 (1868–69), 864; Archives nationales françaises, Section outre-mer [hereafter ANFSOM], Série géographique, Sénégal, XI 30, chief medical officer, Rulland, to governor, 3 January 1869.

18. ANS/H28/AOF/2, governor's decision no. 15 of 2 July 1878; ANS/H28/AOF/4, governor's decision no. 17 of 27 July 1878; ANS/H28/AOF/5, decree no. 16 of 28 July 1878; ANS/H28/AOF/37, *ordonnateur* to governor, 6 August 1878.

19. ACSE, *Journal de la communauté*, entry for 4 August 1881.

20. ANFSOM/FM/SEN/XI/50, Governor General Chaudié to minister of colonies, 26 June 1900.

21. ACSE, *Bulletin général*, 6.42 (1867), 183.
22. ANS/H2/AOF/109, letter to governor, no date provided.
23. ANS/H22, Sanitary Commission meeting, 14 May 1879.
24. ACSE, *Journal de Saint-Louis*, entry for 23 July 1881, 110.
25. ACSE/158/B/Senegal/024, *Soleil*, 5 November 1878.
26. ANS/G10/26, Annual Report 1910, 60.
27. ANS/Senegal/H49, Cabinet's meeting minutes, 11 March 1910.
28. Later on, other ordinances prohibited the urban poor from drying animal skins and fish within the limits of the "faubourgs," or slum areas, during the rainy season between 1 June and 15 December when the outbreaks of yellow fever generally occurred, and from throwing rubbish or even bathing in less than one hundred fifty meters on each side of the Servatius Drive and on Guet N'dar beach. See ANS, ordinance of 23 May 1885; ANS, BOS, municipal ordinances of 21 August 1891, 368, and 28 July 1892, 345.
29. Swanson, "Sanitation Syndrome," 387.
30. For more on the subject, read Philip Strong, "Epidemic Psychology: A Model," *Sociology of Health and Illness* 12, no. 3 (1990): 249–59.
31. Michael Taussig, *Shamanism, Colonialism, and the Wild Man: A Study in Terror and Healing* (Chicago: University of Chicago Press, 1987), 3.
32. ANS, *Moniteur du Sénégal et dépendances*, 1867, 643; ANS/H20/Senegal, minutes of the CPHS meeting, 10–11 January 1868. The duration of the preventive quarantine of observation was seven to fifteen days in 1867, fifteen days in 1878, and twenty-one days in 1881 and thereafter.
33. On 18 July 1882, medical officials in Dakar imposed a twenty-one-day quarantine on ships arriving from the south between Pointe Sangomar and Gabon with an unclean bill of health, and at least a seven-day quarantine of observation on ships without a bill of health. Governor A. Vallon still hoped the measure "would facilitate the operations of commerce while protecting the colony, as much as possible, from an invasion of yellow fever or any other infectious disease." Actually, quarantine measures constituted a major obstacle to commercial activities and a loss of revenues, as we will see later in this chapter.
34. ANS, *Moniteur du Sénégal et dépendances*, 5 December 1882, 225.
35. ANS/H22/Senegal, Ordinance of 20 June 1883 prescribing the measures of sanitary police for Senegal and Dependencies.
36. ANFSOM/Sér. Senegal/XI-28, Ordinance of governor of Senegal and Dependencies, 19 June 1884.
37. ANS/H2/Senegal, decree on the reorganization of the sanitary service in Senegal, 29 August 1884. This decree was similar to the decree signed in November 1883, which protected France against the suspected ships coming from America.
38. ANFSOM/FM/SEN/XI/50A, Sanitary Commission meeting minutes, 6 June 1899.
39. ANS/H2/Senegal, report about quarantines by chief medical officer, 3 May 1889.

40. ANS/H2/Senegal, governor to interior director, no. 139 of 27 May 1889; ANS/H2/Senegal, E. Etienne, undersecretary of state for colonies to governor, no. 778 of 29 June 1889.

41. ANS/H4/Senegal, minutes of the Council of Public Hygiene and Salubrity, 31 May 1890.

42. ANS/H4/Senegal, minutes of the Sanitary Commission meeting, 25 August 1892.

43. ANS/H4/Senegal, minutes of the Sanitary Commission, 1 September 1892.

44. ANS/H46, decree of 29 December 1893 modifying the decree of 29 August 1884.

45. ANS, *Bulletin officiel du Sénégal,* 1897, 343.

46. ANS/H4/Senegal, Chamber of Commerce to Colonial Commission, 11 September 1898.

47. ANS/H24/Senegal, minutes of the Sanitary Commission meeting, 17 May 1899.

48. ANFSOM/FM/SEN/XI/50/A, Deliberations of *Conseil Privé* meeting, no. 12 of 8 June 1899.

49. ANS/H25/Senegal, chief medical officer to governor general, no. 610 of 2 June 1899.

50. ANFSOM/FM/SEN/XI/50A, Sanitary Commission meeting records, 6 June 1899; report prepared by physician Lafage, Chief Medical Officer, and read at the meeting, suggesting more rigorous measures.

51. ANS/H24/Senegal, Sanitary Commission meeting records, 6 June 1899.

52. The Conseil Privé included Governor General Chaudié (president), Bergès (secretary general of government), Cnapelynck (general prosecutor, head of judiciary service), Bunel (commissar of colonies, head of administrative service), Chief Medical Officer Lafage, Raymond Martin (member), Gros (substitute member), and Sasias (archivist secretary). Invited guests for the session held on 8 June 1899 were Colonel Pujol (Superior Commander of Troops), Germain d'Erneville (Chamber of Commerce president, Saint-Louis), Theodore Carpot (deputy mayor filling in for the mayor), Fr. Marsat (mayor of Dakar), Gabard (mayor of Rufisque), and Le Bègue de Germiny (mayor of Gorée).

53. ANFSOM/FM/SEN/XI/50A, Conseil Privé meeting records, 8 June 1899.

54. ANFSOM/FM/SEN/XI/50A.

55. ANFSOM/FM/SEN/XI/50 A, Governor General Chaudié to minister of colonies, no. 1180 of 15 June 1899.

56. ANFSOM/FM/SEN/XI/50A, Note from inspector general of Health Service in Paris to Director of Africa Desk (1st Bureau), 12 July 1899.

57. René Collignon, "La lutte des pouvoirs publics contre les encombrements humains à Dakar," *Canadian Journal of African Studies* 18, no. 3 (1984): 573–82.

PART TWO

Unsettling Narratives

FOUR

Anxiety over Masculinity

*Gendered and Sexual Struggles
in Mwanga II's Buganda, 1884–97*

NAKANYIKE B. MUSISI

THERE IS PROBABLY NO OTHER PERIOD IN BUGANDA'S HIStory so traumatized by anxiety, fear, and discomfiture as 1884 to 1897.[1] Richard Reid and others characterize it as the most violent and tumultuous in the kingdom's history.[2] Several historians view it as misunderstood and call for caution in interpreting Kabaka Mwanga II's rule.[3] Ado K. Tiberendwa asserts that it laid the foundations for the colonization of Uganda.[4] By the mid-nineteenth century, many societies that had been opened up to Arab and European trade, religions, and colonization were afflicted by some form of chaos and painful human experience; Buganda was no exception.[5] Besides, never before was the question of male masculinity the cause of so much uneasiness, embarrassment, and anxiety as in this period. This chapter investigates a topic that has largely been ignored: the extent to which these events were sources of individual and collective anxiety and, above all, what this anxiety represented and the work it performed.

Commencing with a clarification of the term "anxiety," this chapter is divided into four sections. The first section sets the stage by laying out the complex and delicate sociopolitical context within which Mwanga and the Baganda experienced greater fear and anxiety than ever before. The section demonstrates Mwanga's sources of fear and anxiety and his unfruitful and often counterproductive attempts to quell the disquiet.

Thus, the section begins with his assumption of power in 1884 and ends with his overthrow, arrest, and deportation in 1897. The second section demonstrates how Buganda's multiple means of performing masculinities and femininities were at the core of great misunderstandings between the Baganda and their foreign guests and a source of anxiety on both sides. Missionaries' probes into and disapproval of Mwanga's unconventional masculinity, with its fluid institutional and social characteristics, caused them extreme discomfiture and vice versa; the resulting fear, anger, and anxiety culminated in Mwanga's killing of the now so-called and celebrated Uganda Martyrs. The combination of masculinity and femininity visible in Mwanga's behavior—neither homosexual nor heterosexual—was the antithesis of what missionaries felt was appropriate. The third section specifically focuses on women, disclosing how until the arrival of female missionaries in the mid-1890s, the sexuality of Baganda women remained of less interest to missionaries and thus created less anxiety compared to that of men. The fourth section shows the sociopolitical work of a gendered anxiety, arguing that the king's palace and also the missionary communes in Mwanga's capital were sites where fear and panic over masculinity were bred in the private lives of the Baganda, with fatal consequences for some. The section emphasizes the chapter's recurrent theme that different understandings of and practices surrounding gender and sex were at the core of a widespread sense of fear, insecurity, and anxiety in Buganda. I close the chapter with Mwanga's lamentation, one that should be read within the larger context of anxieties over masculinity and a partial victory of one form over the other.

In this chapter, I understand anxiety to be both a signifier and an effect—"a fusion of fear with the anticipation of future evil . . . a feeling of threat, especially of a fearsome threat."[6] Basically, besides being a reaction to an anticipated or imagined situation or event, whether real or not (the effect of danger), anxiety is a state in which certainty has been suspended. This chapter argues that Mwanga's court was a cauldron of bubbling anxieties, fluid and unresolved contradictions, and paradoxes.[7] For the entirety of Mwanga's reign (1884–97), Buganda was in a perpetual state of anxiety. The best Luganda phrase to convey this anxiety is *"obunkenke"* (as in *okubera kubunkenke*)—a condition of being on tiptoe; restless; agitated; in a state of suspicion without trust. Indeed, a sort of benign paranoia (the Baganda make a distinction between *okubera kubunkenke* (being anxious) and *okweralikirila* (being worried). J. F.

Faupel comes close in describing this anxiety as "keeping the Englishmen on tenterhooks."[8] I contend that at the core of this anxiety were spirited cultural tensions and contradictions—a struggle over two competing patriarchal cultures (British and missionary on the one hand and Ganda on the other hand) and, more so, their dissimilar assumptions about power, sexual desire, the body and, above all, constructions of masculinity. A window into this difference is provided by a dialogue between Mwanga and Father Lourdel of the Roman Catholic White Fathers Mission when the kabaka candidly asked the missionary, "Is it true that you forbid the satisfaction of certain *natural desires*?" (my emphasis). Lourdel answered, "Yes, outside the conditions imposed by God," to which Mwanga responded, "But you are asking for the impossible."[9]

While I locate both anxiety and ferment at the royal court and in Buganda at large within the larger political climate in the second half of the nineteenth century in East Africa and the disasters that befell Mwanga, the objective of this chapter is to identify, in the most general sense, the ideological sources behind the anxiety or anxieties in Mwanga's Buganda and to look at this anxiety in a way that those who lived within that ideology could not. Indeed, as Semakula Kiwanuka cautions, the catastrophes that befell Mwanga "are not sufficient explanation" for the emotional crisis and anxiety of the period.[10] Far from being "irrational," the emotions accompanying the historic processes of this period reveal a great deal about the apparatuses of power and sexual politics. Of particular interest is how, in the evolution of the Buganda kingdom, these historic processes were experienced as gendered. Vulnerability to feelings of discomfiture, anxiety, and fear was by no means exclusive to one racial, class, or gender group; rather, it was generally shared across all social strata. Ironically, for Mwanga, anxiety, like anger, could be appeased with material presents.[11]

The chapter's central premise is that Mwanga's Buganda was substantially shaped by repeated occurrences of panic, which bred emotions that had a profound effect on the everyday experiences of the king and his subjects. These emotions were also deeply felt by the Arab-Swahili traders, the missionaries, the members of the Imperial British East Africa Company and, finally, by Captain Lugard and other colonial officials. Yet, at a more substantial level, if we understand anxiety to be merely a condition of okubera kubunkenke we could be missing a crucial point and mistakenly be tempted to see the traders', missionaries', and colonial officials' anxieties as motivated and driven by differing agendas (profit for traders, conversion of souls for missionaries, and territorial and political control for colonialists). I argue that, while this might have some truth to it, in reality each group struggled to secure a niche in a patriarchal and hierarchical social system whose premise was the unequal distribution of power and authority, a system that could only be sustained by a constant defense of the privileges of some of its members and by a constraint of others.[12] I also argue that, to the extent that we may say that "calm/peacefulness/stability" prevailed in the aftermath of Mwanga's downfall, it did so not because a "villain" king departed the scene, but because anxiety, gender and sexual inconsistencies, and contradictions could be curtailed, assimilated, or contained in the new post-Mwanga Buganda by an emerging Buganda Christian oligarchy headed by Apolo Kaggwa and supported by the Christian missionaries and a powerful colonial apparatus. The preservation or potential loss of this new hybrid patriarchal state yielded a new set of anxieties and struggles in the colonial period.

I contend that a problematization of anxiety in Mwanga's Buganda leads us to a useful way of understanding the pervasive masculine anxiety toward female chastity and women's sexuality in general that became endemic by the end of the century. I have discussed some of these gendered anxieties elsewhere.[13] The crisis in Mwanga's Buganda, particularly at the court and more so over his sexuality, requires us to think differently about specific conditions of the late nineteenth century that might have produced gendered anxieties. Expressions and representations of anxiety must be seen as signifiers within a discourse of patriarchy and masculinity. From this perspective, anxiety is taken as a sociopolitical rather a psychic phenomenon.

Procedurally, this requires us to do a number of things: First, to develop an analysis of the productive elements of anxiety in late nineteenth-century Buganda—the functions of its statements (particularly of inclusions and exclusions and anger) and the distribution of power as well as conferred legitimacy or denial thereof. Second, to articulate it beyond an individual (not a private/personal affair) to expose/uncover its discursive function in the production of masculinity. And third, to articulate anxiety as containing enabling element(s)—a resourceful function for the creation of a new and decisively patriarchal Buganda in which the feminine functions (particularly political) became squashed or severely constrained. It is difficult to think of Mwanga and his sex "scandal" in isolation from the social and political tensions that were endemic to his times—the very tensions that produced what Mark Breitenberg has termed "anxious masculinity."[14] Mwanga's anxieties and anxieties over Mwanga were effects of various divisive, contentious, and prickly social and ideological factors—a spectrum of cultural anxieties.

Preamble

From the mid-1880s to the close of the nineteenth century, the inhabitants of Buganda found themselves in an environment that was becoming too complex to fully comprehend. Semakula Kiwanuka, Richard Reid, and others describe it as a kingdom infiltrated by outside forces and less engaged in expansionist wars.[15] Life at the palace was bustling, intense, and tumultuous.[16] In 1884, when Mwanga, following the death of his father, Mutesa I, assumed power, he became, at the tender age of seventeen, Buganda's thirty-first kabaka and inherited a kingdom at the peak of its greatness.[17] Overthrown in 1888 and reinstated in 1890, Mwanga was overthrown again and finally in 1897 and exiled by the British to the Seychelles. In contrast to the positive descriptions early travelers and missionaries gave of Mutesa I, they frequently described Mwanga in unenthusiastic and disparaging terms.[18] Mutesa I had welcomed the Arab-Swahili traders to his court in 1857, the Church Missionary Society (CMS–Anglican Protestants) missionaries in 1877, and the Roman Catholic White Fathers in 1879. Although Muslims preceded both the French Roman Catholics and the British CMS Anglicans in Buganda, their presence within the palace enclave was a continuous source of anxiety for the French White Fathers and CMS missionaries. Mackay of CMS observed that the three groups existed in a permanent state of antagonism.[19] Mutesa somehow managed to contain the situation by playing off the protagonists against one other. Mwanga's lack of success in balancing the conflicts between the competing groups at his court, however, resulted in what he had predicted in 1885: "I shall be the last native king of Buganda."[20] His turbulent and intermittent reign was marked by massacres of Catholic and Protestant converts, civil wars, a near famine, two defeats by Bunyoro, and a disastrous revolt against the British. These were accompanied by rapid changes in gender regime, order, and practices and persistent accusations of sodomy at Mwanga's court.[21]

In 1884, the kabaka's court (*kisakatte*) was a coveted and intriguing space for a sizable number of young boys (referred to as *bagalagala* in Luganda and as "pages" in the missionary literature). It was customary for parents or guardians participating in Buganda's system of political patronage to send their sons to court to receive training for future roles as chiefs or dignitaries (*bakungu*) in the kingdom. Though the CMS missionaries and the White Fathers had now established independent communes inhabited by their mostly young, male followers in Mwanga's capital, the traditional religion of Lubaale continued to pervade the kingdom's political and social life.[22]

At his succession, Mwanga sought to assert authority over his father's chiefs by promoting young men and princesses of his generation to state offices. Kiwanuka states that Mwanga was "determined to be master in his own house."[23] The old establishment resented Mwanga's strategies and took every opportunity to frustrate them. For example, they took advantage of growing fears of European colonial invasion to accuse their Christian rivals of betraying state secrets to the missionaries.[24] In 1885, exploiting Mwanga's gullibility, *Katikkiro* (Prime Minister) Mukasa executed an incoming Anglican bishop, James Hannington—a nightmare Mwanga never recovered from.[25] In November of the same year, having denounced the missionaries, Mwanga castigated his pages as "double-tongued lads."[26] Mwanga executed the leading Christian convert—Joseph Mukasa Balikuddembe—who was one of his best friends. The increase in the number of baptisms that followed the massacres suggests that they bred deepening feelings of anxiety and fear. It became more difficult for Mwanga to anticipate what the Christians thought or planned to do. The occurrence of two fires within the palace added to Mwanga's troubles.[27] In an effort to divert attention from his domestic problems, Mwanga in vain attacked Bunyoro in January 1886. In May and June 1886, frustrated because his efforts to get the Christians on his side were ineffective, and supported by certain traditionalists led by his prime minister, Mukasa, Mwanga finally resorted to outright suppression through murder to engender fear in the Christian and missionary populations.[28] Irrespective of motive, these episodes show that strong masculinist and sentimental emotions toward his pages underlay Mwanga's actions. Nonetheless, his pages' openness to changes was unquestionable.

In addition to increased pressure and tension from the traditionalists and his continuing discomfiture and anxiety about his own circumstances, Mwanga was experiencing remorse about the execution of his Christian allies and friends.[29] Realizing that he could not control the kingdom as long as the old chiefs continued to give him advice, Mwanga opted for extermination of the old guard, though this entailed ignoring his mother's opinion that it would be a political error.[30] To operationalize this strategy, Mwanga recruited and armed the remaining Christian survivors to form a new institution—the "Musket Armed Regiment."[31]

Unsettled by the unfolding events, the old chiefs warned Mwanga that his new regiments could turn against him. In time, as the old chiefs predicted, the new regiments began to resist Mwanga openly with a boldness and insolence that increased his anxiety. In a quick succession of events, Christian and Muslim converts entered into an alliance that overthrew and deposed him in favor of his elder brother, Kiwewa, and divided the chieftainships among themselves.[32] An alliance between Christians and Muslims fell apart within a month. Kiwewa, who refused to be circumcised—which is traditional for Muslims—was deposed, murdered, and replaced by his brother Kalema. To avert a rebellion, Kalema massacred all the princes and princesses.[33] Despite their differences, the three kings—Mwanga, Kiwewa, and Kalema—all "resented and almost feared being dominated by a single political group."[34] Following sixteen months of civil war, the Christian faction finally captured the capital on 11 February 1890 and reinstalled Mwanga on his throne. Mwanga's restoration failed to end the political struggle due to continuing strong traditionalist resistance in the east and a Muslim army in the northern part of Buganda.[35] In December 1890, amid quarrels between the Protestant and Catholic Christian chiefs with one another and with Mwanga, Captain Lugard arrived with a small military force at the head of the Imperial British East Africa Company (IBEAC), which helped the Protestants defeat the Catholics. His restoration of Mwanga as kabaka in February 1892 hastened the declaration of a British protectorate over Buganda in 1894.

Mwanga was finally deposed in 1897 after he tried to revolt. During his final days as kabaka, Mwanga's and the colonialists' anxiety about the potential for conspiracy and insurgency, together with their fear of the unknown, instigated a panic among the colonialists. Lugard used the existence of this panic to justify his plea to the British government to interfere to stop the civil wars. With horror, Lugard stated, "Once Waganda quarrel they must fight to the death or no reconciliation is possible."[36] The CMS's Bishop Tucker warned that, should Her Majesty's government decline to take control over Buganda, the consequences would be disastrous.[37] Disowned by his chiefs, who were now closely associated with the British, Mwanga denounced his prime minister,

Apolo Kaggwa, and his colleagues: "You are no longer my ministers nor my subjects.... You have deserted and offered your services to white foreigners."[38] Taken together, these powerful pronouncements epitomize the prejudices and political fears in each camp. Like Mwanga, each constituency—the colonialists, the Muslims, the missionaries, and the pages—experienced fear and anxiety when they found themselves in a position of vulnerability or in actual danger.

The Europeans and missionaries, for their part, perceived the Baganda as a people with unquenchably brutal tempers which, once let loose, led to absurd and irrational actions. Mwanga, who was situated at the center of this imperial milieu where racist prejudices were widely circulated, interpreted his subjects' acts not only as racially biased but also as betrayal of the highest order. Consider, for instance, his insult of his pages for their dogged commitment to the missionaries and their teachings: "You are disobedient dogs. You call Jesus your King, and look upon me as your brother, because I am black like yourselves."[39] He lived daily with the anxieties that this perception caused him.[40] Moreover, in conjunction with struggles over religion and politics embedded in this chaotic period, Mwanga and those close to him became embroiled in significant struggles over gender and sex that concomitantly affected the social life of the kingdom. The former—religion and politics—have been the focus of much historical attention. The latter—gender and sex, including the innate anxieties they embody—have largely been ignored. This chapter attempts to explicate these anxieties in the context of these larger social and political developments.

Anxieties over Gender and Sex

The structural conditions and constraints within which anxieties about gender and sex were experienced and expressed cannot be ignored. Drawing on the work of social anthropologists who have documented the rites and rituals that surround the transition from one life stage to another in various cultures, I identify three stages in this transition from boyhood to adulthood for both royal and commoner Baganda males. The first stage entailed leaving home. As noted earlier, in conformity with Buganda's complex system of political patronage and as a strategy to get access to or maintain the kabaka's favor, parents, guardians, or patrons sent boys to the royal court, where they underwent training for their futures roles and duties as leaders occupying state offices. Within the court compound, the boys, called *bagalagala* in Luganda and consistently referred to as "pages" in missionary literature (see earlier), inhabited a strictly homosocial space—the *bisakatte* (the royal enclosure).

During the second stage in this transition, the boys underwent training to develop skills essential for their future responsibilities as holders of state offices. Since their roles at court necessitated giving service to the kabaka (or a chief) as well as "attracting his favors,"[41] it could also include participation in warfare. Their training was structured to foster attitudes and behaviors compatible with being dutiful and following orders and routines without question. There was also a strong emphasis on being obedient and compliant.[42] The third stage, analogous to working as an intern prior to graduation, was being deployed as a *mutongole* or a subchief.

The homosocial character of the boys' social environment, as well as its unintended lessons or side effects, promoted male-male competitiveness and facilitated development of intimate bonding that, for Mwanga or other male dignitaries, went beyond sexual gratification. The boys' formal training emphasized physical activities that fostered the boys' control of their sexual and bodily practices and influenced construction of their sexual and gender identity.[43] The boys' future character was also shaped by the hidden curricula in both positive and negative ways. The hidden curricula, for example, fostered the boys' ability to share secrets with friends. Since it is likely that boys who found themselves in a boot camp–like environment without intimate friends would feel lonely or get depressed, this behavior must have been psychologically beneficial. Mwanga expressed deep loneliness just before the second massacre when he was deserted by his pages, who were virtual age-mates. His close friend—the first martyr, Joseph Mukasa Balikuddembe—had confronted him about the homosexual relationship the two had freely engaged in as part of their bonding and as an expression of affection. A zealous Christian convert, Joseph had named the practice as "unclean and detested by God" and demanded that, should Mwanga wish to continue with it, he should "leave . . . my Christians alone and, rather, leave to the Muslims the vileness with which Satan inspires them."[44] Feeling betrayed and deserted, Mwanga was later to lament: "Even Mwafu . . . the only one of my pages who is completely loyal and devoted to me, always ready to obey my slightest wish, even he is absent; and here am I, alone and forsaken. It is a disgrace!"[45]

Other benefits of intimate bonding included learning and practicing problem-solving strategies. Developing intimate relationships was important in establishing trust and expressing vulnerability,[46] especially in a social environment made up of hundreds of boys of relatively the same age. Mwanga's lamentation, cited above, reveals that the world of boy friendship was one in which kindness, love, loyalty, mutual recognition, and support were expected and crucial. Given the social constraints that structured their lives, including the taboo on contact between the two sexes, the boys' only choice was to establish relationships with one another. I draw two important conclusions from this. First, while genital and nongenital bonding could take place in the compound the youths inhabited, they could also be policed and supervised without much difficulty. Second, same-sex and other practical exercises using bodies, together with nurturing and facilitating same-sex emotional intimacies, were embedded in the boys' preparation for political power in precolonial Buganda.[47] In short, these behaviors also formed political work—a royal service.[48] Homosexuality in the palace and, in this case, the king's sexuality with the boys, was a part of a "beneficial" hierarchical system that served as the basis—a springboard—for potential future gain of social, economic, and political power. The boys were sent to the palace to unquestioningly serve the king in whatever manner he would require their service.[49] And should they fail to do so, the sources/guardians/parents of these pages were even ready to give them up to be killed, as one chief expressed to Mwanga after the latter's complaint: "Master, when we gave you our children they were good [meaning obedient]. If now they have become bad, that is not our fault, but the effect of the spell which has been cast upon them. Kill them! We shall provide you with better ones."[50]

The missionaries replaced the bisakatte, as sites in which the kingdom's future leaders were trained, with denominational compounds akin to tight communes. In conjunction with being the locus of the pages' socialization to the new religion, the denominational communes were also sites of gender resocialization. As the pages gathered together daily for Bible study, their sexual behavior was reoriented, tamed, and homogenized to conform to the newly introduced model of hegemonic patriarchy. Significantly, as a result of this reorientation, the boys' sexuality, which had been politically exploited in the bisakatte as a means of achieving office or the favor of the king or his dignitaries, was becoming liberated from state exploitation. Success in establishing communes within palace grounds was essential to the missionary project of creating conditions and terms favorable to introducing a new definition of sex that was intimately linked to the emergence of new emotions and a different way of forming character and training for leadership.

At that time in Buganda, as elsewhere, gender behavior expressed historical, cultural, and emergent social practices that were associated with stocks of knowledge, institutional structures, and ideological leanings that arose out of the recognition of sex differences between males and females.[51] Multiple means of performing masculinities and femininities existed. The missionary project brought with it a qualitatively different gender model that destabilized Ganda practices. As it gained popularity, this gender model—hegemonic masculinity—became dominant. Hegemonic masculinity configured gender practices that embodied and legitimized patriarchy in such a way that no deviation was allowed. It guaranteed the dominant position of men and, notably, the subordinate position of women. Whether young and effeminate or sodomites and homosexuals—all boys were subordinated to it.

This is not to suggest that male dominance did not exist in Baganda prior to missionary arrival. Rather, the moral code embedded in the model of patriarchy prevalent in Buganda consisted of a plurality of prescriptions and proscriptions that governed the multiple ways in which masculinities and femininities were practiced and lived on a daily basis. The argument advanced here is that, in the precolonial Ganda sex/gender system, (1) not all women were subordinated to men, and (2) all men, apart from those of royalty, were gendered female in relation to royalty and were considered to be the king's "wives."[52] These differences were institutionally sanctioned and principally observed. For example, the set of conventions that governed princesses' sexual behavior and private lives differed from the set for commoner women. Princesses were considered honorary men and referred to in masculine terms.[53] The new system of hegemonic patriarchy introduced by the missionaries undermined the Buganda sex/gender system. Emphasizing biological determinism, the missionaries' gender model upheld the notion that every individual man in the patriarchal gender order is automatically in a dominant position and every woman automatically in a position of subordination.

The struggles over and anxieties about gender practices that developed between the Baganda and their foreign guests centered primarily on how male sexual practices were manifested and esteemed and how masculinity must be lived and deployed by the king. Missionary scrutiny of Mwanga's unconventional masculinity, with its fluid institutional and social characteristics, caused them extreme discomfiture. The combination of masculinity and femininity visible in Mwanga's behavior—neither homosexual nor heterosexual—was the antithesis of what they felt was appropriate. Mwanga as a "grand" polygamist had fifteen named wives, two hundred reserve wives, seven hundred concubines, and fifteen hundred maidservants.[54] Moreover, Mwanga's habit of practicing and demanding anal sex from his pages offended the missionaries' notions of morality, normality, and stability; it perturbed them greatly and caused a great deal of anxiety for them. According to Kenneth Hamilton, "the actual sinful (or unenlightened) practices of the *Kabakas*, such as polygamy and same-sex practice, would have fuelled fears of total collapse, lawlessness, and transgressive violence in the European imaginary."[55]

Hence, driven partly by anxiety and partly by ideological and cultural differences, in Buganda, where male power, status, control, and domination were lived according to an alternative sex/gender model, the missionary project focused much of its energy on "civilizing" Baganda notions of masculinity. In addition to condemnation of sodomy, this required promulgation of an ideology that would lead to a reconfiguration of gender practices and relations and manifestly support and privilege the ascendancy and supremacy of male heterosexuality. Thus, the missionaries' success in situating their Western model of education within the palace compound and teaching reading, writing, and technical subjects led to significant cultural and material changes in the lives of all who inhabited the court—the king, the boys, men, girls, and women. Anxiety about "sin" resulting from the pages' exposure to missionary education was aggravated when Mwanga expected them to submit to his "relentless" sexual requests.[56] The existential moral dilemma this instigated in the pages gave rise to panic as well as a desire to achieve righteousness within the Christian moral code. A climax was reached when certain boys, including some whom Mwanga loved greatly and considered close friends, adopted and operationalized the form of normative masculinity the missionaries were teaching.

European observers' opinion that Mwanga's "immorality" caused him to order the massacre of the pages shows that they underestimated the complex political exigencies which lay behind it. Their reductionist and erroneous explanation resulted from their failure to appreciate the complex Baganda sex/gender system and to understand how it was being destabilized and superseded by their narrower system. From reading

Ashe, Mackay, Streicher, Thoonen, and Faupel one gets the impression that both the Church Missionary Society and the Roman Catholic White Fathers missionaries and Baganda Christian leaders became obsessed with evaluating Mwanga's sexual practices in accordance with the premises of hegemonic patriarchy.[57] For instance, one of the major conditions for Mwanga's restoration to the throne in 1888, following his first removal from power, was that he renounce "sodomy" and agree to conform to the sex/gender regime that the missionaries considered acceptable.[58] The same demand was made of him at the second restoration. Besides, it is ironic that the missionaries claimed throughout this period that the Arabs had introduced "sodomy" into the Buganda court and that Mwanga learned "sodomy" from the Arabs. This oft-repeated claim ignores Mwanga's and other Baganda's resistance to missionary gender prescriptions and proscriptions. Nevertheless, the severity of the missionaries' attempts to police, constrain, and tame his sexual practices supports Hamilton's conclusion that "Mwanga was marked and tracked by his sexual practices."[59]

The notion that the Baganda operated on the basis of a single sex/gender model is highly contestable. Henri Médard reports instances of men who preferred boys to women; his work demonstrates the existence of numerous sexual practices in precolonial Buganda.[60] Practices such as the use by a male healer of his external male genitalia in treating his male or female patients indicates that practices observers not conversant with Baganda cultural notions may have considered sexual could have fulfilled purposes such as healing and spirituality; that is, they were not sexual acts. Moreover, to assume as the missionaries did that the occurrence of same-sex behavior was exclusive to Mwanga's court and, thus, the perversity of one man is to ignore accounts of its reported existence elsewhere in eastern and central Africa.[61]

Sense can be made of a number of Mwanga's controversial actions if they are examined in relation to his anxiety about his subjects' perceptions of him as a supreme leader entitled to their confidence. Consider, for example, two events that occurred in quick succession—Mwanga's absolving the Christian pages' behavior, shortly after the massacre, and then arming and permitting them to loot and terrorize the older chiefs; and Mwanga's unexpected decision to wage war against Bunyoro. Because of the pervasive sense of anxiety with which Mwanga lived, he experienced Buganda's defeat by Bunyoro as a personal injury. Mwanga's decision to again take up arms against Bunyoro was thus rational, since defeating them would certainly boost his self-esteem. As an absolute ruler acting within the fluid masculinity of the Buganda sex/gender system, Mwanga felt any disloyalty as an affront to his traditional power and masculinity. Moreover, as kabaka, according to Kiganda culture, Mwanga was entitled to sexual license, and all men as well as all women were considered his wives. But adherents of the newly introduced system of sex/gender relations viewed Mwanga's sexual prerogatives and behavior as kabaka as repellent and perverse. It is not surprising that the Christian pages generated a host of derogatory labels for any male who dared to deviate from the Christian normative masculinity they had so recently adopted for themselves. Mwanga's masculinity was wounded on more than one occasion when his most trusted friend confronted him about what he, as kabaka, saw as his prerogative—an active anal sexual relationship with his pages. Mwanga's sense of his own masculinity was further wounded when, in addition to denying him sex, his pages taunted him over his lack of control.[62]

One can also argue that, in the chaotic period of religious wars that followed the massacre, Mwanga had little scope to explore alternative routes to manhood. He was terrified of being portrayed as a weakling by the Arab-Swahili traders, who often taunted him, and distressed by being characterized as feminine by the Christians.[63] In conformity to the behavior expected of Baganda leaders in those times, Mwanga responded to his anxiety about being seen as an incompetent and feeble ruler by making an effort to conform to the behavior appropriate for a man in the "Christian" sex/gender system. On more than one occasion before his exile he attempted to negotiate and to live within the acceptable boundaries of the missionary characterization of masculinity. Instead of enabling him to gain respect, however, the consequences of his efforts were humiliating and disastrous; further marginalized, he found himself in a politically and psychologically painful position. The only alternative he could envisage was to rebel against what he saw as encroaching on his autonomy. Because of his deep yearning to be recognized as a "man" by others, Mwanga might have conformed to or worked within the new dominant trope of masculinity. But the environment was changing very fast. In 1892 his leading Christian chiefs, reproaching him, as Semakula Kiwanuka reports, "for harboring in his palace notorious characters such as drunkards and homosexuals"[64] and remaining defiant despite his efforts, took it upon themselves to reshuffle the court by bringing in recruits they viewed as a "better set of pages."[65] In an effort to buttress respect for his identity as king, and desiring to demonstrate that he was a leader capable of responding positively to and assimilating emerging opportunities, Mwanga adopted some of the newly introduced and increasingly recognizable masculine traits. He did not wish his legacy to be that of a social and political dupe. Though Mwanga questioned the missionaries' conception and expectations about being a man and the qualities they associated with being a biological male, he displayed the capacity of being open to change. His agency was in vain, but he resisted rather than simply accommodating the messages he received from missionaries and peers about the new version of what it meant to be a man with its emphasis on a particular expression of sexuality, on toughness, and on being less effeminate with fellow boys.

Women

Mwanga's sexuality struggles were inextricably intertwined with structures of power, and so were the politics related to women. The Baganda sex/gender regime incorporated numerous taboos and restrictions pertaining to the female body and sexuality, several of which concealed inherent fears and anxieties.[66] At the highest level of the kingdom, male and female sexuality performed different but equally important roles. In what I have previously called "sexual conspicuous consumption," princesses were granted sexual free license. It is erroneous, however, to presuppose that this sexual license was the prerogative of all women. Because Baganda anxieties about commoner women's sexualities were linked to men's claims on their productive and reproductive labor, commoner women's sexuality was under strict surveillance.[67] The extramarital affair of a married commoner woman could culminate in her death through mutilation; the most her male accomplice could expect was to pay a fine.[68] The norms surrounding men's sexuality emphasized collective and productive clientele roles in the kingdom's political economy.[69] In this context, male-male sexual encounters in the palace could be interpreted as a form of political labor that youth performed along with other duties appropriate to clientele relationships.

Disturbed by many aspects of Ganda female sexuality, the missionaries viewed it as an expression of all that was wrong in Ganda culture.[70] While they shared Ganda anxieties about the overt and covert expression of female sexuality, they did so for different reasons. In what I term the "semen's contamination" theory, the Baganda imposed a three-year sexual ban on a nursing mother. Should a king or chief wish to resume sex with such a mother before the end of the three-year period, a foster mother would have to be appointed.[71] Zealous promoters of monogamy, the missionaries did not share this particular Ganda anxiety. Their support of such a long gestation period, even for commoner women, would have been akin to promoting polygamy.

The narrative the early missionaries developed about Baganda sex/gender practices focuses almost entirely on the male pages. The sexualities and bodies of the women within the confines of the palace's reed fences were apparently of little interest to the missionaries in the early years. Appearing as almost a footnote in the archival record, women seem to have been invisible or nonexistent to the missionaries. There is, for example, little discussion of the issue of polygamy. With the exception of Faupel's reference to "women security officers" who dressed in male attire,[72] there is little discussion of the existence of women "cross-dressers." Yet John Roscoe reports that nude rituals were not uncommon in the *bisakatte* (the women's wing of the palace), particularly at the time a woman's pregnancy was first detected.[73] We learn that Mwanga ordered women and children to be arrested along with the Christian converts who were executed, and that the women were released. We also learn that Mwanga presented a gift of cloth to each woman to appease her; what happened subsequently was not documented.[74] Mackay seems to have been more anxious about his "boy." And, lastly, while the missionaries blamed women smokers for a fire in their compound at the kabaka's court, they did not undertake a campaign against smoking similar to the campaign they unleashed to discredit Mwanga's sexual preferences.[75] The reason given by James Miti and others for the pardoning of Sara Nalwanga (also known as Sara Kitakule), the only woman condemned by Mwanga to the same fate of death as the martyrs, is suspect.[76] Miti and Faupel insinuate that "she was spared because she was discovered to be a relative of the Kabaka."[77] Royals in Buganda were known for killing each other especially when they were suspected of wanting to usurp power. If the rumor of the Christians wanting to place a woman on the throne was to be believed, then Sara would certainly have been a suitable candidate for the job. I suggest that Mwanga spared her because, in his estimation and according to the Ganda gender system, she was "merely" a woman and, according to Alexander Mackay, a CMS missionary who frequented the court, Mwanga "ordered her to be saved, as he wanted to put her in his harem . . . but instead of keeping her, sent her back to us."[78]

Hamilton attributes the missionaries' lack of interest in women's lives to the fact that "there was no consideration of women's holiness, faith, or right to resist the advances of the Kabaka or of the other men at the court."[79] He argues that "the absence of women in the original telling of the martyrs' story serves to reinforce a story of men struggling for power at the cusp of colonialism."[80] In her earlier work, Megan Vaughan argues that female sexuality held little interest for the missionaries because it represented "the happy primitive state of pre-colonial Africa."[81] Advocating caution, Vaughan contends that it was "the maleness" of African sexuality which came to represent "the African." This seems to have been true for Buganda. That the missionaries repeatedly documented the particular "offensive" sexuality Mwanga engaged in with his pages and almost completely ignored the fact that there were large numbers of young women secluded in their quarters at the royal palace supports my assertion that the homosexual practices in Mwanga's court provoked considerable anxiety among the missionaries.

Two points can be made about the near invisibility of women in the missionary archive. First, the missionary project in Buganda was a male project. Female missionaries did not arrive until 1895.[82] This was almost a quarter of a century after the first male missionaries. The reasons for this can be attributed to gender differences which included male anxiety about sending women to faraway foreign territories.[83] With the arrival of women missionaries, the focus of missionary and Christian men's anxieties about Buganda women's sexuality changed to promotion of maternal and child health programs, monogamous marriage, and enactment of numerous new laws and regulations.[84] Second, this silence conceals knowledge about Mwanga's sex life with women in the court. Neville Hoad imputes that, in addition to practicing anal sex with the male pages, Mwanga could possibly have engaged in it with some of the numerous women at his disposal in the palace.[85] If this was the case, as a result of their lack of direct contact with the *bakembuga*,[86] missionary anxiety and panic was linked primarily to behavior in the male wing of Mwanga's palace.

Toward the end of Mwanga's reign, fear and anxiety were becoming widespread that, following British custom, a woman would be placed on the Buganda throne.[87] In the aftermath of an act committed by a princess that shocked many at Mwanga's court, this fear deepened. Despite being baptized by the CMS and married to a Catholic, the princess had accepted an appointment as guardian of the tombs of Kabaka Junju.

But, having refused to live in the shrine, she drove away the medium attending it and burned it down, along with all the amulets and charms displayed there.[88] The traditionalists considered her acts serious felonies that could provoke the wrath of the gods, who would make known their anger by unleashing some form of public calamity.[89] Blaming the missionaries and greatly perturbed by the princess's independent and courageous spirit, Mwanga gave increased credence to the Arab-Swahili traders' rumor that the missionaries wanted a woman on the throne. Ashe, who was at the court, wrote in 1888: "They first of all cleverly worked upon the fears of the king, persuading him that the Christians meant to depose him, and put in his place one of his sisters, who was a Christian, 'for,' said they, 'is not the chief nation of Europe governed by a woman, Queen Victoria and therefore the Christians in Uganda are seeking to establish the same custom here.'"[90] The continuing paranoia about this possibility explains why Kalema, who replaced Kiwewa as kabaka following Mwanga's first overthrow, ordered all the princesses to be massacred alongside the princes. Kalema was convinced that the Christians would raise no objection to the installment of a woman as the ruler of Buganda.[91] Mwanga used this massacre to justify his plea that he be reinstated as kabaka. At this time he also relinquished his earlier position regarding restriction of missionary movements and activities in Buganda. Mackay recorded a pleading letter signed by Mwanga on June 25, 1889. It stated:

> I, Mwanga, beg of you to help me. Do not remember bygone matters. We are now in a miserable plight, but if you, my fathers, are willing to come to help restore me to my kingdom, you will be at liberty to do whatever you like. . . . Consider how Kalema has killed all my brothers and sisters. He has killed my children too.[92]

Notwithstanding the repercussions of the triumph of hegemonic masculinity, some basic features of Buganda society remained unaffected by missionary influence. With respect to the kabaka's succession, for example, the maternal factor remained important in his election. The Catholic and Anglican Christian missions began competing for influence over Mwanga's successor two years before his downfall. The Protestant victory was assured with the baptism of the newborn prince (Daudi Chwa) following resolution of a disagreement between Archdeacon Walker and Bishop Tucker. Archdeacon Walker opposed the baptism because the infant's mother had not been baptized but changed his opinion when Bishop Tucker wrote him a letter to persuade him of the political importance of having the child baptized, even if the mother was still a traditionalist.[93] Despite their ignorance of many Ganda traditions, the process through which the missionaries chose Mwanga's successor reconstituted Kiganda tradition in an innovative way. In conformity with tradition, maternal affiliation remained the deciding factor in selecting the kabaka. At the time of the baptism, the Christian missionaries were so preoccupied with a struggle between themselves, the Christian chiefs, and the British colonialists over how many wives Mwanga would be allowed to take in exile that the particular form of Christian identity bestowed upon the infant was of little concern to them. The number of girls finally agreed upon was three.[94]

Connecting the Dots:
The Sociopolitical Work of a Gendered Anxiety

The missionary world has often been likened to the front line of a battlefield. This was true for Buganda and Mwanga's court, where all the evils of "paganism" were envisioned as residing. Mwanga's court was situated at the center of this front line. But it was also a front line for differences in the articulation of masculinity. A fierce battle for conversion to British and missionary normative masculinity took place within its confines from 1879 to the end of the century. It was not only a battle to win souls but also a battle between competing sets of sex/gender beliefs and practices—a battle of two clashing cultural patriarchal systems. The anxiety and panic generated on this front line was a significant factor in the period's history.

In addition to experiencing anxiety about what was happening to their social and political institutions, the Baganda experienced anxiety about what was happening to themselves. For the converted, anxiety about one's self was closely associated with the idea of personal accountability in this world and in the world to come; it was anxiety about "personal salvation." Significantly, their anxieties and fears about salvation underlay their struggles over gender and sex and, above all, what type of sex a man should engage in. The missionary communes in Mwanga's capital were sites where fear and panic over masculinity were reproduced in the private lives of the Baganda. Mwanga at first permitted a range of Christian activities at the court, but the deep fear of insubordination he began to experience early in his reign led him to put restrictions on missionary movements and, eventually, to order the arrest and execution of Christian leaders and their converts. Mwanga was not alone in being overwhelmed by feelings of anxiety. The ways in which the missionaries and, later on, colonial administrators pathologized Mwanga as naturally violent, impulsive, and ceaselessly restless reveals that they, too, were in a perpetual state of discomfiture about matters pertaining to their own sexual identity and masculinity and fear that their lives were lived in a state of incessant danger. Yet, paradoxically, Mwanga's masculinity, in spite of its aggressive nature, did not measure up to their expectations. In comparing him to his father (Mutesa), who was for all purposes acknowledged as a "real man," Mwanga was pathologized as "a weak, vain and vicious man, a worse and altogether weaker man than Mutesa."[95] Anxiety about the success of their acclaimed civilizing project underlay the veneer of the missionaries' entire Christian and colonial triumph.

Different understandings of and practices surrounding gender and sex were at the core of this widespread sense of insecurity in Buganda, where the new gender practices unfolded under the gaze of Christian men whose role as gender police ensured that men's and women's gender performances adhered to the proscriptions and prescriptions of hegemonic masculinity—under "condition imposed by God," to quote Father Lourdel. These new prescriptions emphatically avoided violating what Michael Kimmel calls "the single cardinal rule of manhood, the one from which all the other characteristics—wealth, power, status, strength, physicality—are derived," which is "to offer constant proof that you are not gay."[96] The version of masculinity the missionaries introduced epitomized and had the distinctive characteristics of the model of manhood that emerged elsewhere in the twentieth century. It reproduced a system of gender-based inequality in Buganda that affected all social classes, including a class of women—the bakembuga—who had not hitherto been subjugated by masculinity. Rather than tolerating the variety of different masculinities and femininities operative in Mwanga's Buganda, the missionary approach prescribed a single monolithic entity or "role" to which all boys and men and all girls and women were expected to conform. In privileging the focus on sex roles, the missionaries inadvertently ignored power and power differentials among the Baganda.

Missionary anxieties about Mwanga's sexuality generated substantial institutional changes, including the restructuring of the palace and the kingship itself. A consequence of this restructuring was marginalization of many palace women from roles in the kingdom's politics in which they had previously wielded considerable power. Moreover, the process of attaining political power was now occurring in circumstances that were radically transformed from those that existed when Mwanga became kabaka in 1884. The missionaries' relentless attack severely destabilized the distinctly authoritarian state that had been fundamental in legitimizing conditions for gender expression which accommodated a plurality of masculinities. Irrespective of Mwanga's sexual transgressions, the kingship remained important because, as Lugard observed, the Baganda were not yet ready to do away with it.[97]

The images the missionaries used to portray Mwanga, who was as intelligent and reflective a man as any of his contemporaries, revealed their negative bias and anxieties. The historical record shows that Mwanga carefully observed, reflected upon, and interpreted missionary stimuli before determining what should be done and operationalizing a response he viewed as appropriate—one befitting the form of masculinity expected of him as royalty. At first, in getting rid of the proto-martyr (Joseph Mukasa), Mwanga had been of the opinion that his masculinity could easily be restored. He sighed to his chancellor (*katikiro*): "You have saved me! Now there will no longer be two Kabakas at this court."[98] To say the least, Mwanga was an arrogant young man who was engrossed in his class masculinity. Was he ever in doubt of his masculinity even in the face of negative valuation and surveillance? Perhaps he was not. He never lost an opportunity to flaunt to the missionaries and his subjects his importance and that he was the man in control. Consider, for instance, his disclaimer on December 6, 1885, regarding the killing of Joseph Mukasa: "If I had him killed, it was not because he prayed to God, but because he insulted me by opposing the order to put the Englishmen to death, and because he informed the white men of my plans. I do not forbid you to practice religion; only prayer, and do not go again to the white men. Besides why do you go there at all?"[99]

Was Mwanga jealous that his pages might be engaging in sexual relations with the missionaries? To Father Lourdel, he confessed that he killed Joseph Mukasa because he insulted him. He continued to say: "He, a simple page, rebuked me! Why did he not ask *you* to come and make me see my fault? From you, Mapera [Lourdel's nickname in Buganda], I would have accepted a rebuke: but from a slave? Never!"[100] Or consider his meeting Ashe, O'Flaherty, and Mackay of the Church Missionary Society in 1884 shortly after he assumed power and telling them that they had "*kyejo*," "a word that may mean anything from unconscious self-complacency to downright insolence."[101] The accusation was based on their failure for not coming to see him earlier when he was enthroned. On another occasion, he called them *bagwagwa* and, with impunity, threatened to harm them, noted by Mackay on November 11, 1884:

> Mwanga then tried his passion. He would kill anyone found at our station. We were Bagwagwa (low savages), who tried to get at his secrets.... Yes, he would put us all in the stocks; and would let word of that go to the coast; and he would challenge England and all Europe to come and rescue us. What could white men do to him?... Had Lukonge ... not killed white men, and had the Queen been able to touch Lukonge? Had Mirambo not killed white men, and had the Queen been able to touch him?[102]

Mwanga was known to speak in proverbs. Was his insinuation of his pages eating "snakes" at the missionaries' compound a sexually loaded accusation, especially when uttered in reference to his favorite Mwafu? Mwanga had burst out: "Am I your *Kabaka*? Or does Buganda belong to the white men? Don't I provide enough meat for you at the palace, or are the snakes you eat at the white men's place more palatable?"[103] Directly chastising Mwafu for a brief absence from his sight, he said: "Did your father send you here to serve me or to learn the religion of the white men?" Turning to an older page who was with Mwafu, he inquired: "Has Mwafu been with you? What business had you with him?"[104] Was he covetous? Mwanga's response to the pages' rejection of his sexual advances (their failure to honor the entitlements encoded in his fluid masculinity) was a gendered response of male aggression. On the one hand, the pages paid with their lives. Yet, on the other hand, in a process aided and abetted by Christian converts, Mwanga paid for his failure to subscribe to the missionaries' version of masculinity by losing his dominion. His sense that he was being encircled in almost every aspect of his public and private life made him particularly vulnerable to feelings of shame and embarrassment. Because it was difficult for him to continue to act honorably as a sovereign monarch in his own kingdom without respect, a sense of discomfiture about his way of expressing his gender identity and anxiety about his ability to maintain authority became commonplace in Mwanga's emotional makeup. Moreover, because Mwanga's agency operated within constrained yet complex and changing structural boundaries, many of the strategies he developed to deal with his experiences of anxiety proved to be counterproductive. At one time or the other, Mwanga sought support from his former nemesis who, surprisingly, accommodated him, perhaps because they were burdened by the same anxieties. No doubt, Mwanga's actions had made them aware of what would happen to them should they not ally with him. While the results were often disastrous, the act of persecution liberated homosexuality at least temporarily from its closet. One witness to the massacre reported: "Before the death of Joseph the practice of unnatural vice was the subject of secret conversation; the Kabaka spoke of those things only with his private servants and with the Muslims, and practiced them like one that steals; but after Joseph's death, they were spoken of in public, and practiced without restraint."[105] In the final analysis, the British colonial policy of "protecting" Buganda entailed advancing a situated normalcy which privileged missionary (read Anglo-Protestant) patriarchal heteronormative definitions of masculinity and femininity. Shortly after Mwanga was deported, anxiety about matters pertaining to sex and gender led the triumphant Christian leaders to enact strict laws, laden with moral and gender bias, to regulate sexual behavior.[106]

To conclude, I revisit the Luganda word *kitalo*, translated by Faupel as "disgrace," in the situation in which Mwanga expressed his feelings after returning from a disappointing hippopotamus hunting expedition before the second massacre. Finding himself abandoned and alone and rejecting any explanations for the pages' absence, he is quoted to have exploded: "Rubbish! . . . I know very well where they are; they have gone off to the white men to study religion. Now I know that the country is no longer mine, but the white men's. Even Mwafu . . . the only one of my pages who is completely loyal and devoted to me, always ready to obey my slightest wish, even he is absent; and here am I, alone and forsaken. It is a disgrace!"[107]

Kitalo is a complex word with multiple meanings. Granted, it can be translated in English as "disgrace" as Faupel did, but also as "what a loss." On learning about the death of a much loved, highly respected community member or the death of an individual with potential, the Baganda frequently use the phrase "*kitalo*." Faupel's choice of "disgrace" to convey Mwanga's meaning reflects missionary ethnocentrism about the morality of some elements of Baganda sexual practices. If we, nevertheless, adopt the second meaning, Mwanga's words can be interpreted as an expression of his deeply felt loss of his own and his kingdom's former existences, including the fluid ways he and the Baganda had expressed their sexual and gender identities. Mwanga was lamenting the loss of his own power, the potential death of his regime, the loss of Buganda's independence, and an injury to his form of masculinity. In all aspects, Mackay captured the Christian victory thus: "All the posts of authority are occupied by Christians, all the land falls into their hands; even the king himself is no more their despotic master and murderer, but a helpless instrument in their hands. God has given them victory."[108] Mwanga's lamentation should be read within the larger context of anxieties over masculinity and a partial victory of one form over the other. The question of homosexuality in contemporary Buganda and Uganda at large continues to evoke both religious and political hot debates and anxiety as gender continues to be largely defined in binary terms of male and female.[109]

Notes

1. Buganda is the name of the kingdom. Its inhabitants are called Baganda; their language is known as Luganda and their culture as Kiganda. The supreme ruler is known as Kabaka.

2. Richard Reid, *Political Power in Pre-colonial Buganda: Economy, Society and Warfare in the Nineteenth Century* (Athens: Ohio University Press, 2002); D. A. Low, *Buganda in Modern History* (London: Weidenfeld and Nicolson, 1971).

3. M. S. M. Semakula Kiwanuka, *A History of Buganda: From the Foundation of the Kingdom to 1900* (New York: Africana Publishing Corporation, 1972); Neville Hoad, *African Intimacies: Race, Homosexuality, and Globalization* (Minneapolis: University of Minnesota Press, 2007); Samwiri Lwanga-Lunyiigo, *Mwanga II: Resistance to Imposition of British Colonial Rule in Buganda, 1884–1899* (Kampala: Wavah Books, 2011).

4. Ado K. Tiberondwa, *Missionary Teachers as Agents of Colonialism: A Study of Their Activities in Uganda, 1877–1925* (Kampala: Fountain, 1998).

5. Bartolomayo Musoke Zimbe, *Buganda ne Kabaka* (Mengo, Uganda: Gambuze, 1939); Low, *Buganda in Modern History*; Kiwanuka, *History of Buganda*; Holger Bernt Hansen, *Mission, Church, and State in a Colonial Setting: Uganda, 1890–1925* (London: Heinemann, 1984); Reid, *Political Power in Pre-colonial Buganda*.

6. H. B. English and H. C. English, *A Comprehensive Dictionary of Psychological and Psychoanalytical Terms* (New York: David McKay, 1958), 34–35.

7. Robert Pickering Ashe, *Two Kings of Uganda* (London: Sampson Low, 1890); Alexina Harrison, *A. M. Mackay: Pioneer Missionary of the Church Missionary Society to Uganda by His Sister* (London: Hodder and Stoughton, 1890); J. F. Faupel, *African Holocaust: The Story of the Ugandan Martyrs* (New York: P. J. Kenedy and Sons, 1962); H. P. Gale, *Uganda and the Mill Hill Fathers* (London: Macmillan, 1959).

8. Faupel, *African Holocaust*, 102.
9. Faupel, 125.
10. Kiwanuka, *History of Buganda*, 196.
11. Harrison, *A. M. Mackay*; Faupel, *African Holocaust*.
12. Ashe, *Two Kings of Uganda*; R. P. Ashe, *Chronicles of Uganda* (London: Hodder and Stoughton, 1895); Harrison, *A. M. Mackay*; Gale, *Uganda and the Mill Hill Fathers*.
13. Nakanyike B. Musisi, "Morality as Identity: The Missionary Moral Agenda in Buganda, 1877–1945," *Journal of Religious History* 23, no. 1 (1999): 51–74.
14. Mark Breitenberg, *Anxious Masculinity in Early Modern England* (New York: Cambridge University Press, 1996).
15. Kiwanuka, *History of Buganda*; Reid, *Political Power in Pre-colonial Buganda*.
16. Ashe, *Two Kings of Uganda*; Harrison, *A. M. Mackay*.
17. Kiwanuka, *History of Buganda*.
18. Harrison, *A. M. Mackay*; Faupel, *African Holocaust*; Ronald Hyam, *Empire and Sexuality: The British Experience* (Manchester: Manchester University Press, 1992); Hansen, *Mission, Church, and State*.
19. Mackay to Wright, 14 July 1879, Church Missionary Society, London, C A6/016, Mackay's Journal 1877–1879, University of Birmingham Archives.
20. As cited in Faupel, *African Holocaust*, 106. Read this as being the last independent kabaka of Buganda, on Buganda terms.
21. Harrison, *A. M. Mackay*; Ashe, *Two Kings of Uganda*; Faupel, *African Holocaust*; Kiwanuka, *History of Buganda*; John Iliffe, *Honour in African History* (New York: Cambridge University Press, 2005); Reid, *Political Power in Pre-colonial Buganda*; Kenneth Lewis Hamilton, "The Flames of Namugongo: Postcolonial, Queer, and Thea/ological Reflections on the Narrative of the 1886 Uganda Martyrdom," (PhD diss., Union Institute and University, 2007); Rao Rahul, "Re-membering Mwanga: Same-Sex Intimacy, Memory and Belonging in Postcolonial Uganda," *Journal of Eastern African Studies* 9, no. 1 (2015): 1–19.
22. D. A. Low, *Religion and Society in Buganda, 1875–1900*, East African Studies no. 8 (Kampala: East African Institute of Social Research, 1957); Low, *Buganda in Modern History* ; Kiwanuka, *History of Buganda*; Hansen, *Mission, Church, and State*; Iliffe, *Honour in African History*. For a more detailed discussion of Lubaale, see John Roscoe, *The Baganda: An Account of Their Native Customs and Beliefs* (New York: Barnes and Noble, 1966 [1911]).
23. Kiwanuka, *History of Buganda*, 194.
24. Kiwanuka, *History of Buganda*; Reid, *Political Power in Pre-colonial Buganda*; Iliffe, *Honour in African History*; Hamilton, "Flames of Namugongo."
25. Harrison, *A. M. Mackay*, 256. Also: Kiwanuka, *History of Buganda*; David Kavulu, *The Uganda Martyrs* (Kampala: Londmans of Uganda, 1969), 22.
26. Faupel, *African Holocaust*, 104.
27. Harrison, *A. M. Mackay*, 275; Hamilton, "Flames of Namugongo," 187; Kiwanuka, *History of Buganda*; B. Nakanyike Luyombya, "A Triangular

Religious Interaction in Buganda, 1844–1900" (MA thesis, University of Birmingham, 1983), 220.

28. J. P. Thoonen, *Black Martyrs* (New York: Sheed and Ward, 1941); Faupel, *African Holocaust*; Kavulu, *Uganda Martyrs*; Iliffe, *Honour in African History*.

29. Harrison, *A. M. Mackay*; Ashe, *Two Kings of Uganda*; Ashe, *Chronicles of Uganda*; Faupel, *African Holocaust*, 125.

30. Low, *Buganda in Modern History*, 29.

31. Ashe, *Chronicles of Uganda*, 90–100; Apolo Kaggwa, *Basekabaka be Buganda* (London: Macmillan, 1953), 142, 143, 274; Zimbe, *Buganda ne Kabaka*, 75–152.

32. C. C. Wrigley, "The Christian Revolution in Buganda," *Comparative Studies in Society and History* 2, no. 1 (1959): 33–48; Martin Southwold, *Bureaucracy and Chiefship in Buganda* (Kampala: East African Institute of Social Research, 1961); Arye Oded, *Islam in Uganda: Islamisation through a Centralized State in Pre-colonial Africa* (New York: John Wiley and Sons, 1974); Michael Twaddle, "The Muslim Revolution in Buganda," *African Affairs* 71 (1972): 54–72; Low, *Buganda in Modern History*.

33. A. R. Tucker, *Eighteen Years in Uganda and East Africa*, 2 vols. (London: Edwin Arnold, 1908), 1:27–28; Kiwanuka, *History of Buganda*, 213; J. A. Rowe, "The Purge of Christians at Mwanga's Court," *Journal of African History* 5, no. 1 (1964): 55–71; Twaddle, "The Muslim Revolution in Buganda."

34. Kiwanuka, *History of Buganda*, 218.

35. Twaddle, "Muslim Revolution in Buganda," 177.

36. Margery Perham and Mary Bull, eds., *The Diaries of Lord Lugard*, vol. 3, *East Africa, January 1892 to August 1892* (London: Faber and Faber, 1959), 242 (entry for 18 May 1892).

37. Tucker to Sir R. Portal, 30 March 1893, White Fathers' Archives, Rome, *Reports* 1894:39.

38. James Kibuka Miti, "A Short History of Buganda, Bunyoro, Busoga, Toro and Ankole," trans. G. K. Rock, unpublished manuscript, Makerere University archives, box number AR/BUG/ 66/2, 1930, 465; Iliffe, *Honour in African History*, 178.

39. Faupel, *African Holocaust*, 122.

40. Ashe, *Two Kings of Uganda*; Harrison, *A. M. Mackay*.

41. Faupel, *African Holocaus*, 172.

42. Apolo Kagwa, *The Customs of the Baganda*, trans. Ernest B. Kalibala, ed. May Mandelbaum Edel (New York: Columbia University Press, 1934).

43. Hoad, *African Intimacies*.

44. Faupel, *African Holocaust*, 83.

45. Faupel, 139.

46. Faupel, 172.

47. Hoad, *African Intimacies*.

48. Faupel, *African Holocaust*, 82, 85.

49. Faupel, 82, 110.

50. Faupel, 147–48.

51. Rahul, "Re-membering Mwanga."

52. Nakanyike B. Musisi, "Women 'Elite Polygyny' and Buganda State Formation," *Signs: Journal of Women in Culture and Society* 16 (1991): 757–86; Rahul, "Re-membering Mwanga."

53. Nakanyike B. Musisi, "Transformations of Baganda Women: From the Earliest Times to the Demise of the Kingdom in 1966" (PhD diss., University of Toronto, 1991).

54. Kagwa, *Customs of the Baganda*; Kiwanuka, *History of Buganda*; Musisi, "Transformations of Baganda Women."

55. Hamilton, "Flames of Namugongo," 205.

56. Faupel, *African Holocaust*, 82–83, 110–11, 132–38.

57. Ashe, *Two Kings of Uganda*; Ashe, *Chronicles of Uganda*; Harrison, *A. M. Mackay*; Henry Streicher, *The Blessed Martyrs of Uganda* (Alexandria Bay, NY: African Missions of the White Fathers, 1928); Thoonen, *Black Martyrs*; Faupel, *African Holocaust*.

58. Faupel, *African Holocaust*; Kiwanuka, *History of Buganda*; Henri Médard, "L'homosexualité au Buganda, une acculturation peut en cacher une autre," *Hypothèses 1999* (Paris: Edition de la Sorbonne, 2000): 169–74 at 173.

59. Hamilton, "Flames of Namugongo," 197.

60. Médard, "L'homosexualité au Buganda," 173–74.

61. Randy P. Conner, *Blossom of Bone: Reclaiming the Connections between Homoeroticism and the Sacred* (San Francisco: HarperCollins, 1993), 37–44; R. P. Conner, David Sparks, and Mariya Sparks, *Cassell's Encyclopedia of Queer Myth, Symbol and Spirit* (London: Cassell, 1997), 1–5.

62. Faupel, *African Holocaust*, 110–11; Hyam, *Empire and Sexuality*, 187.

63. Faupel, *African Holocaust*, 126; Hamilton, "Flames of Namugongo"; Hyam, *Empire and Sexuality*.

64. The Luganda term for this type of relationship is *okusiyaga*. Missionaries initially used the biblical term "sodomy," and it was much later on that the act became referred to as "homosexual" in the missionary literature. See Hoad, *African Intimacies*; Faupel, *African Holocaust*; Harrison, *A. M. Mackay*; Ashe, *Two Kings of Uganda*; Ashe, *Chronicles of Uganda*; Hamilton, "Flames of Namugongo"; Rahul, "Re-membering Mwanga." In this chapter, these terms are used interchangeably.

65. Kiwanuka, *History of Buganda*, 243.

66. Roscoe, *The Baganda*; Rahul, "Re-membering Mwanga"; Musisi, "Transformations of Baganda Women."

67. Karen Sacks, *Sisters and Wives: The Past and Future of Sexual Equality* (Urbana: University of Illinois Press, 1982), 212–13.

68. Sacks, 212.

69. Sacks, 212.

70. Megan Vaughan, *Curing Their Ills: Colonial Power and African Illness* (Stanford, CA: Stanford University Press, 1991), 23.

71. John Roscoe, *The Baganda: An Account of Their Native Customs and Beliefs* (New York: Barnes and Noble, 1966, originally 1911), 53.

72. Faupel, *African Holocaust*, 56.
73. Roscoe, *The Baganda*, 49–50.
74. Faupel, *African Holocaust*, 74; Kavulu, *Uganda Martyrs*, 20.
75. Luyombya, "Triangular Religious Interaction in Buganda," 220.
76. Miti, "Short History of Buganda."
77. Faupel, *African Holocaust*, 75.
78. Mackay, quoted in Faupel, *African Holocaust*, 75.
79. Hamilton, "Flames of Namugongo," 23.
80. Hamilton, 22.
81. Vaughan, *Curing Their Ills*, 21.
82. Church Missionary Society, *One Hundred Years: Being the Short History of the Church Missionary Society*, 3rd ed. (London: Church Missionary Society, 1899), 159.
83. Philippa Levine, *The British Empire: Sunrise to Sunset*, 2nd ed. (London: Routledge, Taylor and Francis Group, 2013).
84. Musisi, "Morality as Identity."
85. Hoad, *African Intimacies*.
86. These were "wives" of aristocratic men, particularly palace wives. For a discussion of the *bakembuga*, see Musisi, "Transformations of Baganda Women."
87. Ashe, *Chronicles of Uganda*, 116; Faupel, *African Holocaust*, 73, 130.
88. Zimbe, *Buganda ne Kabaka*, 75, 252.
89. Luyombya, "Triangular Religious Interaction in Buganda," 220.
90. Ashe, *Chronicles of Uganda*, 116.
91. Kiwanuka, *History of Buganda*, 213.
92. Harrison, *A. M. Mackay*, opp. 373; see also A. R. Tucker, *Eighteen Years in Uganda and East Africa*, 1:27–28.
93. Walker to Wilfred, 35st.7.1898, CMS archives, University of Birmingham.
94. Walker to Father, 11 May 1899.
95. Harrison, *A. M. Mackay*, 255.
96. Michael Kimmel, *Guyland: The Perilous World Where Boys Become Men* (New York: HarperCollins, 2006), 50.
97. Perham and Bull, *Diaries of Lord Lugard*, 121.
98. Quoted in Faupel, *African Holocaust*, 112.
99. Faupel, 123.
100. Faupel, 125.
101. Faupel, 71.
102. Quoted in Faupel, 104–5.
103. Faupel, 139.
104. Faupel, 140.
105. Quoted in Faupel, 125.
106. Musisi, "Morality as Identity."
107. Faupel, *African Holocaust*, 139. Emphasis my own.
108. Harrison, *A. M. Mackay*, 470.
109. For those interested in the current homosexual debates (religious, political, and social) in Uganda, see Rahul, "Re-membering Mwanga"; Kristen

Cheney, "Locating Neocolonialism, 'Tradition,' and Human Rights in Uganda's 'Gay Death Penalty,'" *African Studies Review* 55, no. 2 (2012): 77–95; Masiiwa Ragies Gunda, "Jesus Christ, Homosexuality and Masculinity in African Christianity: Reading Luke 10:1–12," *Exchange: Journal of Missiological and Ecumenical Research* 42, no. 1 (2013): 16–33; John Blevins, "When Sodomy Leads to Martyrdom: Sex, Religion, and Politics in Historical and Contemporary Contexts in Uganda and East Africa," *Theology and Sexuality* 17, no. 1 (2012): 51–74; Prince Karakire Guma, "The Changing Contours of Gay Struggle in Uganda—Resistances and Counter-Resistances," *Pambazuka News* (special issue: *The Struggle for Homosexual Rights in Africa*), 26 February 2014, http://bit.ly/1EBele4; S. Nyanzi, *Alienating Citizens: Exploring the Poetics and Polemics of Foreign Influence over Homosexualities in Uganda*, Makerere Institute of Social Research (MISR) Working Paper no. 14 (Kampala: MISR, 2013); Stella Nyanzi, "Dismantling Reified African Culture through Localized Homosexualities in Uganda," *Culture, Health and Sexuality* 15, no. 8 (2013b): 952–67; Stella Nyanzi, *Politicising "the Sin of Sodom and Gomorrah" in Uganda: Project Statement*, Launch of the 4th African Humanities Program, Makerere University Kampala, 23–25 May 2012; SMUG, *Expanded Criminalisation of Homosexuality in Uganda: A Flawed Narrative Empirical Evidence and Strategic Alternatives from an African Perspective* (Kampala: Sexual Minorities Uganda, 2014); Martin Ssempa, "When Faith, State, and State-Inspired Homosexuality Clash," *New Vision*, 3 June 2005; Sylvia Tamale, "Confronting the Politics of Nonconforming Sexualities in Africa," *African Studies Review* 56, no. 2 (2013): 31–45; Barbara Bompani, "'For God and for My Country': Pentecostal-Charismatic Churches and the Framing of a New Political Discourse in Uganda," in *Public Religion and the Politics of Homosexuality in Africa*, ed. Adriaan van Klinken and Ezra Chitando (New York: Routledge, 2016), 19–34; Prince Karakire Guma, "Narratives of 'Saints' and 'Sinners' in Uganda: Contemporary (Re)presentations of the 1886 Story of Mwanga and Ganda 'Martyrs,'" in van Klinken and Chitando, *Public Religion and the Politics of Homosexuality in Africa*, 197–209.

FIVE

No End to the Trouble

*Decolonization Anxieties and the Evacuation
of White Settlers from Kenya, 1963–64*

WILL JACKSON AND HARRY FIRTH-JONES

IN 2009, AFTER ALMOST A DECADE OF STATE-SANCTIONED seizures of white-owned commercial farms in Zimbabwe, a film, *Mugabe and the White African*, was released to international acclaim. Telling the story of Mike Campbell, an elderly white farmer in Zimbabwe, and his legal challenge to Robert Mugabe's land redistribution program, the film gave an intimate view of the farm invasions through the eyes of Campbell, his family, and other members of the white farming community.[1] Much of the film was recorded covertly. In one scene, footage was filmed through a car window, as Campbell's son-in-law, Ben Freeth, and his wife, Laura, drove past farms that had recently been occupied by war veterans. At one point the couple meet an improvised roadblock: a series of boulders strung out across a dirt road. A group of war veterans is visible beyond the blockade. "OK, they're throwing stones," Freeth says, putting the car into reverse. Laura's voice becomes alarmed as the war veterans begin running toward them. "Drive!" she screams. As the camera shot wobbles and slips, the image dissolves into a blurred mosaic of running figures, bright blue sky, and dark green vegetation.

Sixty-five years before this, the painter Richard Wyndham described his feelings as he traveled in the Anglo-Egyptian Sudan. "I felt for the first time the fear which a civilised being must experience in a landscape that has not changed since the world began," Wyndham wrote, giving a pervasive trope in colonial discourse—of Africa as primeval—a psychological edge.[2] Indeed, Africa in the global imagination has been consistently set up as a place of danger and trepidation, where outsiders—be they missionaries, explorers, colonial administrators, or latter-day journalists and travel writers—have suffered from particular kinds of anxiety and foreboding.[3]

Until the mid-twentieth century, it has been argued, anxieties focused on the natural environment. Under the rubric of tropical neurasthenia, a wide range of symptoms—from depression to nausea to outbursts of passion—were explained by the harmful effects of the sun, the altitude, the heat, the flies, aggravated by the social isolation and the material hardships of colonial life.[4] This, in turn, flowed out of older, eighteenth- and nineteenth-century ideas depicting the exuberance of the tropical environment as destructive of European life.[5] Disease might be manifest in a physical wasting away but "Africa" brought on a moral disorientation as well. Civilization—regnant within the culture of new or "high" imperialism—deteriorated in the enervating tropics. Nature choked off progress.[6]

White settlers who colonized Kenya and Southern Rhodesia during the early twentieth century also imagined their vulnerability with recourse to resurgent nature. Beyond the garden was the jungle; the juxtaposition of the "tamed with the untamed," wrote one settler in Kenya, "at one's very doorstep . . . affected the nerves with an ever-present feeling of insecurity."[7] "In Africa," recorded another, "one may wrest civilisation from the wild . . . but one need never expect security of tenure."[8] "I have always known that in the end this land will take possession once again," wrote a third, "that Nature only waits to reclaim our clearings with regenerated forest and bush."[9] Language such as this expressed the fundamental anxiety of colonialism—of a sense of uncertainty over the legitimacy of belonging in a context where not only the impersonal machinery of a state but the presence of settlers themselves had been imposed on a subject population without its consent.[10]

One prominent historical narrative argues that anxieties over the African environment gave way during and after World War II. In various theaters of the war, whites fought alongside blacks and discovered that they were affected equally by nature. Disease paid no respect to race. Tropical neurasthenia died out. Pith helmets disappeared. After 1945, as Dane Kennedy argued, colonials came to appreciate that they faced a very different, ultimately terminal affliction. "Tropical neurasthenia," in his words, "ceased to offer a meaningful diagnosis of their plight."[11] Anxieties, however, do not simply stop: they change. To track that change, this chapter follows colonial anxieties through decolonization. Its source base is a collection of letters written by British settlers in Kenya to the colonial authorities during 1963 and 1964. These were letters of distress: Kenya became independent on 12 December 1963.[12] Their writers were petitioning for financial assistance to pay for travel out of Kenya or to have their farms or other immovable assets bought out by the British government to be resold at a loss. Together the letters constitute a commentary on decolonization, as refracted through emotions of anxiety and fear.

The intention in what follows is to read these letters ethnographically, as a window onto the emotional moment of decolonization. Historians too often tend to work backwards, as Frederick Cooper has argued, looking for the origins of what we now know and forgetting "all the futures that people once imagined but did not get to see.... Analyses of the end of colonial empires provide a vivid example of the limitations of doing history backwards and the possibilities of studying conjunctures when different futures were in play."[13] For the British, both in Kenya and in Britain, the prospect of Kenyan independence represented great uncertainty. For settlers especially, who had sunk their savings and, indeed, their lives into Kenya, the prospect of decolonization was deeply disturbing. Yet it would be wrong to view these anxieties either as transient—reflective *only* of a moment—or as entirely local—reflective of only one particular colonial context. By zeroing in on 1963–64, the aim here is not to write *about* decolonization so much as to move our perspective toward it. From that vantage we can gain new insight into genealogies of anxiety in Africa that cross the colonial and the postcolonial, enabling connections between images of Africa current in the late nineteenth century and representations current in the early twenty-first.

These letters can be read, moreover, in comparative as well as chronological frames. For on one level they constitute the human record of an evacuation, and can be read alongside other settler evacuations during decolonization in Africa—in Algeria, Congo, Angola, and Mozambique; on another they might be placed alongside episodes of flight far beyond Africa: from Singapore, India, and Egypt for the British (in 1942, 1947, and 1952, respectively) and—for the Americans—from Shanghai in 1948 and Saigon in 1963.[14] Looking forward, they anticipate the emigration of whites from South Africa during the last days of apartheid and the early postapartheid years.[15] In contemporaneous terms, they coincide with a highly charged racial moment within the history of race and immigration in metropolitan Europe.[16] Unlike recent work that has focused on the experience of repatriates after their return to Europe, this chapter focuses on the moment of flight—that is to say, on the struggle to leave. In doing so, it situates decolonization anxieties as part of African no less than European or colonial historiography.[17] To be sure, the emotional experience of Africans themselves is largely missing from these accounts: African hopes,fears, and anxieties are marginalized in a discourse that deliberately presents Africans as intimidating and atavistic. That itself reflects the way that a collective white identity was shaped in part by memories of African violence. It is important to distinguish, however, *between* these fears—and between fear as one emotional category and anxiety as another. Anxiety, as Ranajit Guha argued, is best characterized by uncertainty; fear takes a coherent object.[18] Whereas whites in Africa had long feared a "native rising," the colonial state had always guaranteed its violent suppression. The imminent dissolution of that state conjured the prospect of whites suddenly exposed: Would newly liberated Africans seek revenge on their erstwhile colonizers? Would white life and white-owned land be secure in an independent African state? Anxieties, then, shifted, from a discourse centered on place (the environment) to one centered on people. Africans, not Africa, were configured as invasive—as they continue to be in the British coverage of farm invasions (many of them on white-owned farms) in Kenya in 2017.[19] Yet those seeking evacuation from Kenya in 1963 did not know whether violence on the part of Africans was imminent or a figment of a—now anachronistic—colonial imagination.[20]

Collapsing Categories: Security Risks and White Prestige

The historical literature on Kenyan independence, perhaps surprisingly, has traditionally paid little attention to the white settler population.[21] Studies that have focused on the transfer of previously white-owned land have considered its importance for the negotiations leading to independence and the divisions it wrought within Kenyan nationalism.[22] Fears of a widespread land grab at independence did abound during the early 1960s, but a consensual program of land transfer, subsidized by the British state and organized on a willing seller / willing buyer basis, was preferred over any more radical, redistributive agenda. As Poppy Cullen has argued, "land transfer was significant in promoting continuity [and] in many ways underwrote the emergence of the post-colonial relationship."[23] Yet continuity as well as change is easier to apprehend with the advantage of historical distance. To white settlers, decolonization foreshortened distance; it compressed past, present, and future together. Layers of collective memory congealed around the breakdown of the racial order. From fantasies of frontier violence to the perennial settler agitation over African "insolence" or rebellion to the deeply intimate, domestic killings during Mau Mau, settlers were bound to their pasts as they struggled to envisage their future.

From the moment in 1960 when the British government admitted that majority rule in Kenya was inevitable, white settlers began to write, seeking help to get away. Some wrote to their MPs in Britain, others appealed to well-connected friends in high circles. But most wrote directly to the colonial authorities in Nairobi. Though their circumstances varied considerably, almost all hinted at the possibility of violence at African hands. To those reading these letters, two very different types of applicant appeared to emerge. One was characterized by helplessness. These were the elderly, the sick, the physically infirm, or the destitute. The other was characterized by guilt. They were the "security risks," people for whom there were particular reasons to suspect that a violent attack might be likely. At first, authorities sought to prioritize those people they judged unable to defend themselves if subject to attack. In May 1963, Secretary of State for Commonwealth Relations Duncan Sandys announced a scheme for the evacuation of elderly, infirm, and indigent British citizens from Kenya. The British government granted £700,000 to buy out farms in a program of compassionate farm purchases. A list was compiled of possible cases. The bureaucratic challenge in processing these letters was the need for officials to read every letter on its own terms while evaluating them against each other in judging their suitability for assistance. Officials analyzed the deservedness of applicants by means of a points system; fact-finding missions were conducted into individual cases, while letter writers themselves strived to "establish hardship" in the eyes of the state.[24]

The list, however, was due to close in August 1963, just four months before the scheduled date of independence. To process the repatriation program before independence, officials needed a definitive list of repatriates, one that would be exhaustive and final. Yet new cases kept emerging. Historical time could not be synchronized with biographical time. Individuals who might be fit and well in August 1963 could at any moment after independence begin to exhibit the kinds of distress that had previously warranted evacuation. The last of the British troops were due to leave by the end of 1964; the idea that a compassionate list would provide a conclusive account of those vulnerable to African attacks was contradicted by the fact that the number of the "elderly, infirm and indigent" was bound only to increase.[25]

To be sure, attacks upon white settlers did occur in Kenya throughout 1963 and 1964.[26] Just weeks before independence, sixty-seven-year-old Norman Sherrard-Smith and his wife were attacked while in bed in the early hours of the morning. Sherrard-Smith wrote:

> I was struck on the head, while asleep, and knocked unconscious. My wife, who was awakened by this activity, grappled with the two assailants who fled after inflicting on her quite considerable bodily injuries. I was in hospital for a week—my injuries having been ascertained to be quite extensive cracks of my left temple bone. At the time of writing it is nearly two weeks since the attack and I am still incapable of doing anything about the farm which previously received my constant attention.... Owing to the effect on our health and vigour and minds of our experience it is extremely unlikely that at our age we shall ever be able to resume our farming activities.[27]

In emphasizing his weakened condition since the attack, Sherrard-Smith stressed its psychological effects. "My memory is impaired," he wrote, "[and] I sleep badly. I have a constant ache and dizziness in my head and I walk with a considerable feeling of heaviness." "My wife," he went on, "is exceedingly high strung and we both think with aversion of the time when we must decide to return to sleep in the house of our unfortunate experience."[28]

Significant here is Sherrard-Smith's insight into his and his wife's mental state. The attack he had suffered had caused not only physical injury but an anxiety that made continued farming in Kenya impossible. In this respect, the fact that Sherrard-Smith was elderly added to the pathos of his letter. Africa throughout the colonial period had been imagined as a place where only the fit and robust should venture. Unlike "poor whites," however, whose presence generated profound ambivalence, the vulnerability of the elderly was unambiguously deserving of sympathy. Many elderly settlers who wrote to the government in 1963 described a lifetime of hard "pioneering" toil.[29] That white settlement had been encouraged by the British authorities allowed them to present themselves as victims. The image of the elderly as subject to physical assault carried a particular emotional appeal. Unable to defend themselves, the aged were deserving no matter their political views or past life experiences—and those who assaulted them were deemed especially cruel.

Elderly and infirm settlers were deemed worthy of evacuation because an independent Kenyan state could not be relied on to provide adequate protection, but as officials began to compile a list of likely evacuees, a second category of persons presented itself. These were "security risks"—individuals who had participated in the suppression of Mau Mau and who might be targeted for reprisal.[30] In these cases, the onus was on the applicant to know whether their "anti Mau Mau activities" placed them now in danger. If they thought so, they should pay their own costs in leaving Kenya. Only if they lacked the means to leave would the Treasury be willing to consider them as "special cases."[31] In June 1963, six months before the scheduled date of independence, one such case, Richard Forrester, wrote to Sandys. During the Mau Mau Emergency, Forrester had served as a section commander in the Kenya Police Reserve: his activities, he feared, "would not easily be forgotten in an Independent Kenya." To make matters worse, Forrester had been born in South Africa. As the apartheid state ramped up its repression of African resistance there, Forrester feared that whites with South African connections in Kenya would be especially vulnerable.[32] A year later Forrester wrote again. "Farming over the past couple of years," he wrote, "particularly 1964, has been a nerve-wracking business." The land bordering his farm had been bought by Africans. In the months immediately after independence some of Forrester's livestock had been stolen, his sheep sheds and his stores had been broken into, and a dwelling house, only 200 yards from his own home, had been raided. Furniture had been stolen, handles and locks removed from the doors, and windows broken. A car had been stolen. Africans trespassed at will across his land. Fences were cut down and fence posts stolen for fuel. "Strange Africans go roaming around with packs of dogs hunting everything with two or four legs."[33]

Cases such as these represented a very different category from the elderly and infirm. While aged settlers were seen as offering "easy targets to predatory criminals," attacks on former members of the security forces raised the more troubling prospect that African violence might be rational, even legitimate.³⁴ "As you know," recorded one official, "some of the methods employed [in the screening camps] were of a fairly rough variety."³⁵ Applicants for repatriation described their counterinsurgency work in considerable detail to emphasize the extent of animosity that might be felt toward them. "7,000 Kikuyu passed through my camp," wrote one man, "in addition I organised several other screening camps.... I had a pseudo gang of Mau Mau and spent quite a time as a gangster in the forest with them." African friends had advised him to leave.³⁶ Another former Police Reservist insisted there was "a price on his head."³⁷ "I served as a Senior Police Reserve Officer," wrote another, "for the whole of the Emergency." He worried this might mean "adverse repercussions in the future."³⁸ To investigate the veracity of these claims, British intelligence maintained a list of those they believed might have "attracted attention during the Emergency" and who might consequently be in danger.³⁹

Officials struggled to distinguish, however, between what was a reasonable supposition or an exaggerated, even paranoid, claim. On 19 August 1964—nine months after independence—G. E. C. Robertson, previously in charge of screening at the Mageta Island and Saiyusi camps, wrote to the British High Commissioner. Robertson was worried that documents he had written during the Emergency authorizing the detention of Walter Odede, then president of the Kenya African Union, had been leaked. Just recently, an African acquaintance had told Robertson that he was widely hated for his role in having Odede detained.⁴⁰ Meanwhile, two of Robertson's headmen told him that they had been summoned to Nairobi to give evidence on his activities during and since the Emergency.⁴¹ On a number of occasions, Robertson claimed, Africans had come up to him in public places and told him that the sooner he left the country the better.⁴² Robertson used this evidence to emphasize the need for his farm to be bought out immediately "on Security grounds," but officials at the High Commission looked critically at his claim. "He is rather an odd character," it was noted, and "obviously very highly strung." "I found great difficulty in deciding," wrote an official who spoke to Robertson, "whether the stories he told me are true or whether he has a rather vivid imagination." Robertson, it was recognized, had "almost certainly made enemies" during Mau Mau, and Special Branch had confirmed him as a risk. But doubts persisted as to whether he was exaggerating his role in having Odede arrested. His panicked tone—the Mau Mau suspects he had screened he described as "psychopathic, hard core lunatics"—added to the impression that his testimony was not entirely credible.[43] Whereas in other cases, a long life lived in Kenya emphasized an applicant's deserving status, Robertson, it was observed, had originally been gold mining at Kakamega. He spoke Luo fluently, it was noted. These were intimations not so much of the honest hardworking pioneer as the hard-bitten fortune seeker; that Robertson spoke Luo raised the troubling prospect of a white man too deeply immersed in "native" culture.[44] "Apart from the security position of his case," concluded the official handling Forrester's case, "he is extremely shaky and I would think there are probably medical grounds for getting him out of the country if this can be arranged."[45] Ultimately it was Robertson's frailty, for which his "vivid imagination" was evidence, and not his status as a Mau Mau security case, that justified his evacuation.

The broader interpretive problem here concerned the fact that it was not just those involved in Mau Mau but all Europeans who could be regarded as security risks. As Melissa Steyn has argued, whiteness in the settler societies in Africa must mean something quite different from how it has been characterized in North America and other settler contexts.[46] In America, it is often argued, whiteness is typically characterized as being "unmarked." In colonial Africa, by contrast, where white settlers never made up a majority of the population, whiteness was *hyper* visible, codified into law, engineered through the regulation of social space and given moral force through the white community's adherence to the norms of "white prestige."[47] In that light, decolonization might be understood as the moment when the connotations of whiteness changed dramatically. After Mau Mau—and after the British government's publicly declared commitment to African majority rule—all the moral meaning that whiteness had previously assumed became anachronistic. The myth that Africans believed in the superiority of whites was suddenly exposed, while the uncertainty as to whether an individual was a security risk forced officials to contemplate whether Africans might have good reason to seek revenge. For the British government in London, answerable to public opinion and committed to the safety of kith and kin abroad, the vulnerability of whites remained a matter of official concern. In the sudden absence of a state dedicated to the maintenance of a racial hierarchy, those in charge of the evacuation revived the language of the unsettled frontier: of isolated European, surrounded by hostile forces. Being out of whistle range of a police post was at first the guiding criterion for constituting a security risk, but this was deemed unsatisfactory. There was no guarantee that police posts would be manned after independence. A breakdown in law and order appeared a likely possibility.[48] The elderly and the infirm were especially vulnerable because they would be unable to fight off assailants, but so were those too poor to employ a watchman or to settle elsewhere.[49] Ultimately it was concluded that anybody living alone and who might be taken by surprise should be deemed a security risk.[50] In all these cases, Attorney General Eric Griffith-Jones stressed, the problem was not simply one of material poverty. "We believe that these cases face destitution or violent death or both," he wrote. The emphasis, he continued, must be on security and not compassion, but in reality the two were hard to tell apart.[51]

Government was well aware that the violent deaths of white settlers at the hands of Africans could cause outrage at home. But the British authorities also knew that publicity of the evacuation would damage their position in the eyes of the new Kenyan government. Under no circumstances, urged the governor, should the repatriation of whites be referred to as a rescue operation.[52] To admit to the evacuation would be to concede that the British did not trust the capacity of an independent Kenyan state to protect Europeans. It would also recognize the emptiness of the ideology that had underwritten the colonial presence for half a century: white prestige, the aura that supposedly attached to all Europeans in African eyes, had rested on the idea that an assault on just one white settler jeopardized all who perceived themselves as white. That same logic was at work in the conflation of Mau Mau security risks with a vulnerability that attached to all Europeans. Anxiety in this regard was about the failure of containment. While it reactivated old ideas of isolated Europeans amid hostile "tribes," these ideas were plotted in the language of something entirely new: the prospect of an independent African state. The attempt to make sense of these letters was made even more difficult by the fact that their authors themselves did not know how to interpret the changes that they perceived around them. Would-be evacuees were steeped in the white settler mentality but what gave them alarm in 1963 was uncertain precisely because independence augured something that colonial discourses could neither compute nor contain.

White Vulnerability, African Encroachment

Read together, these letters reveal a clear discursive pattern. Letter writers used whatever evidence they had to show that they had served

Kenya well and that they had invested financial and personal resources into the colony. Some wrote with anger at what they perceived as the betrayal of British politicians in allowing Kenyan independence.[53] But more emphasized their own vulnerability. Together, they describe a typology of African encroachment. Boundaries were breached; livestock were stolen, mutilated, or maimed; unfamiliar Africans trespassed on white-owned land or subversively cultivated it.[54] As other white settlers left Kenya of their own volition or were bought out by government, those who remained found themselves surrounded. The White Highlands were white no more.

The settler home, as various scholars have shown, was always discursively framed through intersections of race, class, and gender. Among letters written by women, many emphasized the absence of protective male figures, lending their descriptions of imminent threat added emotive force. Noreen Hennessy, whose husband worked away from home, refused to countenance living alone after independence "surrounded by Africans in my lonely home." She moved with her son to South Africa.[55] Mary Middleton, whose husband also worked away, described the anxiety of farming alone, set against the ominous presence of African encroachment. A large part of her farm had been occupied by Africans; neither police raids nor protestations to the local authorities had achieved anything, Middleton suspected, because of political pressures:

> My husband wants me to abandon the farm but I honestly cannot do this. We carry a very high grade herd of cattle and as they comprise of a great deal of our savings I refuse to leave. I am of the firm belief that once a farm is vacated that will be the end and there will be no hope whatsoever of selling it. It would be overrun with illegal squatters in 48 hours. . . . I cannot carry on under present conditions and yet unless I can sell I cannot see how I can leave. . . . It seems a rotten way to have to end one's farming years and I hate the very word "compassionate" but it now seems to be my only hope.[56]

Receiving no reply, in February 1964 Middleton wrote again. Her husband had since been moved yet farther away in the course of his work, while the encroachment of Africans onto her farm continued. "On the first day of Uhuru celebrations," she wrote, "my pedigree bull was slaughtered and dragged into the river on the farm. This was done by an illegal squatter on the farm." "I have further heard," she went on, "that pressure is being brought to bear on the compassionate sale of the adjoining farm, the property of a Mr David Wilson who is at present in Scotland with a nervous breakdown. This will then bring settlement of the African population on to our doorstep."[57]

In the South African context, Pierre Hugo has considered how colonial fears might be read—as conjuring images of a bloody and brutal death at the hands of vengeful Africans or as expressing much more prosaic concerns: the loss of status, of wealth or privilege.[58] These letters show the futility of attempting to prize these tropes apart. Anxiety in this respect was about the muddling of fears.[59] Whereas livestock was, on one level, simply that—a capital resource—settlers had deep sentimental attachments to animals, attachments that articulated their "white" identity, as Brett Shadle has shown.[60] One petitioner described her cattle having their legs broken by Africans. Her neighbor had had has his Boran bull's hump cut off, "in which state he found it in the morning—still alive."[61] Another applicant for evacuation wrote:

> We both love Kenya, the climate and the life. Over the years we have purchased a small farm and started a business. Literally everything we possess in this world is either tied up in the business or in the soil on the farm. Neither of which can be picked up at a moment's notice and put on a plane—though we pray to God this will never happen.... The heart-breaking thing is the animals—you cannot put a value on dogs and horses and I just don't know what I would do if I had to leave them all.[62]

The killing of Middleton's bull was disturbing not because it represented the theft of an asset but because of the way it was killed. The slaughter at the river represented not merely the physical encroachment of Africans onto spaces previously marked as white but the encroachment of what had throughout the colonial period been dismissed as mere savagery—African culture—into a space that was at once inescapably political—the question of legitimacy and the law—*and* deeply personal—in this case, the emotional attachment to a pedigree bull. The killing of the bull, moreover, raised the specter of African violence once again. It portended, through the idiom of African ritual, Middleton's own horrific death. In the light of Hugo's argument, demonic and prosaic fears merged. It was the fact that Middleton and her husband could not afford for him to stop working that meant she lived alone. The attempt to prevent a "poor white" problem earlier in the century had always depended on restricting entry to Kenya to those with the financial wherewithal to return to Europe should their ventures fail. The best treatment for tropical neurasthenia was—likewise—getting away. Though an evacuation scheme was only implemented at decolonization, the ability to depart had been a criterion of whiteness throughout the life of the colony. One woman described having to employ five guards at night but continuing to be raided. "Staying here on the farm is becoming unbearable," she wrote, "and . . . the present situation is too much for me."[63] To relieve her nerves, her doctor recommended that she move to the coast, but she lacked the means to install a manager to oversee her farm in her absence.[64]

If anxieties were grounded in the constraints of class, their gendered aspect is less immediately clear. Government officials, to be sure, described women living alone as especially vulnerable, but this was hardly the latest reiteration of a black peril panic so much as an element in the discourse of self-defense. Ultimately the question turned on who could repel a physical assault. None of the categories of isolation, ill-health, infirmity, or—in the words of the governor—"general helplessness" mapped onto a gendered binary that associated women specifically with weakness or vulnerability.[65] Also striking in Middleton's letter is her failure to mention anything of her mental state. Indeed, her only reference to mental illness is to a neighboring *male* settler, recovering in Scotland from a nervous breakdown. When men talked about women, however, or on their behalf, they drew upon the idea of a kind of nerves or nervousness to which only women were susceptible. Sherrard-Smith talked of the mental effects that both he and his wife suffered after being attacked—though he singled out his wife as "extremely highly strung." And he was not the only man to attribute "nerves" to female relatives. "My main concern is my sister," wrote David Jenkins, "who is suffering greatly as a result of the extreme nervous tension which we all have to put up with. There is now no doubt that she will have another total mental collapse fairly soon unless she can leave here . . . or unless we can give her some hope of being able to do so before long."[66] Women themselves, moreover, participated in this gendered language of nerves, conveying their urgent need for evacuation by stressing the intensity of their anxieties. "Having stayed here through the Mau Mau rebellion," wrote Marian Barker, "three nights a week alone, I am now far too nervous to stay here alone even for one night. . . . I am left here without a single relative in Kenya and <u>MUST</u> get out."[67]

Though Forrester could describe farming in 1964 as a "nerve wracking business," men did not describe themselves as nervously inclined or highly strung. Instead, they described a catalogue of worries, depicting in fine detail a deteriorating state of affairs in which declining material fortunes were exacerbated by the anxiety induced by the worsening state of law and order. Peter Sandford at Nanyuki described a litany of problems: the contracting market for the produce of his farm, the difficulties of securing credit for investment, the increasing costs of labor, and the end to school subsidies for his four children, before adding, "on top of all these worries we are faced with the risk of a complete breakdown in the forces of law and order and we cannot let our children wander out of our sight. At night we must bar all doors and windows and unlock the gun safe."[68] For men, law and order was just one element in a repertoire of issues that traversed the economic and the political. Men worried; women suffered nerves. Sandford's final words, meanwhile, augured the prospect of deadly, defensive violence. In his routine of unlocking the gun safe each night he intimated an uneasy sleep ahead, but he also touched on a scenario that stretches from Mike Campbell—whom we also see in *Mugabe and the White African* unlocking his guns—to the *laager*s of the voortrekkers to the defense of Rorke's drift. With their sanctification of the home and the heroism of its defense, colonial settlers in Africa have gone a long way to shaping images of African violence both before the colonial state was established and after its dissolution. Where the state cannot be assumed, "the home"—as a particular gendered, bourgeois construct—must always be both imperiled and required.[69]

Indeed, much of what was powerful about requests for repatriation was in their depiction of signs of menace or threat seen in or around the farm or the home. These expressed both a visceral sensation of physical danger *and* the disintegration of a wider colonial ideology—one built around the domestication of wild nature and the imposition of a stable racial order. The anxieties generated by decolonization were about the dissolution of that order, articulated in a language of encroachment that merged the colonial fear—of violent insurrection—with an imagery of white settlers now isolated in black Africa. One fifty-year-old woman, living with her seventeen-year-old son after her husband had left her, was noted as being "surrounded by members of the Land and Freedom Army." "Incidents" on the farm and nearby were frequent.[70] "I feel desperately anxious over the security situation here," wrote another; "my farm, is surrounded by miles of bush and ... my nearest neighbour is about a mile away out of sight.... Since Uhuru, there has been so much rudeness, drunkenness and trespassing that I feel quite un-nerved at night."[71]

Rudeness and drunkenness were as unnerving as trespass. Hostility induced anxiety because it revealed to whites the lie that their presence in Africa was morally sound and politically secure. It exposed the myth of white prestige. But it also intimated the menace of a criminality unconstrained by the colonial state. "On Uhuru day," wrote Sara MacIntosh from Njoro in February 1964, "we were blackmailed by our labour for 20/0 each."[72] Drunkenness, though it might lead to violence, delegitimized it too. Describing Africans who occupied white farms as drunk—in Zimbabwe in the 2000s as well as in Kenya in 1963–64—expressed a kind of disgust that voided these acts of occupation as political claims. The sudden departure of the colonial state, however, meant that white antipathies could not be themselves validated. One petitioner, writing in June 1964, focused on one particular African police inspector in the district "who is drunk—quite literally—70% to 80% of the time."[73] Four months earlier, another applicant for repatriation had thought the "present Government" was "doing their best" but continued, "they have an almost impossible task with the enormous mass of illiterate and ignorant dragging them down."[74] If these were commentaries on decolonization they were about the novelty of contemplating Africans *in power*—and an inability to distinguish between where men of state ended and "the illiterate and ignorant" began.

The nature of threat presaged by Africans entering white-owned farms was uncertain because what they portended was not clear: Were they symptomatic of a—perhaps temporary—deterioration in law and order? Would criminals be prosecuted, if not as they had been before, at least in line with what whites recognized as "the law"? Or might it be the case that political forces, far from being merely complicit in African trespass and other hostile acts, were actually orchestrating them? Not only did letter writers mention the violence in Congo following independence there; they also referred to events in Zanzibar and Tanzania.[75] Twelve Europeans were killed in Congo, but none were killed in Tanzania or Zanzibar.[76] Massacres of Africans in these places *did* intimate, however, a specter of chronic violence that alarmed Kenya's whites precisely because it brought what had always been imagined as far away—Conradian visions of hearts of darkness—into the immediacy of the here and now. This was both a temporal and a spatial compression: the distant and recent past was reanimated in an imagined future. The word *Uhuru*—freedom in Kiswahili—was loaded both with residual connotations of African violence and with intimations of what postcolonial Africa might imply.

By 1963 white anxieties in Kenya had changed, from a discourse centered on the resurgence of African nature to one focused on the dangers of African people. While medical advances rendered the place safe, the history of colonialism made politics dangerous. The letters of would-be evacuees not only provide a commentary on decolonization through this prism of changing white settler anxieties but also attest to the hollowness of the claim at the heart of settler colonialism: that white settlers could make themselves indigenous. The desire of whites in Kenya to return to a home elsewhere dramatizes the fact that their claim to belong in Africa was dependent on an element of privilege that, in less precarious circumstances, white settlers were always able to deny or disavow. The attempt by white settlers to leave Kenya in 1963 is in this sense no different from the strategies pursued by whites elsewhere in Africa to remain. Leaving is only the final option when other ways of feeling secure—most obviously in the fortification of private spaces in postapartheid South Africa—fail.

Whatever anxieties Africans experienced at decolonization are of course marginal, if not entirely suppressed, in the archival records of settler-colonial repatriation. It is notable, however, that a significant element in the discourse of embattled white landowners in postcolonial Africa is the claim that the Africans they employ would also be adversely affected if, for example, white-owned farms were forcibly seized. Much of this rhetoric assumes a paternalistic relationship of loyalty given and care received, but it does at least point to the fact that the decline of white security was not necessarily matched by a diminishing of African anxiety. The unraveling of colonial patronage presented opportunities for some but difficulties and dangers for others. For many Africans as well as whites, decolonization augured a world—to return to Guha—whose limits were not known.

Nor should the significance of these anxieties be confined to Kenya, or even to settler-colonial societies in Africa. Just as those fleeing Kenya in 1963 reached back into a repository of accumulated colonial fears, they also anticipated in their writing the kind of tropes that would structure white anxieties in Africa after empire. The threat presented by the war veterans at the roadblock in Zimbabwe in 2002 challenged whites in a context where whites could assume no protection from the state. Yet the roadblock has been a persistent trope in Western coverage of Africa *since* decolonization, perhaps the primary symbol of the disorder characteristic of failed states and collapsed regimes.[77] In journalistic reportage, the sighting of an improvised roadblock on a road up ahead evokes the particular anxiety that flows from the Weberian idea of the state as holding the monopoly on legitimate violence. The roadblock was the physical expression of that monopoly; the fact that it could be improvised by nonstate actors—possibly by the most malign and violent forces—meant the state could not be distinguished from the nonstate; the legitimate from the illegitimate. The anxieties that plagued whites in Kenya in 1963—expressed by the question of what precisely was the connection between African politicians and the men and women who occupied white farms or broke down their fences—is part of the same anxiety that characterizes much Western scholarly discourse that attempts to comprehend a postcolonial and characteristically *African* state today.[78]

That the category of the Mau Mau security risk expanded to include all Europeans illustrates the difficulty that both individuals seeking to leave Kenya and the authorities processing their evacuation encountered in knowing who or what was a danger—and who was at risk. Just as the connotations of whiteness were changing, so was the meaning of African violence—or the threat of it. During the colonial period, violence on the part of Africans had always been rendered comprehensible through ideas of irredeemable savagery, chronic backwardness, or the dislocations attendant on the meeting of modernity with tradition. Such colonial common sense ceased to make coherent sense, however, amid the dismantling of the colonial state, signaled most worryingly by the imminent withdrawal of British military personnel. In these conditions it was the prospect of Africans seeking retribution or, more prosaically, the opportunity to seize land or property that gave the figure of the unfamiliar African traversing white-owned land its uncertain—anxiety-inducing—aspect.

Neither those Europeans attacked by Africans during 1963–64 nor those repatriated to Britain or elsewhere were numerous. But the significance of these letters is not in their volume. Essentially these are histories that did not happen. Of the sixty thousand whites in Kenya in 1961, two-thirds had left by 1965. Those who remained, it has been suggested, wanted to do so. They were committed to the new Kenya, as Gavin Nardocchio-Jones has argued, "happy to stay on to help guide the new state through Africanisation toward complete independence."[79] Others have echoed this view. Significant numbers of Kenya's white settlers, Dan Branch suggests, wanted to "make a go of life in the new Kenya."[80] Certainly, it is significant that as many as twenty-five thousand Europeans migrated *to* Kenya during the early 1960s. But it is important to restate that the majority of the whites in Kenya in 1963 did leave, either shortly before or soon after independence. Though historians have a good sense of repatriates' lives back in Britain, the history of settlers' attempts to evacuate Kenya has been overlooked, not least because the records documenting this history were among those concealed by the British government following independence. It is perhaps ironic that it is among the "migrated archives" that we find the histories of those who struggled, and often failed, to migrate themselves.[81] Ultimately the program to evacuate whites from Kenya created the very problem that it ostensibly was designed to resolve. As farms were bought out and their erstwhile owners helped to leave Kenya, more and more settlers found themselves isolated. Encroachment would continue until the very last white settler was bought out. It was around that figure—of the last white person left surrounded—that the anxieties of decolonization coalesced.

Notes

1. *Mugabe and the White African*, dir. Andrew Thompson and Lucy Bailey, 2010.

2. Richard Wyndham, *Gentle Savage* (London: Cassell, 1936), 147.

3. Notable examples from recent popular writing include Tim Butcher, *Blood River: A Journey to Africa's Broken Heart* (London: Vintage, 2008): Paul Theroux, *Dark Star Safari: Overland from Cairo to Cape Town* (New York: Penguin, 2011); and Paul Theroux, *The Last Train to Zona Verde: My Ultimate African Safari* (Boston: Houghton Mifflin Harcourt, 2013). The literature on "Western" discourses on Africa is considerable. Significant contributions include V. Y. Mudimbe, *The Invention of Africa: Gnosis, Philosophy, and the Order of Knowledge* (Bloomington: Indiana University Press, 1988); *Ruth Mayer, Artificial Africas: Colonial Images in the Times of Globalization* (Hanover, NH: University Press of New England, 2002); and MaryEllen Higgins, ed., *Hollywood's Africa after 1994* (Athens: Ohio University Press, 2012). For critical accounts, see Binyavanga Wainaina, "How to Write about Africa," *Granta* 92 (2005) and Chinua Achebe, *Africa's Tarnished Name* (New York: Penguin, 2018).

4. Anna Crozier [now Greenwood], "What Was Tropical about Tropical Neurasthenia? The Utility of the Diagnosis in the Management of British East Africa," *Journal of the History of Medicine and Allied Sciences* 64, no. 4 (2009):

518–48; Dane Kennedy, "Diagnosing the Colonial Dilemma: Tropical Neurasthenia and the Alienated Briton," in *Decentring Empire: Britain, India, and the Transcolonial World*, ed. Durba Ghosh and Dane Kennedy (Hyderabad: Sangam, 2006), 157–81.

5. Nancy Stepan, "Biological Degeneration: Races and Proper Places," in *Degeneration: The Dark Side of Progress*, ed. J. Edward Chamberlin and Sander L. Gilman (New York: Columbia University Press, 1985), 97–120; Mark Harrison, "'The Tender Frame of Man': Disease, Climate, and Racial Difference in India and the West Indies, 1760–1860," *Bulletin of the History of Medicine* 70, no. 1 (1996): 68–93.

6. These representations were not restricted to Africa but extended to "the tropics" as a particular object of the medical gaze. For example: Dane Kennedy, *The Magic Mountains: Hill Stations and the British Raj* (Berkeley: University of California Press, 1996); David Arnold, *The Tropics and the Traveling Gaze: India, Landscape, and Science, 1800–1856* (Seattle: University of Washington Press, 2006). Notions of Africa as place of unraveling did have their own particular genealogy, however. See Philip D. Curtin, *The Image of Africa: British Ideas and Action, 1780–1850*, vol. 1 (Madison: University of Wisconsin Press, 1964); Winthrop D. Jordan, *White over Black: American Attitudes toward the Negro, 1550–1812* (Chapel Hill: University of North Carolina Press, 1968); Ronald E. Robinson and John Gallagher with Alice Denny, *Africa and the Victorians: The Official Mind of Imperialism* (London: Macmillan, 1961); Chinua Achebe, *An Image of Africa: The Trouble with Nigeria* (London: Penguin, 2010).

7. Llewelyn Powys, *Black Laughter* (New York: Harcourt, Brace, 1924), 14.

8. V. A. Carnegie, *A Kenyan Farm Diary* (Edinburgh: Blackwood, 1930), 44.

9. Errol Whittall, *Dimbilil: The Story of a Kenya Farm* (London: A. Barker, 1956), 7.

10. Ranajit Guha, "Not at Home in Empire," *Critical Inquiry* 23, no. 3 (1997): 482–93.

11. Kennedy, "Diagnosing the Colonial Dilemma," 181.

12. For fictional representations, see Robert Ruark, *Uhuru: A Novel of Africa Today* (New York: Fawcett, 1962) and Elspeth Huxley, *Man from Nowhere* (London: Chatto and Windus, 1964).

13. Frederick Cooper, "French Africa, 1947–48: Reform, Violence, and Uncertainty in a Colonial Situation," *Critical Inquiry* 40, no. 4 (2014): 466–78.

14. Mark F. Wilkinson, "The Shanghai American Community, 1937–1949," in *New Frontiers: Imperialism's New Communities in East Asia, 1842–1953*, ed. Robert Bickers and Christian Henriot (Manchester: Manchester University Press, 2017), 244–45; Ian Talbot, "Safety First: The Security of Britons in India, 1946–1947," *Transactions of the Royal Historical Society* 23 (2013): 203–21; Claire Eldridge, "The Empire Returns: 'Repatriates' and 'Refugees' from French Algeria," in *Refugees in Europe, 1919–1959: A Forty Years' Crisis?*, ed. Matthew Frank and Jessica Reinisch (London: Bloomsbury, 2017), 213–50.

15. Richard A. Schroeder, *Africa after Apartheid: South Africa, Race, and Nation in Tanzania* (Bloomington: Indiana University Press, 2012); Johann van Rooyen,

The New Great Trek: The Story of South Africa's White Exodus (Pretoria: Unisa, 2000). On the emigration of whites from Rhodesia before independence, see Josiah Brownell, "The Hole in Rhodesia's Bucket: White Emigration and the End of Settler Rule," *Journal of Southern African Studies* 34, no. 3 (2008): 591–610.

16. Bill Schwarz, "'The Only White Man in There': The Re-racialisation of England, 1956–1968," *Race and Class* 38, no. 1 (1996): 65–78; Elizabeth Buettner, "'This Is Staffordshire Not Alabama': Racial Geographies of Commonwealth Immigration in Early 1960s Britain," *Journal of Imperial and Commonwealth History* 42, no. 4 (2014): 710–40.

17. Elizabeth Buettner, *Europe after Empire: Decolonization, Society, and Culture* (Cambridge: Cambridge University Press, 2016).

18. Guha, "Not at Home in Empire."

19. For two critical accounts, see Tristan McConnell, "Who Shot Kuki Gallmann? The Story of a Kenyan Conservationist Heroine," *The Observer*, 18 June 2017; and Graham Fox, "The Dark and White Side of Conservation," *Africa Is a Country*, 29 August 2017, https://africasacountry.com/2017/08/the-dark-and-white-side-of-conservation-in-kenya.

20. Joanna Bourke, "Fear and Anxiety: Writing about Emotion in Modern History," *History Workshop Journal* 55, no. 1 (2003): 111–33.

21. The only study to focus on settlers themselves as a social grouping is Gavin Nardocchio-Jones, "From Mau Mau to Middlesex? The Fate of Europeans in Independent Kenya," *Comparative Studies of South Asia, Africa and the Middle East* 26, no. 3 (2006): 491–505.

22. Gary Wasserman, *Politics of Decolonization: Kenya Europeans and the Land Issue 1960–1965* (London: Cambridge University Press, 1976); Tabitha Kanogo, *Squatters and the Roots of Mau Mau* (Athens: Ohio University Press, 1987); Keith Kyle, *The Politics of the Independence of Kenya* (Basingstoke, UK: Palgrave Macmillan, 1999); Daniel Branch, *Defeating Mau Mau, Creating Kenya: Counterinsurgency, Civil War, and Decolonization* (Cambridge: Cambridge University Press, 2009).

23. Poppy Cullen, *Kenya and Britain after Independence: Beyond Neo-colonialism* (Basingstoke, UK: Palgrave Macmillan, 2017).

24. For good examples, see The National Archives, United Kingdom [hereafter UKNA] FCO 141/6985, "Proposed Modifications to List of Residential and Smallholders in Category II, June 1963, and UKNA FCO 141/18999, P. F. Walker, British High Commission, Nairobi, to G. H. Grubb, British High Commission, Mombasa, 6 October 1964.

25. UKNA FCO 141/6985, "Integrated Compassionate Farm List," 4 September 1963.

26. UKNA FCO 141/6985, 120; UKNA FCO 141/18999, David Jenkins to John Page, M.P., 13 June 1964.

27. UKNA FCO 141/18999, Norman Sherrard-Smith to the Chairman, Agricultural Sub-Committee, Subokia, 3 December 1963.

28. UKNA FCO 141/18999, Norman Sherrard-Smith to the Chairman, Agricultural Sub-Committee, Subokia, 3 December 1963.

29. UKNA FCO 141/18999, W. Boddy to British High Commissioner, Nairobi, 8 July 1964; R. V. Halstead to British High Commissioner, Nairobi, 6 June 1964.

30. Besides those discussed here, see also FCO 141/18999, G. H. Hawkins report on Lt. Col. W. E. Terry. Terry was, in Hawkins's words, a former "commandant of a detention camp."

31. UKNA DO 170/69, Relief and Repatriation of Distressed British Subjects from Kenya, D. M. R. Skinner to L. E. T. Storar, 2 February 1964.

32. UKNA FCO 141/18999, R. R. Forrester to Duncan Sandys, 4 June 1963.

33. UKNA FCO 141/18999, R. R. Forrester to Sir Richard Turnbull, 15 September 1964.

34. UKNA FCO 141/6985, 17, Record of a meeting with the Secretary of State for the Colonies, Government House, Nairobi, 15 March 1963, Sir Ferdinand Cavendish Bentinck minute.

35. UKNA FCO 141/18999, C. C. Ricketts to F. N. Brockett, 10 September 1964.

36. UKNA FCO 141/18999, W. B. Lambert to Agricultural Board Chair, 24 February 1964.

37. UKNA FCO 141/6986, Governor to Secretary of State for the Colonies, 23 November 1963.

38. UKNA FCO 141/18999, Frank Engelbrecht to British High Commissioner, 22 July 1964.

39. UKNA FCO 141/6986, Governor to Secretary of State for the Colonies, 23 November 1963.

40. UKNA FCO 141/6986, Governor to Secretary of State for the Colonies, 23 November 1963.

Mau Mau and Nationhood, ed. E. S. Atieno Odhiambo and John Lonsdale (Athens: Ohio University Press, 2003), 20–22.

41. UKNA FCO 141/18999, G. E. C. Robertson to British High Commissioner, 19 August 1964.

42. UKNA FCO 141/18999, C. C. Ricketts to F. N. Brockett, 10 September 1964.

43. For more on Robertson, see Caroline Elkins, *Britain's Gulag: The Brutal End of Empire in Kenya* (London: Pimlico, 2005), 192.

44. Priscilla M. Shilaro, *A Failed Eldorado: Colonial Capitalism, Rural Industrialization, African Land Rights in Kenya, and the Kakamega Gold Rush, 1930–1952* (Lanham, MD: University Press of America, 2008).

45. UKNA FCO 141/18999, P. F. Walker to C. C. Ricketts, 21 September 1964.

46. Melissa Steyn, "As the Postcolonial Moment Deepens: A Response to Green, Sonn, and Matsebula," *South African Journal of Psychology* 37, no. 3 (2007): 421–22; Schroeder, *Africa after Apartheid*, 7.

47. On whiteness in Kenya specifically, see Brett L. Shadle, *The Souls of White Folk: White Settlers in Kenya, 1900s–1920s* (Manchester: Manchester University Press, 2015) and Janet McIntosh, *Unsettled: Denial and Belonging among White Kenyans* (Oakland: University of California Press, 2016).

48. UKNA FCO 141/6985, Secret Telegram no. 354, Griffith-Jones (Acting Governor) to Secretary of State, 9 May 1963.

49. UKNA FCO 141/6985, Secret Telegram no. 356, 6 May 1963.

50. UKNA FCO 141/6985, 17, Record of a meeting with the Secretary of State for the Colonies, Government House, Nairobi, 15 March 1963, Secretary of State for the Colonies minute.

51. UKNA FCO 141/6985, 27, E. N. Griffith-Jones to P. D. Webber, Colonial Office, 19 April 1963.

52. UKNA FCO 41/6986, Telegram from Governor MacDonald to Mr Russell, 25 September 1963.

53. For good examples, see all from UKNA FCO 18999: Marian Barker to British High Commissioner, 18 June 1964; Col. D. C. McLeod to Mr. Wilson, 9 March 1964; Winifred H. Nunn to Sir Alec Douglas-Home, 31 December 1963; H. M. Bowker to Duncan Sandys, 14 January 1964.

54. UKNA FCO 18999, R. M. Hoddinott to Duncan Sandys, 17 January 1964. Both for white settlers and for African peasants, *using* the land was the final claim to legitimate occupation. For studies that reveal the nature of African attachments to—and anxieties over—land, see, from a large literature, Kanogo, *Squatters* and Bruce Berman and John Lonsdale, *Unhappy Valley: Conflict in Kenya and Africa* (Athens: Ohio University Press, 1992).

55. UKNA FCO 141/18999, Noreen Hennessy to Colonial Secretary, 27 August 1964.

56. UKNA FCO 141/18999, Mary Middleton to P. Thomas, M.P., 10 December 1963.

57. UKNA FCO 141/18999, Mary Middleton to P. Thomas, M.P., 2 January 1964.

58. Pierre Hugo, "Towards Darkness and Death: Racial Demonology in South Africa," *Journal of Modern African Studies* 26, no. 4 (1988): 567–90.

59. This confusion or muddling of fears should be distinguished from the kind of crystallization Kim Wagner described of the mutiny motif in British India. Kim A. Wagner, "'Treading upon Fires': The 'Mutiny'-Motif and Colonial Anxieties in British India," *Past and Present* 218, np. 1 (2013): 159–97.

60. Brett L. Shadle, "Cruelty and Empathy, Animals and Race, in Colonial Kenya," *Journal of Social History* 45, no. 4 (2012): 1097–116.

61. UKNA FCO 141/18999, Eileen Williams to Richard Hornby, 29 July 1964.

62. UKNA FCO 141/18999, Pat Peters to Mr. Butler, 22 January 1964.

63. UKNA FCO 141/18999, Eileen Williams to Richard Hornby, 29 July 1964.

64. Notably, one Colonial Office memo dating from the start of the repatriation program identified suitable evacuees as those who were both vulnerable due to old age, infirmity, or isolation and too poor to hire a watchman or to resettle elsewhere. UKNA FCO 141/6985, Webber to Griffith-Jones, 3 May 1963.

65. UKNA FCO 141/6985, Secret Telegram no. 351, Griffith Jones (Acting Governor) to Secretary of State, 2 May 1963.

66. UKNA FCO 141/18999, D. K. Jenkins to John Page, M.P., 13 June 1964.

67. UKNA FCO 141/18999, Marion E. Barker to Duncan Sandys, 15 May 1964. For studies into the relationship between gender and discourses of nerves, see Dona L. Davis and Setha M. Low, eds., *Gender, Health and Illness: The Case of Nerves* (New York: Routledge, 1989); Susan E. Cayleff, "'Prisoners of Their Own Feebleness': Women, Nerves and Western Medicine—A Historical Overview," *Social Science and Medicine* 26, no. 12 (1988): 1199–208.

68. UKNA FCO 141/18999, Patrick Sandford to A. P. Hume, February/March 1964.

69. The more recent history of the embattled white settler home after decolonization is most clearly apparent in South Africa, where violent crime and, in particular, incidents of "home invasion" have generated considerable public interest. See, for example, Gary Kynoch, "Fear and Alienation: Narratives of Crime and Race in Post-apartheid South Africa," *Canadian Journal of African Studies* 47, no. 3 (2013): 427–41. On the securitization of the home, see Sheree Rossouw, "Living behind the Barricades," *Mail and Guardian*, 12 January 2001.

70. UKNA FCO 141/18999, Letter by unidentified correspondent sent to Lansdowne, Minister of State, Colonial Office, on behalf of Mrs W. Howden, 25 February 1964.

71. UKNA FCO 141/18999, Vera Bilous to Under Secretary of State for the Commonwealth, 27 January 1964.

72. UKNA FCO 141/18999, Sara MacIntosh to Duncan Sandys, 22 February 1964.

73. UKNA FCO 141/18999, D. K. Jenkins to John Page, M.P., 13 June 1964.

74. UKNA FCO 141/18999, W. B. Lambert to Agricultural Board Chair, 24 February 1964.

75. UKNA FCO 141/18999, M. E. Bishop to C. Osborne, M.P., 20 January 1964; Winifred Hoddinott to Miss Robinson, WVS, 20 January 1964.

76. Buettner, *Europe after Empire*, 232.

77. For one particularly graphic example, see Ryszard Kapuściński, *The Soccer War*, trans. William Brand (New York: Vintage, 1992).

78. For a near-contemporary study that incorporated into its own analysis the misunderstanding inherent in outsiders' analyses of African politics, see Aristide R. Zolberg, *Creating Political Order: The Party-States of West Africa* (Chicago: Rand McNally, 1966).

79. Nardocchio-Jones, "Mau Mau to Middlesex," 499.

80. Branch, *Defeating Mau Mau*, 3.

81. It was only in 2011 that the migrated archives were discovered, catalogued, and released into the public domain. See D. M. Anderson, "Guilty Secrets: Deceit, Denial, and the Discovery of Kenya's 'Migrated Archive,'" *History Workshop Journal* 80, no. 1 (2015): 142–60. On repatriates in Britain, see Buettner, *Europe after Empire* and Elizabeth Buettner, "'We Don't Grow Coffee and Bananas in Clapham Junction You Know!': Imperial Britons Back Home," in *Settlers and Expatriates: Britons over the Seas*, ed. Robert Bickers (Oxford: Oxford University Press, 2010), 302–28.

SIX

Competing Development "Visions"?

State Anxieties and Church Closures in Rwanda

ANDREA MARIKO GRANT

IN FEBRUARY 2018, THE RWANDAN GOVERNMENT CLOSED approximately eight thousand churches and one hundred mosques across the country.[1] The vast majority of the churches were of the Pentecostal or charismatic variety, movements that have seen a dramatic rise in the country since the 1994 genocide. The churches were closed, the government stated, because they failed to comply with new health, safety, and noise regulations. In Kigali alone, more than seven hundred churches and one mosque were shut down.[2] Pastors who defied the closures were arrested.[3] In addition, a new law was proposed that would require all pastors to have theological training before they could open a church. Rwanda's president, Paul Kagame, seemed to wholeheartedly endorse the closures, expressing surprise that the situation had gotten so out of hand. As he commented: "Seven hundred churches in Kigali? Are these boreholes that give people water? . . . I don't think we have as many boreholes. Do we even have as many factories? But 700 churches, which you even had to close? This has been a mess!"[4] In this logic, while boreholes and factories contributed to the country's postgenocide reconstruction and development, churches apparently did not.

I thank Miriam Driessen, Benjamin Chemouni, and Yolana Pringle for their helpful comments on earlier drafts of this chapter.

The "messiness" of the churches—their loud preaching, their supposedly unsafe building conditions—challenged Kigali's image as a tightly controlled "model city"—one defined by order, safety, cleanliness, and silence, a beacon of security in a troubled region.[5] This image extends to Rwanda as a whole, often touted as a development "success story," given its impressive social and economic gains since the genocide. This image has been propped up by Western donors, who have contributed large sums of aid to the country, despite ongoing political repression and human rights abuses. Yet I suggest that the fact that the government intervened in 2018 with such a heavy hand to bring the churches in line revealed a certain telling anxiety about its grip on power. If, by all accounts, the Rwandan Patriotic Front (RPF), led by Kagame, has managed to successfully control public and associational life in the country and impose its particular development "vision" on citizens, why was it bothered by a little "noise"?[6] What made such a large-scale response necessary, and what does it tell us about the nature of the RPF's mode of governance today?

Drawing on fieldwork conducted between 2011 and 2013 and also in 2018, I argue that the closure of the churches must be placed within a longer trajectory of state surveillance and control. I see anxiety as a particularly helpful framework for understanding church-state relations in Rwanda, in large part due to its temporal orientation. In her work on "ugly feelings," literary theorist Sianne Ngai uses Ernst Bloch's distinction between "filled" and "expectant" emotions—with the former including envy, greed, and admiration, and the latter including anxiety, fear, and hope—to underscore how anxiety is anticipatory and future-oriented.[7] Indeed, as Bloch has pointed out, "All emotions refer to the horizon of time . . . but expectant emotions open out entirely into this horizon."[8] Building on this insight—and the idea that anxiety is not necessarily tied to a specific object—in this chapter I explore how anxiety arises when "visions" or plans for the future are thrown into doubt. For what seems to be causing conflict in Rwanda's religious field—both during the time of my fieldwork and up to the present—is a debate about the kind of postgenocide future Rwandans should have, and who does and does not get to have a say in it. While the state enforces its "vision" with a heavy hand, I argue that Pentecostalism provides an alternative: an alternative source of meaning and authority, an alternative kind of citizenship that privileges accountability not to the secular state but rather to God.[9] In this way I take anxiety as multidirectional—the affect that results when the state intervenes to "thwart" one's plans for the future but, in this very act of thwarting, reveals the state's own anxieties (and fragilities).

This chapter focuses on the narrative of one Pentecostal pastor, whom I call Pastor Charles, to better understand the contours of anxiety in Rwanda today. Although focusing on a single narrative may seem limited, I do so because of the exceptionality of Pastor Charles's case: his extraordinary story helps us see both the specific ways in which the state intervenes in social life to control the country's development and the anxieties that result from this intervention. As Pastor Charles's case demonstrates, being considered a good development partner requires not only discursive action—aligning one's nongovernmental organization (NGO) with the priorities of the government's "vision"—but also material action—joining the RPF as a party member and financially contributing to it.

Yet Pastor Charles's case also shows how Pentecostalism provides an important form of what Jonathon Earle (this volume) might call "calm"—an assurance that secular power is no match for God's power, and a belief that the trickery of the state itself will ultimately be revealed. Pentecostalism here holds out new possibilities for imagining and enacting the future, providing hope in difficult circumstances, even if these possibilities never play out according to plan. As Jennifer Cole has pointed out, "The way we imagine the future shapes the mundane strivings of our daily lives, though what we imagine does not always conform to what we create."[10]

I should state from the outset that I did not set out to study anxiety per se. Yet I found it a helpful framework to try to understand what happened to Pastor Charles, particularly in light of the 2018 church closures. The temporality of anxiety allows me to keep in focus two kinds of narratives: a personal narrative of thwarted future, and a state narrative of developmental progress. I am particularly interested in the frictions and convergences between them, and what they can tell us about the nature of the RPF's postgenocide regime. Indeed, given that the RPF seems particularly concerned with controlling not only the country's past and present but also its future, anxiety seems a productive tool to understand the dynamics of its power. Yet the sensitive context in which this work was carried out meant that many aspects of Pastor Charles's story were difficult, if not impossible, to verify without drawing further attention to him. I am less concerned with the "truthfulness" of Pastor Charles's story than with what it can tell us about the kinds of stories that circulate and are conceivably possible in Rwanda today. As Lee Ann Fujii has written, in Rwanda rumors, inventions, denials, evasions, and silences—what she terms "meta-data"—are more important than "truthfulness" as they reveal what can and cannot be said to others.[11] I would add here that when possible, I also try to expand this idea of metadata to include bodily postures and behavior change over time, offering another way for me to read anxiety into Pastor Charles's story.

Before turning to Pastor Charles, however, I first provide some important context: (1) a closer look at the RPF's governance, in particular an outline of its development "vision" for the country and the risks citizens run when they do not support it; and (2) a historical consideration of Christianity in the country and the postgenocide arrival of the "new" Pentecostal churches. I conclude by considering the exceptionality of Pastor Charles's case and what his experiences can tell us about the possibility of Pentecostal critique in the postgenocide period. I also explore how Pentecostalism in the Rwandan context might provide "calm" despite an otherwise insecure and unpredictable social world.

An Impressive Development?

Since taking power after the genocide, the RPF has overseen an impressive period of development and economic growth. Adopted in 2000, its guiding policy has been the ambitious "Vision 2020" program, with the aim of transforming the country into a middle-income, Singapore-style economy by the year 2020.[12] This has seen tangible results: stable GDP growth, poverty reduction, low corruption rates, the political empowerment of women (Rwanda has the highest number of women in parliament in the world), and increased access to education and healthcare. Both the scale and the speed of Rwanda's postgenocide transformations have been remarkable. "There is a view that development is a marathon, not a sprint," Kagame wrote in a 2013 op-ed for the *Wall Street Journal*. "We do not agree. Development is a marathon that must be run at a sprint."[13] This image captures well how development is imagined by Kagame and the RPF: a long-term yet fast-paced process. The RPF has in many ways staked its political legitimacy on the ability to deliver rapid and widespread socioeconomic growth.[14]

Yet, as critics have argued, there have been costs to this "vision." To some, Rwanda's RPF-led postgenocide trajectory can be characterized by "social engineering coupled with sophisticated authoritarianism."[15] This social engineering—which extends to behavior change, spatial reorganization (the "modernization" of the countryside and the redrawing of borders), economic restructuring (small-scale subsistence agriculture giving way to large-scale agribusiness and commercialization), and political repression—is justified in the name of development.[16] The RPF's "vision" is built on the promise that these transformations are necessary in order to bring the country out of its "dark" past and into a bright future wherein genocide will never happen again. Even postgenocide unity and reconciliation are pursued in the name of development, with survivors encouraged to forgive perpetrators so that the country will not be held back by the past.[17] Not only does a well-defined development "vision" oil the wheels of donor funding—international aid makes up approximately 40 percent of the country's annual budget—it serves to "deepen state power."[18] In the Rwanda case, developmental growth and political control "go hand in hand."[19]

What this means in practice is that citizens are expected to contribute to the country's development according to the RPF's terms. Through participation in civic education programs, they are expected to become "ideal development subjects," defined by: "i) possession of knowledge deemed essential for development . . . ; ii) containment of undesirable thoughts, emotions and behaviours; iii) subsuming of individuality to a collective goal; iv) a combative zeal in achieving prescribed targets; and v) loyalty."[20] We could also add here the obligation to be self-reliant (*kwigira*, to rely on oneself alone), to reject passivity and dependency.[21] In this spirit, the government places an emphasis on entrepreneurship, yet only certain kinds of work are understood to be "properly" entrepreneurial. Enterprising citizens who start up businesses selling fruits or vegetables by the side of the road risk having their inventory destroyed or getting thrown in jail, as their work is considered "dirty."[22] During my fieldwork in Rwanda—not only between 2011 and 2013, but also in 2018—on multiple occasions I saw such vendors drop their goods (not only foodstuffs but also clothing and household wares) once they spotted police, and run in the opposite direction, often with officers in hot pursuit. In this way, Rwandans, particularly young Rwandans, are expected to become "orderly entrepreneurs"—creative and resourceful, but willing to be regulated and controlled.[23]

Questions arise, however, about the extent to which this "vision" has delivered its promised results. While development is presented in Rwanda as "*a good unquestioningly benefiting all*," there is evidence instead of rising inequality and a growing rural-urban divide.[24] The private sector, increasingly seen as an important development partner, is dominated by party-statals, large enterprises partly or fully owned and controlled by the RPF, meaning that a politically connected elite profits.[25] Critics allege that the statistics the RPF employs to tout its developmental progress—particularly those related to poverty reduction—are problematic. For example, although the government claimed that poverty was reduced from 44.9 percent in 2010–11 to 39.1 percent in 2013–14, Filip Reyntjens argues that in fact it had not decreased by 6 percent but rather *increased* by the same amount.[26] The discrepancy had to do with how the government calculated the figures, with Reyntjens arguing that the government deliberately misled donors and its own population.[27] The debate was reignited in the summer of 2019 with a report published in the *Financial Times*, provocatively entitled "Rwanda: Where Even Poverty Data Must Toe Kagame's Line."[28] Both Rwanda and the World Bank, which has given more than $4 billion to the country since the 1994 genocide, refuted the *Financial Times*' findings. Kagame, perhaps unsurprisingly, dismissed the piece as "Western propaganda."[29] Nevertheless, important questions were raised about whether Rwanda's economic growth more widely—reported as expanding 8 percent a year over the past decade—has been overstated.[30]

Yet perhaps the irony is that although the RPF relies on its development "vision" to claim a bright future for the country, this vision rests on a certain amnesia about the past. It should not be forgotten that Rwanda before the genocide was considered a "model of development in Africa," performing well according to conventional development indicators and attracting enormous amounts of donor aid.[31] Much like in the postgenocide period, under Rwanda's second president, Juvénal Habyarimana (1973–94), the international aid that flowed into the country served to strengthen the reach of the state, and was distributed in a top-down manner by urban elites who often noticeably disdained the rural poor.[32] This calls into question the extent to which the RPF's vision of development is really as new or transformational as it claims.

A Brief History: Churches and the State

How, then, does the RPF see the role of the churches in its vision for postgenocide development? I suggest that while immediately after the genocide it initially sought to work with the new churches—and, indeed, as we'll see, created the conditions under which they could flourish—it has gradually sought to bring them in line. The culmination here, I argue, was the 2018 church closures, motivated by a growing sense that the churches had gotten out of control; that they had become too unruly, too "noisy"; that they were leading the country down the "wrong" development path, imagining a "wrong" kind of future. I will have more to say about this in the next section.

Before the genocide, Rwanda was heavily Roman Catholic, with more than 60 percent of the population Catholic and more than 18 percent Protestant. Yet when the RPF eventually ended the genocide in July 1994, after the international community had failed to intervene, it treated the Catholic Church with suspicion and outright hostility. Why was this the case? This was because for decades—really, from its first arrival in the country at the beginning of the twentieth century—the Catholic Church had been deeply involved in ethnic politics and had maintained a close connection to the state.[33] Although when it had first arrived in the country it backed the Tutsi elite—believing this would be the most effective strategy for evangelism—with the Hutu Revolution (1959–61) it switched sides, to put it crudely, and began to back the Hutu. In the process, the Catholic Church, along with the Belgian colonial state, helped reify what had been more flexible socioeconomic categories into the ethnic identities of Hutu, Tutsi, and Twa. Under the country's two Hutu Republics, led by Grégoire Kayibana (1962–73), who had been educated in Catholic seminaries, and Juvénal Habyarimana (1973–94), the Catholic Church cozied up to power. Although the country had been beset by periods of ethnic violence from the late 1950s onward—and in 1990, when the RPF invaded from Uganda and started a civil war—church authorities as a whole did not speak out against abuses. Similarly, while the churches, both Catholic and Protestant, were heavily involved in development programs from education to healthcare, these initiatives played out according to the whims of the government and were positioned as apolitical.[34]

This history of playing ethnic politics and a close relationship with the state was to have tragic consequences during the genocide. Sparked by the shooting down of Habyarimana's plane on April 6, 1994, a three-month genocide ensued, wherein roughly 800,000 Tutsi and moderate Hutu were killed. Once again, the churches did not speak out against the violence, allowing some killers to believe "the slaughter actually met with God's favour."[35] Some church officials, lay and clergy, participated in the killings.[36] Churches became massacre sites; some of these sites, such as the Catholic Church of Nyamata, have since been transformed into genocide memorials.

Because of this history, when the RPF took power it was suspicious of the churches—particularly the Catholic Church—and "moved aggressively to bring [them] under its control," in some cases appointing pro-RPF leaders.[37] This mistrust of the mainline churches created a favorable environment for religious entrepreneurs keen on founding independent churches.[38] This call was taken up in large part by returnee Tutsi pastors who began returning to the country after the genocide, following decades in exile in Burundi, Uganda, the Democratic Republic of Congo, Kenya, Tanzania, and indeed, farther afield. Many of them founded "new" Pentecostal or evangelical churches whose adherents called themselves *abarokore* (the saved ones).[39] I use "new" here to distinguish these postgenocide churches from the "old" Pentecostal church, the Association des Églises de Pentecôte (ADEPR), which had arrived in the country via Swedish missionaries in 1940.[40] Unlike the new Pentecostal churches, ADEPR was considered to be Hutu-dominated.[41] This opening of the religious field was unprecedented in the postindependence era: under Habyarimana, for example, the government actively intervened to "quash" any new religious movements, in some cases jailing members of Christian "sects" when they refused to participate in government activities.[42]

When I interviewed converts to these new churches, they had many compelling reasons for converting. Against the formal rituals of the Catholic Church, the new Pentecostal churches—which emphasize personal salvation, close reading of the Bible, miraculous healing, and the importance of signs and wonders—gave believers a new sense of intimate community.[43] Others, as I have argued elsewhere, were drawn by the lively music and sound practices of the new churches.[44] However, despite the comfort and meaning that the new churches have brought to many adherents, particularly in Kigali, critics point out that they may equally be reinforcing ethnic difference.[45] Although ethnicity is banned under the RPF—citizens are encouraged to see themselves as *banyarwanda* (Rwandan), rather than as Tutsi, Hutu, or Twa—many of the new churches in Kigali are made up predominantly of Tutsi returnees. There is a confluence here, then, between the ethnic makeup of the new churches and the makeup of the RPF, which is widely perceived to be dominated by returnee Tutsi, particularly from Uganda.

In sum, the postgenocide religious landscape has seen dramatic transformations. The national census of 2012 found that, out of a population of 10.5 million, 44 percent were Roman Catholic, 38 percent were Protestant, and 12 percent were Adventist, with 2 percent Muslim and 1 percent Jehovah's Witnesses.[46] Although in 1962 Rwanda had fewer than ten recognized religious organizations, by 2017, there were more than a thousand.[47]

Preaching the "Good Gospel" of the Government

Although the 2018 church closures grabbed international headlines and wider media attention, we can now see that they were in fact part of a longer trajectory of postgenocide government control. In 2012, a new law was adopted (N°06/2012) requiring all religious-based organizations (RBOs) to legally register with the government through the Rwanda Governance Board (RGB). RBOs were now required to submit a plethora of documentation (including a statement regarding their "major doctrine") and establish particular administrative "organs" (including one for conflict resolution and another for administrative and financial audit). Even at this stage, it was reported that "several religious groups expressed concern about implementation of the new law and a perceived diminishing separation of church and state."[48] This new law was very much on the mind of Pastor Charles, whose narrative I take up later in the chapter. He too saw it as a way for the government to expand its control of the churches. Since 2014 there has been an ongoing crackdown on "noise pollution" in Kigali, with a number of pastors arrested and fined when they failed to comply with the regulations.[49]

When I talked to an RGB official about the new law in 2012, he told me that it had been formulated to help the churches grow and minimize conflicts within them. To this official, it was only right that churches cooperated with the government. As he told me:

> Nobody can say no to the fact that within the church or within the mosque is the right place to spread a good gospel of the government.... On Friday without any invitation, all mosques in the country are full. On Saturday, all churches of Seventh-Day Adventists, they are full. On Sunday, Catholics and Protestants, they are full. But now call them as a president or as a minister—they'll never come.... So now in Africa, you can't say no to a limited type of working together with the government. It has to be there.

Churches and mosques were expected to encourage citizens to participate in government programs and were considered to be particularly persuasive, given the importance of religion in Rwandans' everyday lives. Yet implicit in this official's comments was the sense that the government's "gospel" was by definition "good"—the official did not suggest that it was within the churches' purview to criticize or speak out against the government if they did not agree with its policies.

Indeed, when citizens do not share the RPF's developmentalist vision, problems arise, and religious figures have been targets of state repression. One example here is the case of a Catholic priest who spoke out against the government's program to eradicate *nyakatsi*, or thatch-roofed houses. The Bye-Bye Nyakatsi program, launched in 2008, was controversial—in some cases it was implemented too soon, as houses were destroyed before replacement housing could be built, leaving some citizens homeless. It seemed motivated in large part by a desire to (forcibly) propel "backward" Rwandans forward—nyakatsi were a symbol of the rural past, and had no place in the country's bright, modern future.[50] In December 2010, Abbé Emile Nsengiyumva, a Catholic priest at the parish of Karenge in eastern Rwanda, spoke out against the program and the government's proposed restrictions on family planning. After the sermon, he was arrested and charged with "endangering state security and inciting civil disobedience."[51] In July 2011, a court in Rwamagana sentenced him to eighteen months in prison.[52] In a better-known recent case, popular Catholic singer and peace and reconciliation activist, Kizito Mihigo, was sentenced to ten years in prison in 2015 for plotting to kill Kagame and inciting hatred against the government. A genocide survivor, he was accused of forming alliances with outlawed opposition groups, the Democratic Forces for the Liberation of Rwanda (FDLR) and the Rwanda National Congress (RNC). Yet many believed a song he had released prior to the twentieth commemoration of the genocide had contributed to his downfall. The song, which suggests that Hutu killed should also be remembered, contradicted the "official" government line and broke a public silence on acknowledging Hutu deaths.[53]

As we saw in the introduction, Kagame justified the 2018 closure of the churches through asserting that they, unlike boreholes and factories, are not productively contributing to Rwanda's development. In later statements, the official line has been that the government is merely protecting citizens from unsafe conditions and from morally bankrupt pastors. A statement about the closures in July 2018 on the government website reads:

> The closures do not infringe on freedom to worship but rather address the alarming proliferation of places of worship in dilapidated

and unhygienic conditions, as well as troubling behaviour of unscrupulous individuals masquerading as religious leaders. The latter have, among other abuses, defrauded innocent followers, broadcast insults against women and other religions, and forced followers to fast to the point of death from starvation.[54]

Through such rhetoric and actions, the government constructs itself as solely capable of protecting citizens' well-being (psychological and physical) and constructs its citizens as passive recipients of this protection, in need of being cared for and unable to care for themselves. Dilapidated churches and misogynist, fraudulent pastors challenge the country's image as a "modern" country with clean and safe streets and little corruption, led by a government that is committed to gender equality. Note too how the government claims it is uniquely able to differentiate between "real" and "fake" pastors, despite its avowed secularity. Indeed, state-run "solidarity" camps (*ingando*) feature philosophy lectures promoting materialism, which, participants complain, in a rare articulation of dissent, teach them that "God does not exist."[55]

For government critics, the 2018 crackdown on the churches revealed RPF anxieties about its own grip on power. David Himbara, once Kagame's economic adviser and now based in exile in Canada, did not mince words, writing that "the real reason Kagame shut down Rwandan churches is fear and paranoia."[56] In a context wherein the media and political life are highly controlled, Himbara pointed out that churches can be understood as "the last open space" where hope and the possibility of change and a better future can be imagined.[57] This is what was so dangerous.

With this background in mind—the particular development "vision" as offered by the RPF and the long history of church-state proximity—we can now turn to Pastor Charles's story. Throughout, I emphasize the anxiety caused by conflicting views of the future and the physical effects this had on Pastor Charles's body. I also demonstrate how the ability to contribute to the country's development seems to be premised on materially contributing to the RPF.

Pastor Charles: Building a Health Center or a Church?

I first met Pastor Charles, a Pentecostal pastor who was a returnee from Uganda, by chance. I was having lunch one day with my friend Pastor Moses, another Pentecostal pastor from Uganda, and Pastor Charles dropped by our table to say hello. Pastor Moses introduced me and suggested that speaking to Pastor Charles would be good for my research. Pastor Charles dutifully handed me his business card. A few days later, I went to visit him at his church.

Pastor Charles's church was located in a poorer area of Kigali, down a dirt road close to a petrol station. The church itself, although large, was bare bones—the wooden timbers holding up the roof were roughly hewn, and the altar at the front of the church was covered in threadbare carpets. I met Pastor Charles in a modest office behind the church; it was neat and tidy, with colorful posters of "crusades" (*ibiterane*) or open-air meetings he had organized over the past few years decorating the walls. On several of the posters I recognized other pastors I knew and had interviewed.

Like many returnee pastors I spoke to, Pastor Charles told me that he had been summoned back to Rwanda by the voice of God. Pastor Charles had grown up in an orphanage in rural Uganda and had given his life to Christ when he was still a young boy. Despite a difficult upbringing, he had managed to attend secondary school and then college in Kampala, and throughout his studies had been involved in various Pentecostal student groups. In 1996, he attended an overnight prayer session at Prayer Mountain, a well-known prayer and pilgrimage location outside Kampala, led by a Nigerian pastor. Here, he heard a voice telling him to "go to preach to Rwanda." Pastor Charles admitted that he had had an ambivalent reaction to this—he was twenty-four years old at the time and didn't see how it would be possible to uproot his life and "return" to a country he had never visited. His parents had fled Rwanda in 1960 and all the relatives he had had in the country had been killed in the genocide. Pastor Charles resisted this voice for several years, but eventually he returned to Rwanda for good in 2003.

Yet even after he returned, Pastor Charles admitted that he still wasn't sure how exactly to follow the voice. As he put it, he didn't know where to begin. So instead of starting a church, he decided to start an NGO—this, to him, was much easier, especially given the development money pouring into the country at the time. The NGO he eventually started in 2003 focused on children's health and education, and soon became successful. It was not a Christian NGO, and positioned itself as more or less secular. One of its main projects was the construction of a health center. Pastor Charles, however, did not forget the voice, and decided that the money he made from his NGO work would go into starting a church. He was able to start his church in 2007, and by the time I met him in 2011, the church had four branches in the city. Unlike the city's most successful megachurches—Zion Temple, Restoration Church, Christian Life Assembly—which were housed in impressive buildings and attracted the (returnee Tutsi) elite, Pastor Charles's church purposely opened branches in poorer areas and preached to those struggling in difficult life circumstances.

We could say that through his work, Pastor Charles imagined a particular kind of future for himself and for Rwanda. Like many other pastors I spoke to, he believed that Rwanda had a special calling from God and that he in turn had been called to help realize this through his church-building and NGO activities. Although the country had almost been destroyed by the genocide, God had a plan for Rwanda's future: to be an example not only for the region, but for the rest of the world. Pastor Charles's actions in the present were working toward achieving this goal. For although the government understood development and the country's future in decidedly secular terms—the result of achieving carefully specified goals at particular intervals—Pastor Charles understood it as a deeply spiritual project. Development, to him, could only occur if it included God—or, better yet, was directed by him.

Despite these initial successes in his NGO and church work, however, Pastor Charles had recently landed in hot water with the government. Yet the trouble was not his church, but the health center. Or, rather, the government accused him of combining his development and spiritual endeavors, which were supposed to be kept separate. Essentially, the story went like this: Pastor Charles's NGO had been awarded quite a significant sum of money—in the tens of thousands of dollars—from a foreign donor to build a health center in a district of Kigali. However, the local authorities accused him of forging documents and of building a church instead. (They later also accused him of embezzling the money.) Pastor Charles, however, insisted that he was innocent, and that he had been building a health center all along. To make this point, during my first visit to his church, he pulled out binders full of documents to defend himself. He showed me receipts for building materials; the registration papers for his NGO; government letters ordering the halt of his NGO's activities; government letters recognizing Pastor Charles as legal representative of his NGO; police summonses; and the title for the land on which the health center was being built. These documents were written in a mixture of Kinyarwanda, English, and French. He also showed me the architectural plans for the site, as well as photos of the buildings that had been under construction. The photos showed small rooms in the process of being built; to my admittedly nonexpert eyes, this kind of construction did not seem consistent with the building of a church. As final proof of his innocence, Pastor Charles showed me a report written by an independent auditor concluding that he had been building a health center, and not a church; it also concluded that he had not misused the funds. And yet, despite this evidence, the government had taken over the health center and was now persecuting Pastor Charles.

Pastor Charles was adamant he had done nothing wrong, yet he remained in doubt regarding why he was being unfairly targeted. Eventually, in response to my persistence, he told me that it might have to do with the fact that he did not give money to the RPF. The RPF expects citizens, who are pressured to become party members, to give "contributions" (sing.: *umusanzu;* pl.: *imisanzu*) not only in terms of labor—participating in mandatory community work such as umuganda—but also in terms of cash.[58] Given the sizable sums that Pastor Charles had managed to raise for his NGO, not only from the foreign donor who gave money for the health center but from other foreign donors for similar projects, he suspected he might have been targeted because he was not sharing his rewards with party officials. And since Pastor Charles also had several churches, the easiest way to go after him was by making accusations through his church. The implication here was twofold: (1) that only party members should be participating in the country's development; and (2) that only party members should be financially profiting from NGO money flowing into the country. Although the RPF prides itself on its transparency and lack of corruption, Pastor Charles was convinced that greedy local authorities were behind his troubles, yet his attempts to go above them and clear his name had been unsuccessful. The future that Pastor Charles had tried to build for himself—as a productive citizen who could contribute to the country's future through not only a "secular" development project but church activities as well—was suddenly thrown in doubt.

More worryingly, Pastor Charles described a wider context of fear and intimidation. He told me that after the government shut down his health center, he suddenly started getting suspicious phone calls from private numbers, asking him to meet. This is a tactic of state intimidation I have described elsewhere, and for Pastor Charles it was the cause of tremendous anxiety.[59] He couldn't say for certain who was calling him, and he still wasn't 100 percent certain that the reason he was being targeted was because of his failure to contribute to the party. Perhaps there was another reason he hadn't considered? How could he trust those around him? Most disturbing, however, was an incident of a fire a few months previous. Pastor Charles had arrived home one evening very late—he had been hosting visiting pastors—and went to sleep. He awoke suddenly a few hours later to discover his house was on fire. Pastor Charles narrowly escaped and was convinced that the fire had been purposely set—how, he asked me, could only one house, nestled tightly between other houses, burn down? This narrow escape had only increased his anxiety as he was now convinced that the government would go to extreme lengths to silence him. The government also seemed to be putting pressure on other foreign donors he worked with through his NGO to cancel collaborations. Funding was suddenly cut off, with little explanation.

Despite his difficulties, Pastor Charles believed that the government's heavy-handed tactics would ultimately backfire. He turned to the Bible to support this idea. He reminded me that when the Christian church was just starting, as described in the Book of Acts, it faced tremendous persecution and difficulties. It was precisely at this moment, however, that the church attracted new believers. So while the state may be acting in reference to the secular world—to maintain its grip on power—it didn't realize that this was having unintended consequences in the spiritual realm. As Pastor Charles told me, "So they [i.e., the government] don't know [what] they are doing [is] for the kingdom of God. Their fighting, it is doing something in the kingdom. Their persecuting the church in Rwanda, is doing something in the kingdom of God." Paradoxically, then, government interference might only serve to strengthen his church and its members. Indeed, Pastor Charles told me that after his troubles with the government, his church had in fact grown. He attributed this to the fact that his conduct throughout proved to people that he was a true man of God.

Less dramatically, we could also see how the deluge of endless documents from various government ministries was another way in which the government tried to intimidate Pastor Charles and provoke, perhaps, anxiety and uncertainty in him. The same ministry that had supported his NGO in one letter wrote in another that it did not recognize it. Evidence itself was called into question. Which document, after all, was "true"? Even a report from a supposedly independent source—the audit—was discounted, as were photographs. The state here claimed ultimate interpretative authority: it alone was able to weave together these various documents and craft a damning narrative. Yet in carefully safeguarding these documents, placing each document in a binder in chronological order, Pastor Charles was able to show the inconsistencies of the state, the changeability of its various "moods." And, indeed, perhaps by keeping this careful record Pastor Charles was able to find (however fleetingly) some kind of "calm." While the state told one narrative about him and his NGO activities, the documents themselves held out the possibility of another kind of story being told; they held out the possibility of finding a more sympathetic audience in the future.

Revealing Government Agents?

For the rest of my fieldwork, I would meet Pastor Charles periodically to check in on how he was doing; or I would run into him at cafés in the city, where he would often be sitting alone, seemingly deep in thought. When I would meet Pastor Charles, he would tell me about his plans for other projects. He wanted to start a mental health clinic because many Rwandans were still traumatized, he said; he wanted to start a reconciliation project involving theater in secondary schools to target the youth; he wanted to start a pen pal project between Rwandan secondary schools and Canadian schools (here I offered to put him in touch with a friend who was a secondary school teacher, but things never materialized). He wanted to publish a book based on his experiences. Despite his difficulties, he still imagined himself as a productive participant in building Rwanda's future. Or perhaps he thought that if he proved himself through other development projects, he would be able to make up for the health center fiasco.

I left Rwanda in December 2012 but returned in September 2013. When I met up with Pastor Charles again, he had news to share. In the time I'd been gone, the foreign donor, unsurprisingly, had demanded to know what had happened to its money. If the government had taken over the project—which it essentially had—then the donor wanted its money back. This had given rise to a situation, Pastor Charles told me, where someone needed to be blamed. That person was Pastor Charles. He was arrested and detained for nine days. He was eventually released, and an investigation was conducted into the matter. In the end he faced several charges and a total of eight years in prison.[60] Yet, after a convoluted process wherein Pastor Charles told me he had become convinced his lawyer was corrupt and actively working against him, all the charges were dropped. Pastor Charles was again back to running his church, though he was on even shakier ground. As he told me, "I'm not certain that I'm safe. I'm not certain. I'm not confident. Because the people who ... are behind this are still there. They've not gone anywhere." Even here, Pastor Charles only had suspicions about the identities of his tormentors; he didn't know for certain who they were, and his anxiety intensified because he could not definitively point to the root cause of his problems.

In one of our meetings I asked Pastor Charles if he felt that his fellow pastors had supported him throughout his ordeal, and he said that they had, although they were limited in what they could do. Some of them, after all, faced similar problems. Pastor Charles mentioned, in fact, Pastor Moses, the pastor who had introduced us. Pastor Moses was also in a difficult situation (which he had shared with me), having built a church in an area the government wanted to resettle to build high-end housing. Pastor Moses refused to leave. In the end, he told the government that he might be willing to sell, but the amount they offered him was insultingly low—less than a fraction of its real worth (at least according to an independent evaluation that Pastor Moses had commissioned). Pastor Charles knew of at least one other case wherein the government had forcibly confiscated a pastor's land.

As Chris Huggins has noted, under the RPF's Vision 2020 plan, the land and property of thousands of citizens in urban areas have been expropriated by the government without adequate compensation.[61] Urban policies—undertaken with an aim to "modernize" Kigali—seem to benefit the urban elite and lead to increased precarity for the urban poor.[62] There have been cases of senior government officials taking interest in particular areas of land and enlisting the help of local authorities to pressure residents into selling the land at less than market value. In one case Huggins examines that took place in Masaka sector, a rural area close to Kigali, not only were residents threatened with imprisonment, but one resident who resisted the land purchases was informed that he had "genocide ideology."[63] Their crops were later destroyed and state officials—such as the Office of the Ombudsman—were unwilling to intervene given the high profile of the senior government officials involved. In the end, the residents were forced to sell their land for far below its worth. The similarities here with Pastor Charles's case were striking, down to the indirect, insidious ways in which the state intervenes to thwart citizens' futures—in this case, dreams of owning land and cultivating it on their own terms.

Meeting Pastor Charles during my second trip, I could see the physical effects of the ordeal. His disposition was more anxious, more fearful; his voice weaker, less forceful. He had become resigned and spoke less of other plans for future projects. One of our conversations occurred again at his church. Before I arrived, I tried calling Pastor Charles to see where exactly I should meet him (in the church itself, in his office), but he didn't answer. When I arrived, I found him sitting outside his church in a white plastic chair in the shade, his back to the wall of the church. He explained that he didn't have his phone with him. He now always turned if off or left it at home when he met someone as he was convinced that the government was listening in. This was different from our first meeting at his church, where he had been interrupted several times by phone calls and had answered them enthusiastically.

Throughout it all, Pastor Charles insisted he had survived only because of his faith in God. God had been particularly important in revealing the "real" intentions of others, he said. While this notion that God revealed "pagans" or the devil's agents among churchgoers was a common theme in other Pentecostal churches I attended, in Pastor Charles's case, it took on a different meaning. Here he meant that God revealed to him when people who came to his church pretending to pray were really government agents. He told me too that the reason he was unmarried—which was quite unusual for a Pentecostal pastor of his age—was that he could not trust that women were genuinely interested in him, and were not government spies. Two relationships, he told me, had broken down because he realized the women had "political" motives. In the postgenocide period, it seems, state power operates not only through practices of repression and control but equally through practices of deception and disguise, through the production and circulation of emotions such as suspicion, paranoia, and anxiety.[64]

In her work on Protestant NGOs in Zimbabwe, Erica Bornstein has shown how they cultivated a "politics of transcendence": by claiming their work was oriented toward the "kingdom of God" and "markets," they were able to frame their provisioning of social and material aid as politically neutral, even though it in fact directly benefited a weak Zimbabwean state unable to provide these services.[65] In Rwanda, since development is heavily controlled by the RPF, the possibility of positioning involvement in it as politically neutral is all but impossible. The logic seems to be that development that does not involve contributing to the party is not really development at all. The future being built must conform to the "vision" laid out by the RPF. Those who, like Pastor Charles, dare to imagine otherwise are punished through channels both "official" (endless documents, legal procedures) and "unofficial" (suspicious phone calls, threats, attempts on one's life).

In the face of state repression, however, Pastor Charles's faith did not waver. He may have grown more anxious, but he maintained an underlying calm—a belief that any action in the world would have effects in the spiritual realm, and a trust that God would reveal the lying of the state itself. The kind of future he imagined was one wherein citizens were able to "contribute" to the country's development on their own terms (regardless of party affiliation), one wherein they understood development itself as ultimately a spiritual project—as a way to rebuild the nation in the image of God. In a way similar to what Kevin O'Neill has described for neo-Pentecostals in postwar Guatemala, Pastor Charles believed that it was through his Christianity that he could help combat the problems of postgenocide Rwanda—through prayer and fasting, and building both a health center and a church—no matter how much the government attempted to curtail his actions.[66]

The problem was that the RPF wanted the country to be rebuilt in its own image—even if, in trying to impose this "vision," it revealed a certain fragility. For the more the RPF tried to "trick" Pastor Charles, the more he relied on God; further, the more the RPF practiced its trickery, the more the actions of the state itself were cast not as godly, but rather as of the devil, opening up the possibility, through the logic of spiritual warfare, that Christians would be morally justified in combatting the state. This, after all, is the danger: if, as Ruth Marshall has argued, Pentecostal theology is ultimately antidemocratic because it imagines a world in which the other must be "overcome" through conversion, then the state was running the risk of putting itself in such a position—of being identified with "the demonic that needs to be destroyed for salvation and redemption to occur."[67] It was this anxiety, I suggest, that in part motivated the state to take such dramatic measures against the churches in 2018.

"Frictionless" Development: Pentecostal Politics and State Anxieties

Although in this chapter I have focused on the ways in which some Pentecostal leaders understood faith in a way that contradicts the RPF's developmentalist logic, in some ways church leaders such as Pastor Charles might be exceptions. As I have documented elsewhere, in other more public ways the Protestant churches spiritually legitimize the RPF regime, giving thanks for its rule after the genocide.[68] For example, at the inaugural Rwanda Thanksgiving Day (or *Rwanda Shima Imana*) I attended in 2012 at Amahoro stadium in Kigali—along with 23,000 Rwandans—high-ranking Protestant authorities called on the audience to thank God for various government programs, including *gacaca* (community courts established to try cases of genocide) and *mutuelle de santé* (health insurance). Preaching the "good gospel" of the government, indeed.

As we have seen, this collusion between the state and the churches has long roots in Rwanda. As much as the RPF claims a break with the corrupt policies of the former Hutu regimes, this break seems to be in name only—in practice, troubling continuities persist. As Timothy Longman notes, "the churches' practice of urging support for the current regime, despite its involvement in major human rights abuses, is reminiscent of the blind support churches offered to the Kayibanda and Habyarimana regimes."[69] He argues that in order to contribute meaningfully to the reconstruction of the country, churches must "begin to speak with a prophetic voice inspired by the Word of God rather than political considerations. Ultimately, Rwanda needs strong, prophetic, independent churches to develop a brighter future."[70]

While Pastor Charles's case would likely not count as prophetic—he was not proclaiming loudly against the regime's human rights abuses or political repression, although he did so in private conversations—I suggest that it does point to a certain Pentecostal politics that cannot be ignored. In charting out alternative understandings of the future—or, more dramatically, in claiming that faith in God allows the trickery of the state to be revealed—Pastor Charles challenges the RPF's "vision" and suggests that there are ways other than secular development of imagining the future. Despite the Rwandan state's strength, he insists instead on its weakness—its seemingly petty desire to silence citizens when they dare to imagine development otherwise, its anxious intolerance of a little "noise." Yet the kind of politics that we might read into Pastor Charles's case should not be understood as directly resistant to the state—the dynamics I explore in this chapter suggest a more "quiet" or indirect form of politics than a framework of resistance would allow.[71] After all, as Harri Englund has argued, claiming that religious or occult practices are acts of political resistance ultimately "diminishes" religion's "practical import" and "imaginative resources."[72] It is precisely the "imaginative resources" of Pentecostalism in Rwanda that I tried to sketch out in this chapter, its ability to offer "visions" of the future that might ultimately prove more compelling to large swaths of citizens. No matter how much the government attempts to intimidate citizens, using anxiety as a political tool, God provides another source of power and calm.

Shutting down chuches, appropriating a health center: in these actions that seemingly attempt to communicate strength, the RPF's own anxieties about its grip on power come to light. Despite its façade of certainty, its apparent conviction of the rightness and legitimacy of the development future it has mapped out for the country, in quashing any and all alternative visions, the RPF reveals an anxiety that these alternatives might hold some weight, that citizens might be questioning whether or not "development" has truly trickled down to them, that they might be envisioning futures otherwise, and relying on God to do so. Impressive development statistics, after all, aren't so convincing when citizens can't find employment or when their land is forcibly confiscated. Furthermore, there is the irony that even when citizens act in a way that the RPF promotes—Pastor Charles, after all, demonstrated self-reliance and an entrepreneurial spirit in setting up his NGO and securing donor funds—the RPF ultimately seems to feel threatened. Hence the requirement that those who contribute to the country's development must be party members, presumably so that they can be kept in line.

It takes political work to make development appear "frictionless"—and, at least to international donors, the RPF has been largely successful in selling this narrative. Yet the heavy-handed church closures and the appropriation of a health center suggest chafing, raising the uncomfortable possibility that the Rwandan population isn't being led into a "bright" future so willingly. Since the RPF has staked its claim for political legitimacy on its ability to deliver this future, suggestions otherwise are a cause of deep concern and anxiety, a noisy "truth" it would rather silence than acknowledge.

Notes

1. Ignatius Ssuuna, "Rwanda Restricts Fasting as 8,000 Churches Closed," *Christianity Today*, 7 August 2018, https://www.christianitytoday.com/news/2018/august/rwanda-churches-closed-fasting-restricted-rgb-religion-law.html.

2. Collins Mwai, "700 Churches Closed in Kigali over Standards," *New Times*, 28 February 2018, http://www.newtimes.co.rw/section/read/229466.

3. Edmund Kagire, "Six Pastors Arrested in Rwanda for Opposing Shutdown of Churches," *East African*, 6 March 2018, https://www.theeastafrican.co.ke/news/ea/Rwandan-pastors-arrest-closed-churches/4552908-4330346-101ks8xz/index.html.

4. Johnson Kanamugire and Edmund Kagire, "President Kagame Shocked by High Number of Churches in Rwanda," *East African*, 3 March 2018, http://www.theeastafrican.co.ke/news/President-Kagame-shock-high-number-churches-in-Rwanda/2558-4326622-6lxyde/index.html.

5. Tom Goodfellow and Alyson Smith, "From Urban Catastrophe to 'Model' City? Politics, Security and Development in Post-Conflict Kigali," *Urban Studies* 50, no. 15 (2013): 3185–202.

6. We could see the crackdown as part of an ongoing "politics of silence" in Kigali, whereby the state forcibly quashes any kind of "noisy" dissent. See Tom Goodfellow, "The Institutionalisation of 'Noise' and 'Silence' in Urban Politics: Riots and Compliance in Uganda and Rwanda," *Oxford Development Studies* 41, no. 4 (2013): 436–54.

7. Sianne Ngai, *Ugly Feelings* (Cambridge, MA: Harvard University Press, 2005).

8. Ernst Bloch, *The Principle of Hope*, vol. 1, trans. Neville Plaice, Stephen Plaice, and Paul Knight, Studies in Contemporary German Social Thought (Cambridge, MA: MIT Press, 1995), 74–75. Quoted in Ngai, *Ugly Feelings*, 210.

9. Barbara Bompani and Caroline Valois, eds., *Christian Citizens and the Moral Regeneration of the African State* (London: Routledge, 2017); Kevin Lewis O'Neill, *City of God: Christian Citizenship in Postwar Guatemala* (Berkeley: University of California Press, 2010).

10. Jennifer Cole, *Sex and Salvation: Imagining the Future in Madagascar* (Chicago: University of Chicago Press, 2010), 5.

11. Lee Ann Fujii, "Shades of Truth and Lies: Interpreting Testimonies of War and Violence," *Journal of Peace Research* 47, no. 2 (2010): 231–41.

12. In 2017, the country launched the seven-year "National Strategy for Transformation" (NST1), to encompass the years 2017–24. It was designed to see the country "cross over" from Vision 2020 to Vision 2050. See Republic of Rwanda, "7 Years Government Programme: National Strategy for Transformation (NST 1): 2017–2024," accessed 16 January 2020, http://www.minecofin.gov.rw/fileadmin/user_upload/NST1_7YGP_Final.pdf; World Bank Group and the Government of Rwanda, *Future Drivers of Growth in Rwanda: Innovation, Integration, Agglomeration, and Competition* (Washington, DC: World Bank, 2019), accessed 28 February 2020, https://openknowledge.worldbank.org/handle/10986/30372.

13. Paul Kagame, "Rwanda and the New Lions of Africa," *Wall Street Journal*, 19 May 2013, sec. Opinion, http://online.wsj.com/news/articles/SB10001424127887324767004578485234078541160.

14. Benjamin Chemouni, "The Politics of Core Public Sector Reform in Rwanda," ESID Working Paper no. 88 (Manchester: University of Manchester, 2017).

15. Scott Straus and Lars Waldorf, "Introduction: Seeing Like a Post-conflict State," in *Remaking Rwanda: State Building and Human Rights after Mass Atrocity*, ed. Scott Straus and Lars Waldorf (Madison: University of Wisconsin Press, 2011), 13.

16. Straus and Waldorf, 8–10.

17. Andrea Purdeková, "Civic Education and Social Transformation in Post-Genocide Rwanda: Forging the Perfect Development Subjects," in *Rwanda Fast Forward: Social, Economic, Military and Reconciliation Prospects*, ed. Maddalena Campioni and Patrick Noack (Basingstoke, UK: Palgrave Macmillan, 2012), 192–209.

18. Laura Mann and Marie Berry, "Understanding the Political Motivations That Shape Rwanda's Emergent Developmental State," *New Political Economy* 21, no. 1 (2016): 120.

19. Mann and Berry, 120.

20. Purdeková, "Civic Education and Social Transformation," 195.

21. Benjamin Chemouni, "The Political Path to Universal Health Coverage: Power, Ideas and Community-Based Health Insurance in Rwanda," *World Development* 106 (2018): 87–98.

22. Mann and Berry, "Understanding the Political Motivations," 136–37; see also Catherine A Honeyman, *The Orderly Entrepreneur: Youth, Education, and Governance in Rwanda* (Stanford, CA: Stanford University Press, 2016).

23. Honeyman, *Orderly Entrepreneur*.

24. Purdeková, "Civic Education and Social Transformation," 204.

25. Mann and Berry, "Understanding the Political Motivations," 131; see also Nilgün Gökgür, "Rwanda's Ruling Party-Owned Enterprises: Do They Enhance or Impede Development?" (Universiteit Antwerpen, Institute of Development Policy and Management, 2012), http://EconPapers.repec.org/RePEc:iob:dpaper:2012003.

26. Filip Reyntjens, "Lies, Damned Lies and Statistics: Poverty Reduction Rwandan-Style and How the Aid Community Loves It," *African Arguments* (blog), 3 November 2015, https://africanarguments.org/2015/11/03/lies-damned-lies-and-statistics-poverty-reduction-rwandan-style-and-how-the-aid-community-loves-it/. See also An Ansoms et al., "Statistics versus Livelihoods: Questioning Rwanda's Pathway Out of Poverty," *Review of African Political Economy* 44, no. 151 (2017): 47–65.

27. Reyntjens, "Lies, Damned Lies and Statistics."

28. Tom Wilson and David Blood, "Rwanda: Where Even Poverty Data Must Toe Kagame's Line," *Financial Times*, 13 August 2019, https://www.ft.com/content/683047ac-b857-11e9-96bd-8e884d3ea203?segmentId=63bac0e6-3d28-36b1-7417-423982f60790.

29. Tom Wilson, "Rwanda's Kagame Dismisses FT Story as Western Propaganda," *Financial Times*, 15 August 2019, https://www.ft.com/content/eba24b0e-bf2c-11e9-b350-db00d509634e.

30. "The Devil in the Details: Has Rwanda Been Fiddling Its Numbers?," *The Economist*, 15 August 2019, https://www.economist.com/middle-east-and-africa/2019/08/15/has-rwanda-been-fiddling-its-numbers.

31. Peter Uvin, *Aiding Violence: The Development Enterprise in Rwanda* (West Hartford, CT: Kumarian Press, 1998), 1.

32. Uvin.

33. This history is only briefly sketched out here. For fuller accounts, see J. J. Carney, *Rwanda before the Genocide: Catholic Politics and Ethnic Discourse in the Late Colonial Era* (Oxford: Oxford University Press, 2014); Tharcisse Gatwa, *The Churches and Ethnic Ideology in the Rwandan Crises, 1900–1994* (Bletchley, UK: Paternoster, 2005); Ian Linden, *Church and Revolution in Rwanda* (Manchester: Manchester University Press, 1977); Timothy Longman, *Christianity and Genocide in Rwanda* (Cambridge: Cambridge University Press, 2010); Laurent Mbanda, *Committed to Conflict: The Destruction of the Church in Rwanda* (London: SPCK, 1997).

34. Uvin, *Aiding Violence*.

35. Alison Des Forges, *"Leave None to Tell the Story": Genocide in Rwanda* (New York: Human Rights Watch Paris, 1999), 246.

36. For example, Father Athanase Seromba was accused of ordering the bulldozing of his parish in Nyange, leading to the deaths of more than two thousand Tutsi. The first Catholic priest to later be tried at the International Criminal Tribunal for Rwanda (ICTR), he was sentenced to fifteen years in prison.

37. Timothy Longman, "Limitations to Political Reform: The Undemocratic Nature of Transition in Rwanda," in *Remaking Rwanda: State Building and Human Rights after Mass Atrocity*, ed. Scott Straus and Lars Waldorf (Madison: University of Wisconsin Press, 2011), 28; see also Gerard van't Spijker, "La rivalité des alliances: Les églises après le génocide rwandais," in *Concurrences en mission: Propagandes, conflits, coexistences (XVIe–XXIe siècle)*, ed. Salvador Eyezo'o and Jean-François Zorn (Paris: Karthala, 2011), 1–14.

38. Van't Spijker, "La rivalité des alliances."

39. There is a longer historical trajectory of *abarokore*: followers of the East African Revival of the 1930s also called themselves *abarokore*, as did those who participated in a second abarokore movement within the Protestant churches in Rwanda in the 1980s.

40. "Old" here refers not only to ADEPR's longer historical presence in the country, but also to the sense some postgenocide Pentecostal converts had that some of ADEPR's teachings—particularly as related to dress and service structure—were conservative and outdated. Women, for example, were expected to cover their hair and wear skirts that extended below their knees.

41. Josephine Sundqvist, "Reconciliation as a Societal Process: A Case Study on the Role of the Pentecostal Movement (ADEPR) as an Actor in the Reconciliation Process in Post-genocide Rwanda," *Svensk Missionstidsskrift* 99, no. 2 (2011): 157–95.

42. Longman, *Christianity and Genocide in Rwanda*, 92–93.

43. See also Anne Kubai, "Post-genocide Rwanda: The Changing Religious Landscape," *Exchange* 36, no. 2 (2007): 198–214.

44. Andrea Mariko Grant, "Noise and Silence in Rwanda's Postgenocide Religious Soundscape," *Journal of Religion in Africa* 48 (2018): 35–64.

45. Kubai, "Post-genocide Rwanda"; Gerard van't Spijker, "The Churches and Genocide in Rwanda," *Exchange* 26, no. 3 (1997): 233–55.

46. NISR and MINECOFIN, "2012 Population and Housing Census: Provisional Results" (Republic of Rwanda, 2012).

47. Republic of Rwanda, "Note on Regulating Faith Based Organizations in Rwanda," 28 July 2018, http://gov.rw/newsdetails2/?tx_ttnews%5Btt_news%5D=1965&cHash=192e92c6213bc0ff46617c86e114a7d1.

48. U.S. Department of State, "Rwanda 2012 International Religious Freedom Report" (U.S. Department of State, 2012), https://2009-2017.state.gov/j/drl/rls/irf/2012religiousfreedom/index.htm?year=2012&dlid=208184#wrapper.

49. Times Reporter, "Police Arrest Nine over Noise Pollution," *New Times*, 13 October 2014, http://www.newtimes.co.rw/section/article/2014-10-13/181880/; see also Andrea Mariko Grant, "Pentecostal Sounds and Silences in Rwanda," *The Immanent Frame* (blog), 4 June 2019, https://tif.ssrc.org/2019/06/04/pentecostal-sounds-and-silences-in-rwanda/.

50. Shyaka Kanuma, "Trials and Tribulations in Nyakatsi," *Rwanda Focus*, 10 January 2011.

51. "World Report 2012: Rwanda," Human Rights Watch, https://www.hrw.org/world-report/2012/country-chapters/Rwanda.

52. "Rwanda: Freedom in the World 2012," Freedom House, accessed 11 September 2014.

53. David Mwambari, "Music and the Politics of the Past: Kizito Mihigo and Music in the Commemoration of the Genocide against the Tutsi in Rwanda," *Memory Studies* 34 (2019): 1–16; I discuss an earlier controversy Mihigo was involved in here: Andrea Mariko Grant, "Ecumenism in Question: Rwanda's Contentious Post-genocide Religious Landscape," *Journal of Southern African Studies* 44, no. 2 (2018): 221–38. Mihigo was later released through presidential pardon in 2018, along with more than two thousand other prisoners, including opposition leader Victoire Ingabire. Tragically, Mihigo was arrested in February 2020 for allegedly trying to cross the border into Burundi. Taken to Kigali and imprisoned, he was found dead in his cell several days later. The "official" cause of his death was suicide, but some believed he had been killed by the government.

54. Republic of Rwanda, "Note on Regulating Faith Based Organizations in Rwanda." The second charge—of broadcasting insults against women—referred to the case of Pastor Nicholas Niyibikora, who had delivered a sermon on the Christian radio station Amazing Grace at the end of January 2018 that was widely condemned for its misogyny. In response, the Rwanda Utilities Regulatory Authority (RURA) revoked the station's license. The station's owner, American evangelist Gregg Schoof, was arrested in October 2019 when he tried to hold a press conference—without the proper authorization—during which he planned to criticize the government for shutting down his radio station. He was swiftly deported.

55. Andrea Purdeková, "Rwanda's *Ingando* Camps: Liminality and the Reproduction of Power," Oxford Refugee Studies Centre Working Paper Series, no. 80 (Oxford: Refugee Studies Centre, 2011), 27.

56. David Himbara, "Kagame, I Put It to You That the Real Reason You Closed over 700 Rwandan Churches Is Not Lack of Hygiene—It Is Your Fear of Freedom," *Medium* (blog), 5 March 2018, https://medium.com/@david.himbara_27884/kagame-i-put-it-to-you-that-the-real-reason-you-closed-rwandan-churches-is-not-lack-of-hygiene-bf57b8d325cd.

57. Himbara, "Kagame, I Put It to You."

58. Andrea Purdeková, "'Even If I Am Not Here, There Are So Many Eyes': Surveillance and State Reach in Rwanda," *Journal of Modern African Studies* 49, no. 3 (2011): 482.

59. Andrea Mariko Grant, "Quiet Insecurity and Quiet Agency in Post-genocide Rwanda," *Etnofoor* 27, no. 2 (2015): 15–36.

60. I am being deliberately vague here about the charges against him.

61. Chris Huggins, "Land Grabbing and Land Tenure Security in Post-genocide Rwanda," in *Losing Your Land: Dispossession in the Great Lakes*, ed. An Ansoms and Thea Hilhorst (Woodbridge, UK: James Currey, 2014), 141–62.

62. Vincent Manirakiza and An Ansoms, "'Modernizing Kigali': The Struggle for Space in the Rwandan Urban Context," in Ansoms and Hilhorst, *Losing Your Land*, 186–203.

63. Huggins, "Land Grabbing and Land Tenure Security," 154–55.

64. Mateusz Laszczkowski and Madeleine Reeves, "Introduction: Affect and the Anthropology of the State," in *Affective States: Entanglements, Suspensions, Suspicions*, ed. Mateusz Laszczkowski and Madeleine Reeves (New York: Berghahn Books, 2018), 1–14.

65. Erica Bornstein, *The Spirit of Development: Protestant NGOs, Morality and Economics in Zimbabwe* (New York: Routledge, 2003), chapter 4.

66. O'Neill, *City of God*.

67. Ruth Marshall, *Political Spiritualities: The Pentecostal Revolution in Nigeria* (Chicago: University of Chicago Press, 2009), 14.

68. Grant, "Ecumenism in Question."

69. Timothy Longman, "Christian Churches in Post-genocide Rwanda: Reconciliation and Its Limits," in *The Healing of Memories: African Christian Responses to Politically Induced Trauma*, ed. Mohammed Girma (Lanham, MD: Lexington Books, 2018), 73.

70. Longman, 73.

71. For important work that explores Christianity as a site of contestation and resistance to hegemonic power, see Jean Comaroff, *Body of Power, Spirit of Resistance: The Culture and History of a South African People* (Chicago: University of Chicago Press, 1985); Karen Fields, *Revival and Rebellion in Colonial Central Africa* (Princeton, NJ: Princeton University Press, 1985).

72. Harri Englund, "Rethinking African Christianities: Beyond the Religion-Politics Conundrum," in *Christianity and Public Culture in Africa*, ed. Harri Englund (Athens: Ohio University Press, 2011), 8.

PART THREE

Alternative Temporalities

SEVEN

"Right Now, I Don't Know What the Future Might Bring"

Hope, Anxiety, and Despair in the Burundian Crisis

SIMON TURNER

IN APRIL 2015, THE BURUNDIAN PRESIDENT, PIERRE NKURUNziza, declared at the ruling party's congress that he would run for a third presidential term in the elections scheduled for July that year. The president's decision is widely believed to be unconstitutional and in contradiction to the Arusha peace agreement of August 2000, and people took to the streets of the capital city, Bujumbura, to demonstrate against the "troisième mandat." The situation escalated over the next weeks and months, as police cracked down on the demonstrators, and the youth wing of the ruling party, the *imbonerakure*, was involved in intimidation, violence, and abductions—often in collaboration with the secret police. Independent media were closed—their premises often being burned down—and many journalists went underground or fled the country. Purges within the army were meant to keep the army more loyal to the president. Dozens of people lost their lives or disappeared.

By mid-May 2015, more than one hundred thousand people had fled Burundi to neighboring countries, even though only a few people had lost their lives at that point. By the end of the year, 210,000 had fled the country. The majority live in camps in Tanzania and Rwanda, while roughly twenty thousand live in Rwanda's capital, Kigali. The majority of the Burundians living in Kigali are Tutsi from Bujumbura, and they left Burundi with the intention of staying only a few weeks until the troubles had calmed down. But as the conflict continued, they had to revise their plans and make the tough choice either to return to an uncertain future in Burundi or to remain in Rwanda without many options of "making a life."

Based on fieldwork in 2015 and 2016 among Burundian refugees in Kigali who left Burundi in 2015, and drawing on previous fieldwork among Burundians who were displaced by the war from 1993 to 2005, this chapter explores how they navigate in relation to crisis, uncertainty, hope, and anxiety. When futures become unpredictable—as is the case in times of crisis—they create uncertainty and hence hope and anxiety. While hope turns uncertainty into positive potentiality,[1] anxiety is concerned with the potential for negative futures. On the one hand, the indeterminacy of the crisis creates hope that the situation may soon get better and the refugees will be able to return home. On the other hand, the indeterminacy creates anxieties that conditions will only get worse, and that the refugees will remain in Kigali without options for a proper future. Meanwhile, they are trying to make difficult decisions on whether to return or not, anticipating what the future might bring them. Doubt is strongly present in their attempts to believe.[2] Finally, the ethnography reveals how the conflict has morphed over time as the sense of uncertainty has been replaced by a sense of certainty—the certainty that the situation will not get any better. This chapter explores how this change affects their anxieties and argues that anxiety appears to be giving way to despair.

In the next section I attempt to disentangle the related concepts of hope, anticipation, anxiety, despair, and doubt before giving an ethnographic glimpse into the ways in which a handful of my interlocutors struggle with these emotions. I explore how some are struggling with the dilemmas of return while others turn—in part—to God to make it possible to "live with" despair. I claim that they turn "in part" to God because they distinguish between themselves as Christians and as human beings when reflecting on their hopes for the future.

Studying Anticipation

Anxiety as an emotion differs from fear, for instance, in the fact that it is an "unease about something with an uncertain outcome" (*Oxford English Dictionary*). In other words, anxiety is concerned with future potentialities[3] and is linked to feelings of anticipation. How do we study something that has yet to come—that is simply anticipated—and something that is uncertain?

Since the 2000s, anthropologists have shown an increasing interest in studying futures, as opposed to anthropology's usual emphasis on memories. Arjun Appadurai, for instance, calls for anthropology to "repatriate" aspirations to the domain of culture.[4] We have seen a literature on aspirations,[5] potentialities,[6] and hope.[7] A common argument in this focus on futures is that the actions of individuals and groups are not simply the product of their pasts (although these certainly play a role, as I will argue below) but that people also act according to perceived potential futures.

Pierre Bourdieu argues that anticipation is to assess the forthcoming (à venir) in a prereflexive manner. It is to have "sense for the game" and—if we remain in the metaphor of the game—it is to place oneself where one expects the ball to be in the near future. "This means that the objective probabilities are determinant only for an agent endowed with the sense of the game in the form of the capacity to anticipate the forthcoming of the game."[8] In other words, one's practical knowledge, one's habitus, must be in line with the game in order to predict the immediate future. He argues further that there may be some uncertainty but that it must be limited or regulated in order that anticipation can function. "In order for the particular relationship between subjective expectations and objective chances which defines investment, interest or *illusio* to be set up, the objective chances have to be situated between absolute necessity and absolute impossibility" (213). The great strength of Bourdieu's writings is his theories on how structures reproduce themselves. What, however, happens in situations of rupture or crisis? He is not so explicit on this, but he does mention that this is when time becomes an issue; waiting, regret, nostalgia, boredom, or discontent (209). He also talks of the "lumpenproletariat," for whom it makes no sense to invest in the game, as the odds are so small. In these situations, it becomes difficult to maintain a social life. Ghassan Hage argues with Bourdieu's *Pascalian Meditations,* that social death may be the result of being deprived of *illusio.*[9] In other words, if we are not able to have reasonable anticipations of the future, we lose our place in the world. However, as much as uncertainty about the future may prevent the full functioning of a habitus, it may also produce something new.

The literature on hope often takes its point of departure in situations of uncertainty, arguing that uncertainty does not just produce precarity and "stuckness" but also carries with it the potential for alternative futures and therefore produces hope.[10] In my own work among Burundian clandestine refugees in Nairobi in the early 2000s, I explored a situation of indeterminacy and uncertainty that was productive of hope and aspirations, as opposed to the refugee camps that they had left, where certainty crushed all hope.[11] In this chapter, I follow up on the themes of uncertainty and hope by exploring how the crisis in Burundi is constantly shifting between uncertainty and certainty and how affects such as hope, anxiety, and despair relate to these different kinds of crisis.

Just as there is a focus on indeterminacy and uncertainty, studies of hope and aspirations have often been carried out in situations of crisis or conflict. Nauja Kleist and Stef Jansen argue that "productive entry points can often be found in moments of exception, in difficulties to establish routine, in crises."[12] Daniel M. Knight and Charles Stewart point out that "crises turn ordinary daily routine inside out and expose the seams of temporality to view."[13] In other words, it is in these situations that futures (and pasts) need revising and that therefore give the anthropologist a privileged access to how futures are made. I take a similar starting point, as the shifting character of the crisis in Burundi affects my respondents' ability to think of futures. The events in 2015 forced Burundians to rethink their life paths as well as their ideas about the future of the country.

Stef Jansen distinguishes between transitive hope, as hope that has objects ("I hope that there will be peace next year"), and intransitive hope, as hopefulness or affect ("I am hopeful that the future will be better").[14] The latter is similar to the kind of hope that has been developed by Christian theologians such as Jürgen Moltmann.[15] In this view, one must not hope for something in particular but simply be hopeful. In fact, to hope for something particular would ruin the general state of hope. Many scholars—including myself—have similarly approached hope as intransitive and have in particular perceived of hope as related to uncertainty[16] and indeterminacy.[17] Inspired by Ernst Bloch's ideas of hope as future-oriented and hence indeterminate,[18] hope is a means to understand and explore anticipation and how individuals orient themselves towards unknown futures, rather than simply build on their pasts. Studying hope may, in other words, be a means to study futures.

While we may accuse anthropologists of being too optimistic in their emphasis on hope,[19] this chapter explores the other side of hope: anxiety. We may argue that anxiety and hope are two sides of the same coin.

They are each other's Janus face. Both are oriented toward a future, looking for signs of what the future might bring. If hope is a disposition, we look for signs of improvement, however precarious the present might be. Anxiety is also related to the future—but inversely: the situation may seem fine right now, but we fear it may turn sour, so we look for signs of this future. In situations of crisis, when the future is uncertain and anticipation as practical knowledge in Bourdieu's sense makes little sense, anticipation may go both ways—and often will oscillate between hope and anxiety.[20] Just as intransitive hope has no object, we may argue that anxiety, as opposed to fear, has no object. While one fears war or thunderstorms or losing a job, anxiety is more of a "mood" that has no direct object on which to pinpoint its sense of discomfort—a Kierkegaardian "grundstemning."

Although rarely theorized, hope is often opposed to despair in common language. Despair may be understood—for now—as the other binary opposite of hope. In this sense, I operate with two binaries; on the one hand, we may oppose hope and anxiety, while on the other hand, hope may be opposed to despair. While the first binary operates within a situation of uncertainty—one being positive and the other being negative—the second binary opposes indeterminate futures to determinate (negative) futures. Hope and anxiety are thus emotions that can run in tandem, while despair marks the end of hope. If hope and anxiety are concerned with anticipation, despair is the only emotion that is left when one is bereft of anticipation. I observed this movement from anxiety to despair among Burundians in Kigali, as time passed by and hope dwindled. In the following ethnographic analysis, I explore the relationship between these three affects and explore how they relate to the shift in the nature of crisis in Burundi.

Crisis, Anxiety, and Hope in Burundi

In order to understand the emotion work of Burundian refugees in Kigali in relation to the present conflict in Burundi, we need to see it in the context of the political climate leading up to Nkurunziza's decision to run for a third term. Burundi had been through decades of ethnic and political tensions. Through most of the 1970s and 1980s, ethnic and political tensions remained restrained by an oppressive one-party regime, which made ethnicity a taboo. From 1993 to the early 2000s, the tensions were "open," as Burundians like to say,[21] when the ethnic tensions were articulated by the Hutu rebel movements, ethnicity was put on the table, and the country experienced a devastating civil war. With the Arusha agreement in 2000 and the following peace process and political reforms, ethnicity remained de-tabooed, and the population experienced a sense of being able to speak openly about ethnicity and other political issues.[22] This was witnessed most strongly in a multitude of vibrant media—mostly radio stations—where a growing number of journalists spoke openly about politics and political power holders. In other words, it was in this context, where Burundians sensed that "we can make a difference" and that "we have a voice," that the present crisis should be understood. The Arusha agreement brought with it a sense of hope among broad sections of the population.[23]

Antoine, a man in his forties who had held various positions with international agencies and who had fled to Kigali in neighboring Rwanda, where I met him, explains the "mood" at the time and how this mood changed. He explains how, even before the president announced his intention to run for a third term, people were anticipating it—creating anxiety but also anticipation of change and hope that one could prevent it from happening. It was, in other words, not an inevitable fact that he would run for a third term, or that he would succeed, as it would have been in many neighboring countries where the room for open critique of power holders is limited.[24] "Before the president announced his intention to run for the presidential elections," Antoine said, "everyone was asking themselves what would happen. The media and civil society were posing the question of whether or not he would run for a third term" (my translation).

Rumors began circulating, and people began discussing whether this was actually in contradiction with the Arusha accords. "With the discussions about the Arusha Accords and the constitution and the radio and TV programs, we realized that this would not be easy." Antoine describes a situation where the media and civil society were scrutinizing possible scenarios and fearing what might happen, if the president should decide to run for a third term. It was a mood of tension and anxiety, where "people"—helped along by a host of media—were trying to predict various outcomes, often through rumors. But it was also a time of great engagement by civil society and the media, debating the constitution and criticizing the potential decision of the president. So, while there were anxieties, there were also optimism and hope. The mere fact that they were debating these issues in the media and that various actors, from the Catholic Church to human rights organizations, were criticizing such a decision, was a sign, in Antoine's mind, that one could influence the outcome of politics. The mood Antoine is describing is part of a larger transformation of Burundian society that had taken place since the end of the armed conflict in the early 2000s. As opposed to Rwanda, where the postgenocide regime has taken a course of careful social engineering, tight control of security, and limited political freedoms,[25] Burundi took almost the opposite approach.[26] Supported by international donors, independent media blossomed and the Arusha agreement paved the way for a consociational model of power sharing with a complex system of ethnic quotas in the legislature, the executive branch, and the judiciary.[27] While ethnicity had been a taboo in Burundi under previous regimes, it was now out in the open and openly debated. Interestingly, one of the effects of removing the taboo on ethnicity was that the political fault lines that had previously run along ethnic lines, now cut across ethnicity. Thus, the political tensions were most often among Hutu-dominated parties that had previously belonged to one or another rebel movement. This is not to say that Burundians could and would now speak openly about ethnicity and that all tensions had disappeared. In her fine-grained ethnography of political uncertainties among urban youth in Bujumbura around 2010, Lidewyde Berckmoes shows how they were still struggling with the position of ethnicity.[28] Furthermore, while the press was indeed free and independent, the political regime in place repeatedly attacked the media, passing laws that limited their freedom, imprisoning journalists, and generally harassing them. Similarly, political corruption had been widespread, and human rights activists had been threatened.[29] At the level of the everyday, Berckmoes demonstrates how optimism was mixed with anxieties about the political future. The youth whom she studied were constantly navigating these uncertain futures, at times allying with the ruling party and its youth wing, the imbonerakure, and at times allying with the opposition, juggling a mixture of livelihood opportunities and ideological convictions. In other words, the period after the Arusha accords and the end of decades of oppressive regimes and almost a decade of a devastating war was marked by an opening of the political field and a mixture of hope and anxiety.

This mood changed, according to Antoine, after the president's announcement that he would run for a third term. "It all started with the president proclaiming to run for a third term at his party's congress. Everyone was gripped by fear [La peur avait gagné tout le monde], and there were many rumors." Here, we see how fear is perceived as a force that can grip (*gagner*) the population. And I would argue that what Antoine calls fear (*peur*) is similar to anxiety because it is associated with uncertainty. By the president proclaiming his candidature, nothing has yet happened; nobody has been killed or imprisoned. But it creates an uncertainty about the immediate future. What will happen now? Which way will the coin flip? This is what creates rumors—rumors being a means to anticipate futures in situations of uncertainty[30]—and this is what creates anxiety.

While the situation after the presidential declaration was uncertain and rumors circulated, there was also hope, as people took to the streets to demonstrate against the decision. The attempt to topple the president through a coup d'état brought a short sense of relief, of hope that things would change for the better. However, when the coup failed, this hope evaporated, according to Antoine. "Fear prevailed in our minds. The threat was tangible. Fear grew in our hearts. The coup had given us hope. But it failed." With great pathos, Antoine conveys how the sense of fear surrounding the president's proclamation must be seen in relation—and opposition—to the relative optimism that existed in the period leading up to the events. What disappeared was hope, he claims. Instead, people were left with "fear in their hearts."

He then goes on to explain the general sense of fear at the time. These fears also drew lines back to memories of past violence. "If, for instance, the party in power organized a party, the imbonerakure would terrorize the population. But we also had a sense of fear, thinking of what happened to our neighboring country, Rwanda. We began to think that the imbonerakure could carry out organized massacres, making reference to Rwanda." In other words, the president's decision to run for a third term created uncertainty about the future, but it was the memories of past violence (against the Tutsi) that turned uncertainty into anxiety. Burundians "read" the past—and the past of Rwanda—into present events, so that parties organized by the ruling party were read in the light of the Rwandan genocide.

Antoine is perhaps exceptionally adept at conveying these sensibilities. His French is fluent, his confidence is high, and he is obviously a man who is used to demanding respect. He is also a man who is enthusiastic and extrovert, and who talked for two hours nonstop when I met him again the following year. Others may not be so eloquent, but they also express this shift and the anxieties that followed—a shift from being partially hopeful about uncertain futures to being anxious about these futures.

Life in Kigali—from Anxiety to Despair

Approximately twenty thousand Burundians are registered as refugees in Kigali, while another sixty thousand live in refugee camps in Rwanda.[31] Large numbers arrived shortly after the demonstrations against the third mandate started in Bujumbura, while some arrived even before the demonstrations in anticipation of the potential danger. And while some returned after a short while, the majority remained and more have arrived since. We have no exact figures on the composition of the group, but from my fieldwork it appears that the vast majority of those who settled in Kigali rather than in the camps have come from Burundi's capital, Bujumbura, and often—but not exclusively—from what is called "les quartiers contestataires." These are the parts of the city where many demonstrations took place and where the following terrorizing of the population by the imbonerakure, the police, and the intelligence service (Service National de Renseignement, SNR), commonly known as "la documentation," has been particularly fierce. These are also areas of Bujumbura that historically have been "Tutsi" and often lower middle class (as opposed to the wealthy Tutsi areas such as Kinindo that remained relatively peaceful throughout the crisis). Others had fled areas of Bujumbura that were ethnically mixed or predominantly Hutu and where the majority were loyal to the government. In these areas, the imbonerakure militias have a free hand to harass anyone suspected of not supporting the president's third term. All the refugees I met were Tutsi. Assessing their class position is difficult, in part because they had lost most of their belongings and their positions due to flight, and in part because respondents were reluctant to talk about their economy. However, the majority had at least secondary education, spoke good French and often some English. They had lived in houses with electricity, often had owned cars, and some still did, and were either self-employed or worked in government offices, for NGOs, or for private companies in managerial positions. In Kigali, they had refugee papers and the right to seek employment on a par with Rwandans. The Rwandan state provides primary schooling for free, and the United Nations High Commissioner for Refugees (UNHCR) provides basic health services for children under twelve and adults over sixty-five. Two social categories emerged in my fieldwork. One consisted of young men and women, often in their twenties, who arrived on their own. Being young, urban Tutsi, they felt targeted by the regime. Often, they had been students or new graduates in Burundi, so their families would not lose an income by sending them to Kigali. In Kigali they lived with relatives, acting as babysitters, or in rented rooms together with other young Burundians. Often, they were desperately poor in Kigali. The other group consisted of families in which one of the parents would often remain in Burundi to secure an income. They were often more economically stable—although this also changed as the conflict dragged out and the second parent fled to Kigali, abandoning their jobs in Burundi.

There was a lot of anxiety among the refugees whom I met. Their anxieties were related to the situation in Burundi and what it might become in the near future. Meanwhile, they were also anxious about their situation in Kigali.[32] They seemed aware that their present situation in Kigali was not viable. They appreciated the hospitality of the Rwandan government and were grateful that the Rwandan secret service could guarantee their security, because it was superior to the Burundian secret service in their view. In particular, journalists and others who assumed that they were personally targeted by the Burundian regime would tell me stories about Burundian spies in bars and hotel lobbies, and that the Burundian spies had been caught out by the Rwandan secret service. Some Burundians claimed that they avoided contact with other Burundians in public spaces in Kigali, as they could be spies. Mostly, they stayed at home to avoid such encounters. Even going to church was a challenge, as men would film the congregation with their mobile phones, they claimed. "I look down and try discretely to cover my face," a woman explained, as she would not miss out on church services. Burundians also appreciated that they were able to send their children to school in Kigali. However, they had no income in Kigali and saw no future for themselves there. Despite their gratitude, they rarely expressed any desire to stay in the city. They felt that the people were "cold" and aloof (while local Rwandans complained that the Burundians were loud and partied too much in Kigali). One woman told me that the weather was bad: "It's so cold and windy here." Similarly, nostalgia for Burundi would often be expressed in quotidian terms of the climate and the food.

Often, it was not by chance that they had wound up in Kigali. Many had relatives or old neighbors and friends in Kigali and had used these networks when they first arrived. After the Hutu revolution in Rwanda in 1959, large numbers of Tutsi fled Rwanda for

Burundi, where they settled in Ngagara just outside Bujumbura.[33] While some returned to Rwanda in 1994, others remained in Burundi. The present refugees in Kigali often drew on these networks of relatives and friends when arriving in Kigali. They all explained, however, that they quickly outstayed their welcome. As what was supposed to be a few weeks' stay until the danger blew over turned into months and months, they had to find their own homes and their own means of income. I heard countless stories of even very close relationships between siblings or with in-laws becoming strained to a point where they ceased to function. In other words, the refugees were guaranteed the right to be in the city and enjoyed general personal security, but they had unstable income if any, no social relations to draw on, and hence no ambition to stay.

Neither could they, however, see any options of returning to Burundi in any foreseeable future. This left them with the difficult task of trying to make critical decisions on whether to remain in Kigali or return to Burundi with shaky knowledge of the futures in either case. They were weighing their personal safety against their possibilities of making a meaningful future—and in both cases under very uncertain conditions. In what follows I outline two examples of these decision-making processes.

Anxious Decisions about Return

I did my first fieldwork in Kigali in August 2015, shortly after the failed coup d'état and when the conflict seemed to be reaching a stalemate. The situation was, however, still volatile, and there seemed to be great uncertainty about the future, although hopes were fading: Would the East African community intervene? What about other international actors such as the AU, the EU, and the UN? Did President Nkurunziza control all the officers in the army? Where were the coup makers? Was a rebel movement establishing itself in Rwanda—secretly supported by Rwanda's omnipotent President Kagame? These and other questions circulated among the Burundian refugees in Kigali and in the social media, leading to hopes for change but also anxieties that the situation might deteriorate further.

I met Boniface in August 2015. He was in his early twenties and had been studying law in Bujumbura. I met him at his home, which was unusual, as many Burundians were either afraid to reveal where they lived for fear of spies or were embarrassed about their modest living conditions that did not fit their class position in Burundi. The house was modern and big with well-kept lawns, leather sofas, and a giant flat-screen TV. Outside was a small car with Burundian number plates. He was staying with a Burundian family, in which the father was in Bujumbura in order not to lose his job while the mother and children had found safety in Kigali. This kind of arrangement, in which family members weigh the pros and cons of predicting insecurity against the risk of losing livelihoods, is very common in Kigali.

Boniface's own flight story is rather dramatic. While families in cars usually could leave Bujumbura and drive to Rwanda with some ease, young men from the "quartiers contestataires," traveling by public transport heading to Rwanda, ran risks of being stopped at roadblocks and accused of being rebels. Although there were direct busses from Bujumbura to Rwanda, they would take alternative routes to avoid being questioned about their travel to Rwanda. Boniface took a bus to Kivu in DRC and from there to Rwanda. As they were leaving Bujumbura, he was stopped at a roadblock and ordered to leave the bus because they could see on his papers that he was from Mutakura, which is one of the "quartiers contestataires" where demonstrations took place in 2015. Fortunately, other passengers intervened, and he was able to stay on board.

He explains that he has no income and no network in Kigali, and talks about going back to Burundi. But he also explains that it would be difficult for him as a young man who has been to Rwanda to live in Mutakura. "I will have to stay somewhere else at night," he says. The following exchange reveals his sense of being left without choice—of stuckness:

> Simon: And here you live with?
> Boniface: I am with my friend. But here, life is not easy. We are obliged to turn back to Bujumbura. We don't have choice.
> Simon: Life is expensive.
> Boniface: Very expensive and we don't have choice.
> Simon: How do you see the future of your country?
> Boniface: In this situation, I see nothing.
> Simon: Do you think that there will be a war or genocide?
> Boniface: Perhaps a war but not genocide

He goes on to explain that the president is trying to divide the population and is accusing the Tutsi of the troubles. But areas like Mutakura, where Boniface comes from, are ethnically mixed, he claims. So, there will be no genocide. There might, however, be a war, as the population is also getting armed. "The imbonerakure are not the only ones with weapons."

> Simon: Do you say that you have to go back to Bujumbura?
> Boniface: Yes, we don't have other choice. Here we have no food, no water, everything we have to buy it.
> Simon: If you go back, you will go to Mutakura or?
> Boniface: Back to Mutakura. I will live difficultly, but I will stay there, sometimes I am obliged to spend the night somewhere, or I move . . . we can spend holiday somewhere and after you come back home.

From here, we talk about the insecurity in the country, the extrajudicial killings, and so on, only to return to his own present dilemmas.

> Simon: So, what do you do here?
> Boniface: Nothing.
> Simon: You don't have a small job?
> Boniface: Nothing.
> Simon: It is difficult. You don't have any plan?
> Boniface: Sh . . . What kind of plan?
> Simon: I don't know. Ehh. Plan for studies or applying for a job or join the rebellion?
> Boniface: Aaaheem! It is what remains: join rebellion maybe. It is the only one option that remains.
> Simon: To join the rebellion is dangerous, you can be killed!
> Boniface: It is the same.

What we sense here is a man who sees mostly dead ends. Some of the answers are demonstratively short—as if to punctuate his point: "There is nothing" or "it is the same"—and there is no need to waste words on explaining. Several young men told me in 2015 that they were ready to join the rebellion. This number had dwindled in 2016 when no rebellion had emerged and none had any hope that it would. Most of the young men who made these claims seemed neither very convincing nor very convinced by they own statements, however. Perhaps they really intended to join a fictive rebel movement, but they might also have been making such statements as an expression of the hopelessness of their situation and the scarcity of options they had. Similarly, Boniface's claims to return to Bujumbura seemed rhetorical, as if to demonstrate to me the hopelessness of his situation. Earlier in our conversation, he had explained in detail the dangers of being a young man in Mutakura. In other words, his statement that "we are obliged to return back to Bujumbura. We have no choice" appeared to me as an expression of his dilemmas more than a decision to return.

The following day, Boniface and I are taking the bus together to visit his friend, Innocent. On the way, he mentions—*en passant*—that by the way he will be going back to Burundi the next day. He can get a lift with the woman he lives with, and she has to return to her work in Bujumbura. This comes as a complete surprise to me. I had not imagined that his talk about return could be so concrete or produce results so soon. Innocent seems surprised as well and tries to convince him not to go, but he reassures us that he will not go to Bujumbura but will stay in a small town on the way. The next day, I received a WhatsApp message that he had crossed the border, and later that day, I received another one that he was in Bujumbura. I am still in touch with him via WhatsApp, and he has now finished his law degree.

Richard is also in his twenties. He finished a bachelor's degree in psychology but never managed to get his diploma before he was forced to leave the country. I am at his home—a one-room house in a backyard. As so often before when we have talked, he starts fretting about his future options and the choices he has to make soon. He feels that he cannot get a job in Kigali because he has no proof of his degree, and the university will not send his diploma or give it to a friend or family member. He has to collect it in person, apparently. One minute he is saying: "I'll go! It can't be that dangerous. I just have to get the diploma, and then leave the country quickly again." Next minute he is saying: "I cannot return. It's too dangerous. I won't risk my life for a piece of paper!" At one point, he is sitting on his floor, banging his knees with his fists, as if he is physically distraught by the impossibility of his choice. Richard remained in Kigali, and I met him still in Kigali the following year. He still had not got the diploma and was trying to find jobs without it.

Boniface and Richard were weighing the pros and cons of remaining in Kigali versus returning to Burundi. The decision to leave the country in the first place was not a simple question of violence forcing people to leave. They were weighing livelihoods against the risks of losing their lives, and they were making these appraisals according to future possibilities. In other words, they were anticipating violence that could possibly/potentially hit them, and weighing this against the income that they could possibly lose. Finally, they were making these decisions as families, as one or both of the parents might remain in Bujumbura, sending the rest of the family into safety in Kigali. The cases of Richard's and Boniface's dilemmas prove that these anticipations and assessments continued when they were in Kigali. They saw no future in Kigali but equally feared that the situation in Burundi would not improve and the options for return would only get slimmer. For them, there was also a temporal aspect to further complicate the decision-making: the longer they stayed in Rwanda, the more skeptical the Burundian authorities would be if they were to return. A young man from certain parts of Bujumbura was viewed with suspicion, but a young man from these areas who had lived for months in Rwanda was even more suspicious in the eyes of the SNR. When I returned in 2016, I could see that these fears had proven true. None of the Burundians in Kigali were contemplating return, and more significantly, the fathers and mothers who in 2015 had remained in Burundi and commuted back and forth to see their families on weekends and bring them cheap foodstuffs from Burundi had mostly relocated to Kigali as well. The few who had decided to remain in Burundi only rarely paid visits and never brought goods or food.

Richard and Boniface confront the following choice. On the one hand, if they stay in Kigali, they have no future. They may survive, but they will not have a meaningful life. If they return, on the other hand, they face either a meaningful future or death. In other words, Kigali was safe but without hope, while Burundi to some degree offered some hope, but this window of hope was narrowing by the day. Their dilemmas illustrate the relationship between hope, anxiety, and despair. If they stay in Kigali, they may be safe, but they will be left only with despair. They will in Bourdieu's terms be socially dead, walking among others in Kigali while not being part of Kigali. If, however, they return to Bujumbura—either as civilians or as rebels—they take part in *illusio*; they play the game and hence hope that they may win—although chances are pretty high that they will lose and die.

This choice between two evils creates anxiety as an embodied emotion. Richard cannot solve the dilemma through language and bangs his knees with his hands, shaking his head. Boniface repeats the hopelessness of the situations in single-word answers to my enquiries, as if argumentation cannot resolve his anxiety. And then he ups and leaves the country without further deliberation, as if the decision were random. Uncertainty is more than making choices; it creates anxiety as a mood.

Hope in Hopelessness

In my discussions with Burundian refugees, they would express anxieties that the conflict would turn "ethnic" and that the imbonerakure and the Hutu population would start hunting down Tutsi in general. They all agreed that so far the violence was not ethnic and was about politics—but they also were aware that the president was trying in his public statements to turn it into a conflict between the Tutsi elite and the Hutu "people." This was clearly visible on Twitter through the tweets made by his porte-parole Willy Nyamwitse. Meanwhile, the violence had not yet turned ethnic and there was hope that this conflict was different from the last one. Boniface explained that both Hutu and Tutsi were involved in the "anti–troisième mandat" demonstrations, and several interlocutors explained to me that the peasants were no longer so naïve as they had been in the 1990s—thanks to the years of democratic debate—and that they would not take the bait that the president and his advisors were throwing to them. They explained that in the 1990s, political entrepreneurs used ethnicity as an instrument to manipulate gullible peasants and set Hutu against Tutsi, and this was no longer the case—they hoped. In August 2015 my interlocutors were unsure whether the conflict would go from bad to worse or whether it would come to an end by means of external pressure and negotiations or by force through a rebellion.

When I returned a year later, the good news was that the conflict had not turned into an ethnocide. The bad news was that negotiations had broken down, the East African Community and African Union had shown no genuine interest in solving the crisis, and no rebel movement had materialized. In the year that had passed, the number of refugees had risen. By July 2016, an estimated 1,100 people had lost their lives in the conflict,[34] and the total number of Burundian refugees registered by UNHCR was over 260,000, up from 175,000 in August 2015. The number of Burundians in Rwanda had risen from almost 70,000 to almost 80,000 in the same period.[35] Uncertainty had to some degree given way to certainty; but this was a negative certainty of no future. Richard was no longer in doubt about whether or not to go back to Burundi. Returning to Burundi was not an option. Meanwhile, life in Kigali was still lonely, cold, and expensive.

"Right Now, I Don't Know What the Future Might Bring"

I had been interviewing Esther, a middle-aged, middle-class Burundian woman at a café on the outskirts of Kigali, about the difficult choices that she had needed to make when deciding to leave Bujumbura and seek refuge in Kigali. These were decisions that had to predict potential dangers and weigh them against the difficulties of making ends meet in exile. At the end of the interview, while I was still digesting the travails that this woman had been through, my assistant asked her, "In terms of your future? Do you see any hope?" After a short pause, Esther answered, "If you see what is happening at the moment, there is really no hope. Earlier, we hoped that the African Union and the European union would react—but in vain. So as a human being I don't see any hope, as things are getting worse by the day. As a Christian our hope lies only in God." I heard almost the same words from numerous Burundians—mostly women in her situation: middle-class mothers who were not involved in politics or activism and who were simply trying to provide the best possible options for their families, given the circumstances.

> Simon: Do you think you will be here for a long time? Or do you want to return to Burundi?
>
> Agnes: If you look at it with the eyes of a human being, you'll see that it will really be a long time. Earlier, we didn't think that the issues [les choses] would go on for so long. We really do not have any hope. But if you look at it with the eyes of a Christian, I know that everything is possible in God. I don't know how it will happen, but I hope that everything will be alright. But with human eyes we have no hope.
>
> Simon: No hope!
>
> Agnes: Yes, but as I told you; I believe. I have faith in God. But I wonder for the others who do not believe. It's difficult.

Claudette is another middle-aged, middle-class woman with children whom I met in 2016.

> Simon: Do you have hope that the situation will change in Burundi?
>
> Claudette: Now, I don't know. With hope in God perhaps. Earlier, we thought that in a month we would return, and now a year has passed! We hope that, thank God, we will return.
>
> Simon: One has to keep up hope.

Claudette: Yes, but our wish is really to return. Home is home [A la maison c'est à la maison].

Esther, Agnes, and Claudette show how their perceptions of the future have changed over the past year. To start with, they were convinced that the crisis would be over in a matter of weeks or months. However, now they realize that it is not going to disappear in any foreseeable future. Secondly, they distinguish—quite sharply—between their Christian and their human perceptions of the future.

How are we to understand these contradictory statements? On the one hand, they are ritually paying allegiance to their Christian heritage, and we should therefore take only their second claim seriously; they see no hope. Like many of the people I interviewed, they were Catholic and attended church regularly. However, for these women—as for most of the others—attending church was also part of being a good, conservative member of the community.[36] In other words, while they had faith and went to church, they were also pragmatic and knowledgeable about the political situation and the role of, for instance, the African Union. Therefore, they also knew that "as a human being" there is no hope. However, rather than dismissing their claims to Christian hope as empty rhetoric, I suggest that we may find the truth of their anxieties about the future in exactly these two counterpositions: as a Christian and as a human being. They seem to be saying that even if there is no hope and only despair is left, they have a duty to act "as if" they were hopeful. Although they see no hope as a concrete, achievable goal, they maintain that they must remain hopeful, thus making an important distinction between "having hope" and "being hopeful." Similarly, we might make the distinction between having fear and being anxious.

The Burundians in Kigali had originally chosen to flee to Kigali for a while, simply to survive while they waited for the situation in Burundi to calm down. They did not see a future in Kigali, and the focus of their attention—their hopes and their anxieties—lay in Burundi. As the situation in Burundi did not calm down, however, they had to readjust their anticipations and their hopes and anxieties.

When I visited Burundi in August 2015, hope was already narrowing and giving place to despair. With the closure of the independent media, and with the last activists leaving the country as I arrived, there was an increasing sense that the president had free rein to do what he wanted. Returning to Burundi was perhaps an option, but this was a race against time, as the longer time they spent in Rwanda, the more suspicious the Burundian regime would be of them, suspecting them of being terrorists, hiding with Kagame in Rwanda. Hope that the international community would intervene was dwindling. The only option seemed, at that point in time, to remove Nkurunziza by force. When I returned a year later, uncertainty and indeterminacy had given place to a sense that the present situation would not change in any foreseeable future. The conflict had not exploded into genocide, but neither had the situation got any better.

In this situation, there seemed to be a discrepancy between claiming to be optimistic and having any concrete ideas about how things could change to the better. People were usually very vague when asked about the future. When I asked in 2015, many would simply say, "There will be war." Some would say, "If I knew where to go, I'd join the rebellion today." When I dug more into this, it turned out that they had no idea about warfare or what the battle should concretely achieve. It seemed more like an expression of the wish to "do something" than a concrete future option. It gave them hope.

Most often, however, people did not have any clear idea of what would or could happen in the future. This was even more pronounced in 2016. Perhaps they were clinging to what Jansen calls intransitive hope or what Hage has termed hopefulness, despite the lack of transitive or object-oriented hope. Perhaps only despair existed, and this is how they were able to express this despair.

Conclusions

In this chapter, I have explored the related emotions of hope, anxiety, and despair in situations of crisis and violent conflict. By following Burundian refugees over a year, I was able to explore how they negotiate such uncertain and unpredictable circumstances and how emotions of hope, anxiety, and despair changed accordingly. Not being able to predict futures gave rise to hope that their present situation would come to an end. However, the flipside was anxiety from not knowing what the future would bring, once the present situation was over. This anxiety led to great difficulties in making decisions on whether to return to Burundi or to remain in exile. With no clear picture of what the future might bring and what might be the consequences of one's actions, the Burundians in Kigali had no "sense of the game," as Bourdieu would put it, and made decisions that appeared random. Not being able to master the game and position oneself in relation to "the forthcoming" resulted in a sense of not being able to take control over one's life—and this lack of control led to a general sense of anxiety.

While anxiety—as a general state of being—seemed to have a grip on my interlocutors, the unpredictability of the present also gave them some hope. In August 2015, this hope was to some degree embodied in regional and international organizations, but it was increasingly being transferred to rebel movements that had yet to see the light of the day. In July 2016, this hope had all but disappeared, as the regional negotiations had failed miserably and no rebel movement had materialized. Despair seemed to have taken the place of anxiety, leaving little space for concrete hopes. The only hope that was left was the Christian injunction to be hopeful.

Notes

1. Vincent Crapanzano, "Reflections on Hope as a Category of Social and Psychological Analysis," *Cultural Anthropology* 18, no. 1 (2003): 3–32; Mathijs Pelkmans, ed., *Ethnographies of Doubt: Faith and Uncertainty in Contemporary Societies* (London: I. B. Tauris, 2013); Simon Turner, "'We Wait for Miracles': Ideas of Hope and Future among Clandestine Burundian Refugees in Nairobi," in *Ethnographies of Uncertainty in Africa*, ed. Elizabeth Cooper and David Pratten (Basingstoke, UK: Palgrave Macmillan, 2015), 173–92; Henrik Vigh, "Wayward Migration: On Imagined Futures and Technological Voids," *Ethnos* 74, no. 1 (2009): 91–109, https://doi.org/10.1080/00141840902751220.

2. Pelkmans, *Ethnographies of Doubt*.

3. Henrik Vigh, "Crisis and Chronicity: Anthropological Perspectives on Continuous Conflict and Decline," *Ethnos* 73, no. 1 (2008): 5–24.

4. Arjun Appadurai, "The Capacity to Aspire: Culture and the Terms of Recognition," in *Culture and Public Action*, ed. Vijayendra Rao and Michael Walton (Stanford, CA: Stanford University Press, 2004), 59–84.

5. Appadurai, "Capacity to Aspire"; Arjun Appadurai, *The Future as Cultural Fact: Essays on the Global Condition* (New York: Verso, 2013).

6. Vigh, "Crisis and Chronicity."

7. Crapanzano, "Reflections on Hope"; Nauja Kleist and Stef Jansen, "Introduction: Hope over Time—Crisis, Immobility and Future-Making," *History and Anthropology* 27, no. 4 (2016): 373–92, https://doi.org/10.1080/02757206.2016.1207636; Hirokazu Miyazaki, "From Sugar Cane to 'Swords': Hope and the Extensibility of the Gift in Fiji," *Journal of the Royal Anthropological Institute* 11, no. 2 (2005): 277–95, https://doi.org/10.1111/j.1467-9655.2005.00236.x.

8. Pierre Bourdieu, *Pascalian Meditations* (Stanford, CA: Stanford University Press, 2000), 211.

9. Ghassan Hage, "'Comes a Time We Are All Enthusiasm': Understanding Palestinian Suicide Bombers in Times of Exighophobia," *Public Culture* 15, no. 1 (2003): 65–89.

10. Elizabeth Cooper and David Pratten, eds., *Ethnographies of Uncertainty in Africa* (Basingstoke, UK: Palgrave Macmillan, 2015); Turner, "'We Wait for Miracles'"; Morten Axel Pedersen, "A Day in the Cadillac: The Work of Hope in Urban Mongolia," *Social Analysis* 56, no. 2 (2012): 136–51.

11. Turner, "'We Wait for Miracles.'"

12. Kleist and Jansen, "Introduction: Hope over Time," 380.

13. Daniel M. Knight and Charles Stewart, "Ethnographies of Austerity: Temporality, Crisis and Affect in Southern Europe," *History and Anthropology* 27, no. 1 (2016): 1–18 at 3.

14. Stef Jansen, "For a Relational, Historical Ethnography of Hope: Indeterminacy and Determination in the Bosnian and Herzegovinian Meantime," *History and Anthropology* 27, no. 4 (2016): 447–64.

15. Jürgen Moltmann, *Theology of Hope: On the Ground and the Implications of a Christian Eschatology* (London: SCM, 1967).

16. Turner, "'We Wait for Miracles.'"

17. Miyazaki, "From Sugar Cane to 'Swords'"; Pedersen, "Day in the Cadillac."

18. Bloch, *Principle of Hope*.

19. There is also a danger that the author's own normative ideas of hope as emancipatory are projected onto the field (Kleist and Jansen, "Introduction: Hope over Time," 373 and 378).

20. There are similarities with Pelkmans's ideas of doubt. Doubt and belief, he argues, go hand in hand (Pelkmans, *Ethnographies of Doubt*).

21. Simon Turner, *Politics of Innocence: Hutu Identity, Conflict and Camp Life* (Oxford: Berghahn Books, 2010), 164.

22. Marc Sommers and Peter Uvin, *Youth in Rwanda and Burundi: Contrasting Visions*, USIP Special Report 293 (Washington, DC: United States Institute of Peace, 2011); Simon Turner, "The Waxing and Waning of the Political Field in Burundi and Its Diaspora," *Ethnic and Racial Studies* 31, no. 4 (2008): 742–65.

23. Peter Uvin, *Life after Violence—A People's Story of Burundi* (London: Zed Books, 2009).

24. Andrea Purdeková, Filip Reyntjens, and Nina Wilén, "Militarisation of Governance after Conflict: Beyond the Rebel-to-Ruler Frame—the Case of Rwanda," *Third World Quarterly* 39, no. 1 (2018): 158–74, https://doi.org/10.1080/01436597.2017.1369036.

25. Scott Straus and Lars Waldorf, "Introduction: Seeing Like a Post-conflict State," in *Remaking Rwanda: State Building and Human Rights after Mass Violence*, ed. Scott Straus and Lars Waldorf (Madison: University of Wisconsin Press, 2011), 3–25.

26. Simon Turner, *Mirror Images: Different Paths to Building Peace and Building States in Rwanda and Burundi* (Copenhagen: DIIS, 2013).

27. René Lemarchand, "Consociationalism and Power Sharing in Africa: Rwanda, Burundi, and the Democratic Republic of the Congo," *African Affairs* 106, no. 422 (2007): 1–20; Miyazaki, "From Sugar Cane to 'Swords'"; Stef

Vandeginste, "Transitional Justice for Burundi: A Long and Winding Road," paper presented at the international conference "Building a Future on Peace and Justice," 2010.

28. Lidewyde H. Berckmoes, "Elusive Tactics: Urban Youth Navigating the Aftermath of War in Burundi" (PhD diss., Vrije Universiteit Amsterdam, 2014).

29. Human Rights Watch, *Closing Doors? The Narrowing of Democratic Space in Burundi* (New York: Human Rights Watch, 2010), hrw.org, news release, 23 November 2010; Human Rights Watch, *"We'll Tie You Up and Shoot You": Lack of Accountability for Political Violence in Burundi* (New York: Human Rights Watch, 2010), hwr.org, news release, 14 May 2010.

30. Allen Feldman, "Ethnographic States of Emergency," in *Fieldwork under Fire: Contemporary Stories of Violence and Survival*, ed. Carolyn Nordstrom and Antonius C. G. M. Robben (Berkeley: University of California Press, 1995), 224–52; Simon Turner, "Corruption Narratives and the Power of Concealment: The Case of Burundi's Civil War," in *Corruption and the Secret of Law: A Legal Anthropological Perspective*, ed. Monique Nuijtens and Gerhard Anders (Aldershot, UK: Ashgate, 2007), 125–42.

31. United Nations High Commissioner for Refugees (UNHCR) figures, December 2016.

32. This uncertainty also affected my fieldwork, and I changed my ticket and my plans several times because of these uncertainties. I had, for instance, planned to travel to Bujumbura from Kigali but was warned against being in Burundi on the 26th August when the president would officially be inaugurated. It was thought that perhaps opposition groups would use this symbolically laden date to launch an attack of some sort. Furthermore, many Burundians were reluctant to speak to me at all, fearing that I might be working for the Burundian government.

33. Ngagara started as a refugee camp but later became a suburb of Bujumbura with many Rwandans marrying Burundians and a large number of the inhabitants taking up positions as functionaries in the then Tutsi-dominated Burundian state (including the army).

34. International Crisis Group, "The African Union and the Burundi Crisis: Ambition versus Reality," Briefing no. 122/Africa, 28 September 2016, https://www.crisisgroup.org/africa/central-africa/burundi/african-union-and-burundi-crisis-ambition-versus-reality.

35. UNHCR.org. In May 2018, the figure was 390,000.

36. This is quite different from the "born-again" Christians whom I met in Nairobi a decade earlier. These young Hutu men and women, eking out an existence at the bottom of society, laid their future in the hands of the various charismatic churches to which they belonged. The churches distributed hope among the refugees (Turner, "'We Wait for Miracles'").

EIGHT

"Obuganda Buladde"

Power, Anxiety, and Calm in Postcolonial Buganda

JONATHON L. EARLE

Akaalo ka Buganda ka dda; akaalo kaaliko nnanyiniko. Obote n'akaleka—yali wa maanyi. N'abaali abamaanyi baakaleka.

The village of Buganda started long ago; it has its owner. Even Obote left it—yet he was powerful. All others with power will leave it too.
—Kampala, sung near the royal tombs following their destruction by fire, 18 March 2010[1]

THIS CHAPTER EXPLORES THE FICTIONS OF CALM IN THE postcolonial eastern African kingdom of Buganda. In March 2010, the royal tombs where the bodies of Buganda's four preceding kings were interred were destroyed by fire. The destruction of the Kasubi Tombs (*Amasiro ga ba Ssekabaka*) evoked uproar and demonstrations of protest throughout southern Uganda. Baganda patriots accused the central government of organizing the obliteration of the Tombs by arson. At the site, thousands of protesters participated in spirit possession practices, during which communities recounted moments in the past when the kingdom of Buganda allayed social anxiety in the region. Through songs, posters, and the public pronuncation of Buganda's ostensibly powerful past, the possessed at Kasubi worked to create curative space: an arena within which communities imagined monarchical alternatives in Museveni's Republic.

Drawing on ethnographic fieldwork that I conducted during the disturbance, this piece examines the vocabularies of calm and anxiety in contemporary Uganda. Whereas previous studies on the state in Africa have employed the categories of anxiety to describe the postcolonial experience, this study shows the extent to which modern protest in Uganda is shaped by larger reflections on the production of social calm. To develop this argument, I begin by outlining the existing literature on anxiety in postcolonial Africa, before turning directly to the theme of anxiety and calm in the intellectual and political history of colonial Buganda. Afterward, I interrogate the history of Buganda's kingdom in postcolonial Uganda and conclude by exploring the productions of calm surrounding the fire.

Historiographies of Anxiety in Colonial Buganda

Critics of the state in Africa have long used the nomenclatures of anxiety—and its epistemological corollaries, including nervousness, depression, trouble, or uncertainty—to describe the conditionality of colonial and postcolonial politics across the continent. For writers such as Frantz Fanon, the colonial state in Africa failed to extend social or psychological reassurances to its communities. The state, by contrast, often roused societies' deepest anxieties.[2] In response to the force of military and political violence in late colonial Algeria, Fanon used *The Wretched of the Earth* (*Les damnés de la terre*) to describe anxiety in colonial society in three ways. First, he argued that the increasingly attenuated status of French settlers in Algeria, whose positions in society were challenged by the Front de Libération Nationale, produced expatriate communities that were apprehensive about their statuses in postwar Algeria.[3] Next, the possibility of independence was itself a moment of uncertainty as activists asserted competing religious claims in their effort to both control the state and fill administrative vacancies that were once occupied by French officials. As Fanon noted: "This merciless fight engaged upon by races and tribes, and this aggressive anxiety to occupy the posts left vacant by the departure of the foreigner, will equally give rise to religious rivalries."[4] Finally, for Fanon, the expectations and reach of the modern state's legal system and its demand for labor and resources caused indescribable psychological anxiety, depression, and suicidal tendencies among the state's citizens.[5] The state, with its historical proximity to industrial capitalism, was fundamentally a force of anxiety in the lives of communities.

The intersection of anxiety and state formation in Africa, however, was not simply the preoccupation of politically mindful psychiatrists. In no area has the theme of anxiety been more powerfully addressed than in popular novels on the colonial and postcolonial state. These works include Chinua Achebe's *Things Fall Apart* (1958), Ngũgĩ wa Thiong'o's *Weep Not, Child* (1964), Okot p'Bitek's *Song of Lawino* (1966), and, more recently, Tsitsi Dangarembga's commentary on gender and social production in postcolonial Zimbabwe, *Nervous Conditions* (1988), the title of which is an adaptation of Jean-Paul Sartre's introduction to *The Wretched of the Earth*.[6] For Dangarembga, the fabrication of colonial histories and society in 1980s Zimbabwe propelled young women to experience profound uneasiness.[7]

In the eastern African kingdom of Buganda, as well, writers used the vocabularies of anxiety and worry to describe the emotional landscapes of the mid-twentieth century. In Luganda, one word that writers used to capture the anxieties of the 1950s was *obugubi*, or being in a condition of "darkness; hardship, pressure, difficulty; uncertainty."[8] The intransitive verb *–bonaabona* was further used to describe the act of experiencing anxiety as suffering, misery, or trouble.[9] When the Protestant constitutional thinker Eridadi Mulira, for instance, sought to explain the long history of a series of riots and protests in B/Uganda during the late 1940s, he talked about "trouble."[10] For Mulira, "trouble" was the inevitable consequence of historical change.[11] Anxiety in colonial society, he concluded, was the outcome of unprecedented progress, social strain, and political unrest.[12]

Mulira's preoccupation with anxiety, however, was not unique in southern Uganda. And in his reflections on progress and anxiety he drew from concepts that were already in circulation among missionary writers and Ganda elites by the 1910s. In Uganda's early twentieth-century missionary ethnographies, commentaries on social anxiety reinforced the necessity of Christian manners and conversion. For the Protestant anthropologist John Roscoe, Ganda greetings revealed the extent to which hidden anxieties were interwoven in the tapestry of daily life in the kingdom. The common greeting, *otyano sebo*, he noted, was principally concerned with Ganda fears of sickness or death: "in *otyano* the letter *o* is without doubt the pronoun 'thou,' *tya* is the verb 'to fear,' while *no* is simply an enclitic which adds to the politeness of the word; the literal meaning must have been 'Have you any cause for fear?' to which the reply would be in the negative, 'ah! ah! no.'"[13] Roscoe argued further that similar language was used to evaluate anxiety or uncertainty in the home. To assure members of the community that a home was not under a curse, respondents specifically noted that "there was no cause for fear or anxiety."[14] In turn, he concluded that ordinary greetings revealed apprehensions surrounding the birth of children and the succession of village and clan leaders.[15]

Prime Minister Apolo Kaggwa, preeminent historian and the foremost Ganda administrator in early colonial Uganda, was a prolific commentator on Ganda culture. In his history of the customs of Buganda he reflected at length on the role of extended greetings and the important role that prolonged meetings played in abating public anxiety and fear following the death of a king. In his writing on "death customs," Kaggwa explicitly challenged Roscoe's observation regarding the amount of time required to orchestrate a royal burial: "When the king died his body lay in state for about four weeks and all his relatives came to mourn. (Roscoe says that the body was kept only for a day or two)."[16] The extended ceremony, in addition to including periods of formal greetings, provisioned a series of conferences where the cause of a king's death was determined, an heir was appointed, and the king's body was anointed.[17] Why Kaggwa specifically challenged Roscoe on the point of periodization is a topic beyond the scope of this chapter. What we can begin to see, though, is the extent to which Kaggwa continued to advocate for long seasons of time to mediate social change. In doing so, he sought to convince Baganda to withhold undue judgment of a kingdom that was undergoing considerable change under his administration.

By the early 1900s, as Kaggwa's commentary shows, the language of anxiety underscored the intersection of nineteenth-century cultural practices in Buganda with Victorian expectations surrounding the interment of dead bodies and royal burial practices. In the written remarks of missionaries and Ganda Protestants in *Mmengo/Uganda Notes*, a periodical published by the Church Missionary Society, commentators noticed the anxiety with which kings (given the title *kabaka* in the Buganda kingdom and *omugabe* in the Ankole kingdom) approached their forbearers' tombs. When a young Kabaka Daudi Chwa visited the tomb of Kabaka Muteesa I, his grandfather, one missionary observer noted that organizers were especially anxious to include the sacrifice of a fatted bullock and the cooking of plantains.[18] Edward Kahaya, the omugabe of Ankole in 1911, expressed similar anxieties surrounding the proper reburial of his father, Omugabe Ntale. As one writer observed:

"Ntale died some twelve years ago, but was only hastily buried by some peasants, and for some time the people have been anxious to bury his remains with due pomp and ceremony."[19] In both instances, aspiring colonial kings struggled to appease the guidance of clan heads on the one hand, who regulated burial customs, with missionary demands for cultural change on the other. As one missionary noted with concern: "'Old things are passed away; behold, all things are become new' is a true saying of most if not all things in Uganda. But old customs die hard, and especially when strong superstitions are attached to them."[20] Missionaries failed to understand the extent to which older practices surrounding burial customs—especially their spiritual or ancestral components—facilitated public equilibrium and social calm during periods of succession in the long history of littoral politics.[21]

Beyond royal committal practices, the anxieties of the time were a regular topic of conversation among administrators who worried about modeling the virtues of colonial progress. Apolo Kaggwa was often in a state of anxiety over the future of his son Blasio, whom Kaggwa wished to see master the piano and British etiquette.[22] Communities throughout the kingdom were anxious about Buganda's colonial labor economy and the pressure to learn Swahili in missionary schools,[23] while British administrators were anxious to find more effective ways to connect Uganda and London through steamships and railway.[24]

The development of colonial society propelled extensive historical debate. By the 1940s, partisan historians, such as Haji Sekimwanyi, James Miti, and Father J. Ddiba, were fervently debating the extent to which colonial settlement undermined the political power of women, clan heads, and public healers.[25] Debates about political calm and stability often centered around the question of the religious conversion of Buganda's powerful nineteenth-century state builder, Kabaka Muteesa I. Prior to assuming the name Muteesa, or one who causes peace or calm, Buganda's king's name was Mukaabya, or one who causes suffering or tears.[26] Ganda historians throughout the 1940s and 1950s were keen to identify the precise moment during which Buganda's king assumed his second name. For writers such as Mulira and his father-in-law, the prolific historian Hamu Mukasa, Mukaabya's name was changed only after he had converted to Christianity.[27] By contrast, for Muslim historians such as Sheikh Ali Kulumba, Muteesa's political makeover had occurred following his conversion to Islam.[28] By returning to the nineteenth century, partisan historians sought to claim a special relationship with the genealogies of political calm at a moment of foreseeable change.

For Great Lakes activists, as David Schoenbrun has convincingly argued, the invocation of calm was part of envisioning normative politics from at least the sixteenth century onward.[29] Indeed, by the early twentieth century, Luganda proverbs tended to underscore the virtues of social calm, patience, and public healing, of which anxiety was a short-lived corollary. One proverb noted: "Abonaabona n'omulwadde: si ye amuskira" (The one who endures suffering with the patient; S/he does not inherit the ailment).[30] By the 1980s, though, Ganda communities were hardly debating the precise chronology of Muteesa I's conversion. By contrast, recent activists have more commonly evoked a past within which Buganda was a powerful kingdom throughout the nineteenth century. In doing so, contemporary writers and activists have aimed to connect the policies of the Museveni government with the republican vision of President Milton Obote, who, as I will now discuss, dissolved Uganda's kingdoms in 1967.

Imagining Calm in Postcolonial Buganda

It has been approximately fifty years since Uganda attained independence. Since then, the country has undergone extensive political and economic change. In 1966, at the end of a short-lived alliance between Buganda's royalist party, Kabaka Yekka (the King Alone Party), and Prime Minister Milton Obote's republican movement, Uganda People's Congress, Obote ordered Uganda's army under the command of General Idi Amin to apprehend Kabaka Muteesa II, Uganda's first president. Muteesa II had been unwilling to return Buganda's northern frontier to its precolonial owner, the kingdom of Bunyoro.[31] In response, Obote argued that Muteesa had violated his constitutional responsibility to protect the Republic of Uganda against political tribalism. Buganda's king fled Kampala during the attack and journeyed to London, where he died in the late 1960s, after spending his final years living in council housing in Surrey Quays. Following the exile of Muteesa, Obote constitutionally abolished Uganda's hereditary monarchies in 1967. Uganda's kingdoms remained abrogated until 1993, when President Yoweri Museveni reinvested the state's kingships as cultural institutions, allegedly without constitutional or political power.[32]

General Idi Amin marshaled Uganda's military in 1971 to successfully remove his former commander, Milton Obote, from power. Amin's

Second Republic lasted for nearly a decade. At multiple levels, Uganda's Second Republic constituted a moment of paradox and ambiguity.[33] In consequence, it was a season of particular social anxiety—especially by the late 1970s.[34] Early in his administration, Amin declared an economic war on Uganda's Asian communities, through whom the state's colonial economies had been largely organized. Amin demanded the mass exodus of the country's Asian population. As Anneeth Hundle has shown, 55,000 Indians lived in Uganda when the expulsion began; after a period of approximately three months, however, there were only 3,000 to 5,000.[35] Amin, in turn, was challenged to allay public uneasiness with what was to follow. The national press worked to articulate Amin's calming and assuring counsel: "The General told the people that if they want to buy an hotel they will have to fill in forms 'without fear.' If they do not have money the Government will see how it can assist them."[36]

For Christians, the advent of a Muslim presidency conjured the anxieties of the past. It recalled a moment in the mid- to late nineteenth century when Christian and Muslim neophytes struggled to control regional politics.[37] Beyond expulsion and religious practices, the uncertainties of the period were both deeply gendered, as Alicia Decker has powerfully demonstrated,[38] and encumbered by the challenge of cultural production. From the expansion of regional beauty pageants to the proliferation of historical markers and provincial museums, the Amin government anxiously labored to attract tourists and market its legitimacy.[39] Following General Amin's presidency, Uganda was ruled by seven administrations between 1979 and 1986. Each administration was removed by force, excluding the current administration of Yoweri Museveni.

The lack of continuity in postcolonial Uganda has resulted in bleak analyses, in which writers and state builders have raised concerns about the unlikelihood of stability in the region. Scholars of eastern Africa have suggested that, following the early 1960s, "Uganda itself was one of the greatest single sources of political instability, social dislocation and economic disruption in the Great Lakes region of sub-Saharan Africa."[40] The Ganda historian Phares Mutibwa has argued that "the Buganda Factor," or the perennial conflict between Uganda's central government and the kingdom of Buganda, has driven the recurrence of constitutional crises in postcolonial Uganda.[41] Shortly after President Museveni secured military control of Kampala after a five-year conflict with the Obote military, Mutibwa suggested that "Museveni has a golden opportunity, with the people's goodwill behind him, to lift Uganda finally out of its abyss of agony."[42] Since the cultural restoration of Uganda's hereditary monarchies in July 1993,[43] Buganda's relationship with the central government has been mostly stable. However, over the past five years, this relationship has become increasingly capricious.[44] Mutibwa no longer effuses his earlier optimism. He writes that there "is no doubt that the relations between Mmengo [capital of Buganda] and the NRM [National Resistance Movement] Government (including and above all Museveni himself) are no longer as warm as they used to be," with the "relationship between Mmengo and the NRM Administration [becoming] blurred every day."[45]

In an address in 2014, to abate the perceived "revival" of Ganda patriotism over the past several years, Museveni cautioned ministers of the government of Buganda that "when a cultural institution mixes with politics that is sine qua non with its death." He contended that Buganda should emulate the kingdom of Japan, whose emperors, unlike the rulers of the Qing dynasty, survived because they removed themselves from the arena of national politics following World War II.[46] The forces of global trade drove Museveni's comparative history. He adapted China's late nineteenth-century economic and political history, with which he became familiar while preparing to work with Chinese delegates.[47]

Earlier, in the mid-1980s, to cast a nationalist vision over the royalist gaze of the kingdom's ministers and subjects, activists in the NRM returned to the late 1950s. "When Uganda attained independence in 1962," observed one NRM document, "it was one of the most promising states to emerge at the time."[48] Beyond possessing both a buoyant economy and highly educated civil service, Museveni argued, Uganda boasted "a population of hard-working, God-fearing men and women tilling some of the best land in East Africa." It was fully expected that "Uganda would grow into a strong, prosperous and proud nation," whose postcolonial prospects were bedeviled by Presidents Obote and Amin. To recapture Uganda's bygone glory, Museveni reinforced the importance of a national political culture, a republic that assimilated and controlled the state's inferior "sub-cultures."[49] This was (and is) the logic of Museveni's cultural kingdoms: customary monarchies without political bite.

As my interviews throughout Buganda over the past sixteen years have shown, it is commonly argued that the Museveni government has undermined the moral authority of the kingdom's public shrines in order to weaken the political force of Ganda patriotism.[50] By the late 1980s, early in his administration, for instance, Museveni notified Ugandans that "a lot of our political work entails" showing communities that Buganda's ancestral spirits, *balubaale*, are incapable of causing or curing social or physical ailment.[51] By sanitizing or supplanting the sovereignties and spirits of Buganda, Museveni's vision was superficially modernist, an attempt to move Uganda away from a Hobbesian "State of Nature" into the pasture and order of a "national coalition of democratic, political and social forces, that could, at least, bring some motion in the centuries-old stagnation."[52]

But despite the official nomenclatures of Museveni's government, Buganda is a political kingdom for many communities in southern Uganda. Buganda's king and its parliament's activists influence how communities navigate national politics, while local communities look toward Mmengo (the kingdom's capital) for their own reasons. Debates and protests surrounding the deforestation of Mabira,[53] land allocation (*ebyaffe*, Buganda land nationalized by President Obote),[54] the movement of kings in the public sphere,[55] the repeated closure of Buganda's national radio station,[56] the federal decentralization of economic resources and political authority (commonly referred to as Federo),[57] the rise of neoconservative politics,[58] and postelection violence all raise important questions about the sustainability of Uganda's current political economy.[59]

In ways that sharply contrast with Museveni's historical vision, *Katikkiro* (Prime Minister of Buganda) Charles Peter Mayiga used his recent book to show readers that "history reveals that the people of Buganda carefully choose when to draw their swords, and when to negotiate."[60] Written by a practicing Catholic, Mayiga's history incorporates the earliest motto of the colonial Catholic periodical *Munno*: "Katonda ne Buganda, Omwoyo Gumu n'Emmeeme Emu" (God bless Buganda, with her people together as one in spirit). By drawing from B/Uganda's Catholic past, Mayiga wished to reinforce "Buganda's nationalism, which seems immutable."[61] Today, patriots look toward the past, a time in Buganda's political history when "the Kingdom enjoyed sovereignty and military might."[62] In popular discussions, this is a period that typically begins with the reign of Muteesa I (r. 1856–84) and ends with Muteesa II's (r. 1939–69), two political bookends that encompass Ganda authority in the region. Communities continue to use the language of local power, knowledge (*–maanyi*) and, as I will now show, calm, to talk about the

FIGURE 1. Kasubi Tombs, September 2005. © Jonathon L. Earle

status of Buganda in national politics. The continuity and resurrection of Buganda's monarchical histories are recalled as activists use material culture, prayers, and possession to imagine a kingdom that is calm, *Obuganda buladde*.

Possession, Calm, and the Burning of the Royal Tombs

On the evening of 16 March 2010, during a period of particular agitation between the government of Buganda and the central government over the closure of the royalist radio station CBS (see above), the kingdom's royal tombs in Kasubi, Kampala, were destroyed by fire.[63] The tombs were recognized as a UNESCO world heritage site, and housed the bodies of Buganda's four preceding monarchs (fig. 1). The tombs also contained historical artifacts, including furniture brought by Protestant missionaries in the late nineteenth century and a mounted leopard that belonged to Kabaka Muteesa I. The fire evoked immediate outcry in Buganda and instigated rumors and accusations on the streets of Kampala and throughout the kingdom.[64] Thousands of Kabaka Muteebi's loyal subjects, wearing *kkanzu* (traditional long tunics) and bark cloth, to signify tradition and loss, poured into Kampala, bringing with them poles and grass for the tomb's reconstruction (fig. 2).

FIGURE 2. Mourners wearing kkanzu robes, near Kasubi, during a day of national mourning declared by the Kingdom of Buganda, 26 March 2010. © Jonathon L. Earle

Local and prominent activists, who suspected state-sanctioned arson, cast President Museveni as the leading conspirator. At Kasubi, demonstrations against Museveni were fanatical. Through the performance of songs, disillusioned youth compared Museveni to a rotten fish and Buganda's monarch to a life-giving herb: "Kabaka Ssere—bwali ssere amaze okwanya; Kaguta [Museveni] ngege—bwali ngege emaze okududa" (Kabaka is like an herb that has multiplied; Museveni, like a perch that has gone bad).[65] On this same day, President Museveni unexpectedly arrived at Kasubi with his security forces. He was unwelcome, and Ganda youth organized a barricade to prevent his visit. Oral interviews suggest that the blockade was organized by the same youth whom I observed singing and dancing earlier in the day, performers who had concluded that Museveni, while once a hopeful president, was now an overcooked and rotten fish. To remove their obstruction, Museveni's presidential entourage shot and killed two to three protesters and wounded approximately five others.[66]

From the floor of the Lukiiko (parliament), members cautiously expressed concern toward the ruling government. One youth organizer remarked: "Today, we should not talk but weep; because we always say, 'Whoever makes the Kabaka shed tears, I shall make them shed blood.'"[67] More insightfully, one prominent chief summarized the long history of Buganda's relationship with Uganda's postcolonial presidents:

> We love our president, no doubt, but why does he think that we don't love him, and then brings the army with him when he visits? I have seen many leaders in this country—Amin sometimes rode a bicycle. We loved Museveni, to the extent of loving the ground upon which he walked, but why does he now send the army before he visits? He would first have gone to the *kabaka* or *katikkiro* to express his condolences, but how could he come to say "sorry" as other bodies were falling down? What do you expect your hosts to think? *You*[!], his spies, tell his Excellency that we have a complaint: Why do you have to first beat-up your hosts before visiting them? If there is anything the president is uncomfortable with concerning Buganda, let him say it, because we have loved him and cannot understand why it has come to this. Long live the *kabaka*![68]

This chief reflected on etiquette, the proper sequences of power and order. In Buganda, Uganda's presidents were expected to respect the kingdom's hierarchy. In the past, political visits to royal tombs were not unannounced, they required considerable negotiation over intent and responsibility; the arbitration of state power was often tied to the acquisition of knowledge obtained at royal burial sites. By using the military to secure his visit to the tombs, Museveni failed, like his republican predecessors, to demonstrate that he and his government were (and are) guests entertained by a generous host, a kingdom whose patience was (and is) being worn thin by poor manners.

Following the death of Ganda protesters and the convening of the parliament of Buganda, President Museveni issued a public apology. His speech addressed the government's fraught relationship with monarchical and customary politics. Amid accusations that the NRM had orchestrated the arson, Museveni reminded his audience that it was the NRM, following Uganda's civil war during the 1980s, that "liberated Kasubi and other Royal sites from the forces that had confiscated them and then, we handed them over to the Royal families of the different Kingdoms." The president, in describing the moral character of his accusers, lamented: "What incredibly wicked elements we have in Uganda!" If the point was not clear enough, Museveni then used the Epistle to the Galatians (6:7) to argue that "this type of wickedness will have plenty of evil on themselves."[69]

Museveni's comments underscored the burden of the past and the politics of heritage in contemporary Uganda, a theme that scholars including Derek R. Peterson have begun to assess.[70] At one level, the Tombs had been placed under the control of the government of Buganda. However, Museveni also noted that the "Kasubi tombs are a national and international heritage." In this same speech—given in English, Uganda's national language—Museveni employed Runyankore (the language of Ankole) and Luganda (the language of Buganda) to talk about older royal practices of extinguishing fires. Museveni argued that the government's effort to fight the fire was opposed during the evening of the burning. Due to the obstruction of young Ganda patriots, who resisted government intervention due to customary beliefs, he argued, the fire could not be properly contained. The result was a national tragedy. Museveni adapted a Swahili idiom to describe Ganda youth, "*Mambo ya ujinga tuu*," a phrase that means "things of ignorant seeds," or "only ignorant things." The idea suggests that, due to ignorance and immaturity, naïve youthful activists often act foolishly. In Buganda, Swahili is contentious, and has been long devalued due to its associations with settler policies in Kenya (and Closer Union debates) in the colonial period and military politics in postcolonial Uganda. Today, Museveni's use of Swahili as a national lingua franca has been viewed with suspicion in Buganda—a way of undermining the linguistic integrity of Buganda and the attempt to prevent the use of Luganda in national public life.[71] By using Swahili nomenclature to criticise Ganda youth, Museveni sought to reconceptualize the parochial boundaries within which the Tombs and their activists conjured spiritual authority and power.

Indeed, in the wake of the burning, spirit possession practices accompanied protest and lamentation throughout Buganda and Kasubi.[72] On the compound, small groups of protesters convened to facilitate possession, which entailed singing around small fires that were used to invite regional spirits. Like the spirit priest Kigaanira Kibuuka, a prominent activist who advocated for Buganda's monarchy from various trees in the mid-1950s,[73] the possessed climbed adjacent trees (fig. 3).[74] Activists, who were disheartened, looked for insight, relief, and justice

FIGURE 3. Possessed activist in tree, Kasubi, 18 March 2010. © Jonathon L. Earle

from *balubaale* (local or regional deities) and their priests. As possession practices were performed, dissenters recalled the tragedies of state building in postcolonial Buganda, and explored the ways in which possession might empower communities to engineer political and cultural critique. At Kasubi, antiphonic songs reminded Baganda that despite social rupture and Museveni's politics, the spirits were powerful purveyors of political insight:

> Leader: Trouble, trouble
> People: We have been troubled since morning
> Leader: Lubaale is powerful these days
> People: We have been troubled since morning[75]

Through the rituals of possession, communities obtained political knowledge and the understanding of specialists. Priests assured their devotees that balubaale would not rest until the identity of the perpetrator of arson was publicly revealed. As one interlocutor noted, "Ebintu biri bisobola okulaba abayokyezza wano" (The powers can see those who have burned this place).[76]

Known for its ability to track down and reveal guilty parties, the *jjembe* (spirit) Kalondoozi frequented possession rituals at Kasubi. Choirs enveloped fallen and gyrating women and men possessed by Kalondoozi, singing: "[The spirit] is tracking down; even if the guilty is far away, [they] will be tracked."[77] Beyond the confines of Kasubi, priests in Masaka (Buddu) launched an intelligence probe. Aired on the Kampala-based news program NTV, one spirit declared that it would not fail to apprehend Museveni: "For some forty years he has spoilt our things and we have already caught him." Confident of its ability, the spirit informed audiences that should it fail, "I will never again come on the head and possess another."[78] After the spirit's medium was no longer possessed, he notified Baganda that power and knowledge (*–maanyi*) must be used to protect culture and custom: "This is where we, the believers of culture and custom, are now—we have to show power in catching that enemy."[79]

The practice of possession was part of a larger reflection on the production of calm. This was at least to some degree the logic of appealing to Kalondoozi. With Kalondoozi at work, communities in Buganda could remain poised before the challenges ahead. In the Luganda press, editors devoted entire sections to exploring the history of Buganda's resolve.[80] Local dissenters and members of Buganda's Lukiiko compared the fire to the dissolution of their monarchy in 1966 and 1967. Owekitiibwa (Honorable) Apollo Makubuya openly compared the Kasubi inferno to the government's military attack on the Lubiiri (royal palace) in 1966, and suggested that the federal status of Buganda was the only solution to a marriage characterized by ridicule and torture.[81] In ways that mirrored Makubuya's comments, laborers who cleared the tombs' ashes sang about Buganda's ancient and recent past, recalling the fate of Uganda's violent presidents. One song reminded mourners about President Obote, who, though once powerful, is now deceased: "Akaalo ka Buganda ka dda, akaalo kaaliko nnanyiniko. Obote n'akaleka—yali wa maanyi. N'abaali abamaanyi baakaleka" (The village of Buganda started long ago; it has its owner. Even Obote left it—yet he was powerful. All others with power will leave it, [too]).[82]

Throughout Kampala, vendors used computers and design software to produce and distribute, impromptu, memorabilia that recalled an earlier, calm period in the life of the kingdom. One placard I obtained portrayed a somber Kabaka Muteebi II covered in barkcloth and a leopard skin,

FIGURE 4. "The Former Glory of Buganda," March 2010. Jonathon L. Earle Papers

signifying spiritual and political authority and authentic Ganda culture (fig. 4). Local artists used Photoshop to place Muteebi in front of the royal tombs, before and during the fire. Muteebi's father, Kabaka Muteesa II, is placed on the right section of the card in black-and-white tint. With penetrating eyes, now without a home (tomb), Buganda's martyred king in colonial regalia stares at the viewer; he embodies calm regal composure and resolve. A competent and gregarious Muteebi, depicted in the lower left corner of the image, shows viewers that a king remains on the throne. He must work to embody calm and restore the former glory of Buganda, "*Agali Amakula Gabuganda*," a magnificence dated to 1835, the reign of Kabaka Ssuuna, who is often remembered for successfully welcoming Buganda's first international traders from the Swahili coast.

A few days after the fire, near the compound of the tombs, a middle-aged man handed me a small laminated poster (fig. 5), copies of which were displayed in taxis around Kampala. The poster's representation was simple. It showed Kabaka Muteebi II sitting on one of Buganda's royal seats. The throne is Victorian in design. Its arms and back are covered in upholstered leather. Above the back of the chair is the national crest of Buganda, carved in wood, with spears, shield, and lion. Buganda's king sits comfortably, slightly reclined. He gently gazes

FIGURE 5. Kabaka Ronald Muwenda Muteebi II, "Buganda is Calm," 2010. Jonathon L. Earle Papers

toward the photographer, wearing a white kkanzu and navy sports coat with a golden striped pocket square, a blending of Arab and European garments. The collar of the kkanzu is blue, the hue of the national flag of Buganda. The designer(s) of the poster matched this color to create a cerulean canvas for the background of the reproduction. Muteebi's arms rest leisurely in his lap, with his hands interconnected. On his left wrist is a digital Timex. Below the king, the following inscription is printed: "*Obuganda Buladde*"—"Buganda is calm."

Conclusion: Calm and the Study of Anxiety

Amid the burning of the royal tombs, the performance of calm, seen in the activism of Kalondoozi and the production of political placards, empowered communities to publicly challenge the state. It was not from a position of perceived political anxiety that royalists mobilized and pursued possession, however tumultuous the moment might have been. To the contrary, Baganda at Kasubi saw themselves as members of a calm kingdom, a tranquil partner in a long and rocky marriage with an unstable spouse.

The portrayals of calm in 2010, though, had earlier precedents in Ganda intellectual history. Whereas previous literature on the postcolonial state in Africa has underscored the power and production of anxiety, the long conjuring of calm in Buganda challenges scholars of the state to rethink the complexities of kingship—and the extent to which activists solicit precolonial kingdoms to create normative discourses of calm and stability. In colonial and postcolonial Buganda, discourses surrounding anxiety were common. But they were common precisely because there were broader and more penetrating conceptions of calm and stability guiding normative politics.

Notes

1. Copies in author's possession, Kasubi Video/34/00A Kasubi Grounds, 18 March 2010.
2. Frantz Fanon, *The Wretched of the Earth*, trans. Constance Farrington (New York: Grove, 1963), 165.
3. Fanon, 43–53.
4. Fanon, 160.
5. Fanon, 253–92.
6. Sartre reflected: "The status of 'native' is a nervous condition introduced and maintained by the settler among colonized people *with their consent*" (Fanon, *Wretched of the Earth*, preface, 20).
7. This is clearly seen in the following section: Tsitsi Dangarembga, *Nervous Conditions* (Seattle: Seal, 1988), 201.
8. John D. Murphy, *Luganda-English Dictionary* (Washington, DC: Consortium Press for Catholic University of America Press, 1972), 34.
9. Murphy, 28.
10. E. M. K. Mulira, *Troubled Uganda* (London: Fabian, 1950).
11. Mulira, 13.
12. Mulira, 12–15 (progress); 16–22 (social strain); 23–43 (political unrest).

13. John Roscoe, *The Baganda: An Account of Their Native Customs and Beliefs*, 2nd ed. (London: Frank Cass, 1965), 42.

14. Roscoe, 42.

15. Roscoe, 54.

16. Apolo Kaggwa, *Ekitabo Kye Mpisa Za Baganda (The Customs of the Baganda)*, ed. May M. Edel, trans. Ernest B. Kalibala (New York: Columbia University Press, 1934), 108.

17. Kaggwa, 109–10.

18. C. W. Hattersley, "The Kabaka's First Visit to Mtesa's Tomb," *Uganda Notes*, December 1906, 182–85.

19. *Uganda Notes*, June 1911, 94–95.

20. Hattersley, "Kabaka's First Visit to Mtesa's Tomb."

21. Jean-Pierre Chrétien, *The Great Lakes of Africa: Two Thousand Years of History*, trans. Scott Straus (New York: Zone Books, 2003), 121–37.

22. *Uganda Notes*, October 1904, 142; January 1909, 16–20.

23. *Uganda Notes*, February 1902, 9; September 1903, 47.

24. *Uganda Notes*, November 1908, 164.

25. The best review of this literature remains John A. Rowe, "Myth, Memoir, and Moral Admonition: Luganda Historical Writing, 1893–1969," *Uganda Journal* 33 (1969): 17–40, 217–19; Michael Twaddle, "On Ganda Historiography," *History in Africa* 1 (1974): 85–100.

26. The political genealogies of Muteesa's names are addressed more fully in Jonathon L. Earle, *Colonial Buganda and the End of Empire: Political Thought and Historical Imagination in Africa* (Cambridge: Cambridge University Press, 2017), chapter 4.

27. Ham Mukasa, "The Rule of the Kings of Buganda," *Uganda Journal* 10 (1946): 136–43.

28. Ali Kulumba, *Ebyafayo By'obusiramu mu Uganda* (Kampala: n.p., 1953).

29. David Schoenbrun, "A Mask of Calm: Emotion and Founding the Kingdom of Bunyoro in the Sixteenth Century," *Comparative Studies in Society and History* 55 (2013): 634–64.

30. Ferdinand Walser, *Luganda Proverbs* (Berlin: Reimer, 1982), no. 88.

31. For further discussion, see Shane Doyle, "From Kitara to the Lost Counties: Genealogy, Land and Legitimacy in the Kingdom of Bunyoro, Western Uganda," *Social Identities* 12 (2006): 457–70.

32. Mikael Karlström, "The Cultural Kingdom in Uganda: Popular Royalism and the Restoration of the Buganda Kingship, Volume I" (PhD diss., University of Chicago, 1999).

33. Holger Bernt Hansen, "Uganda in the 1970s: A Decade of Paradoxes and Ambiguities," *Journal of Eastern African Studies* 7 (2013): 83–103.

34. See Richard J. Reid's discussion in *A History of Modern Uganda* (Cambridge: Cambridge University Press, 2017), 53–99.

35. Anneeth K. Hundle, "Exceptions to the Expulsion: Violence, Security and Community among Ugandan Asians, 1972–79," *Journal of Eastern African Studies* 7, no. 1 (2013): 164–82 at 166.

36. "All Asians Must Go: President's New Phase in 'Economic War,'" *Uganda Argus*, 21 August 1972, 1.

37. John Rowe, "Islam under Idi Amin: A Case of Déjà Vu?," in *Uganda Now: Between Decay and Development*, ed. Hölger Bernt Hansen and Michael Twaddle (Athens: Ohio University Press, 1988), 267–79. For additional discussion on the politics of public healing during the Amin period, see Marissa Mika, "Fifty Years of Creativity, Crisis, and Cancer in Uganda," *Canadian Journal of African Studies* 50, no. 3 (2016): 395–413.

38. Alicia C. Decker, *In Idi Amin's Shadow: Women, Gender, and Militarism in Uganda* (Athens: Ohio University Press, 2014).

39. Derek R. Peterson, "Introduction: Heritage Management in Colonial and Contemporary Africa," in *The Politics of Heritage in Africa: Economies, Histories, and Infrastructures* (Cambridge: Cambridge University Press, 2015), 1–36 at 23.

40. Michael Twaddle and Hölger Bernt Hansen, "The Changing State of Uganda," in *Developing Uganda*, ed. Hölger Bernt Hansen and Michael Twaddle (Athens: Ohio University Press, 1998), 1.

41. Phares Mutibwa, *The Buganda Factor in Uganda Politics* (Kampala: Fountain, 2008).

42. Phares Mutibwa, *Uganda since Independence: A Story of Unfulfilled Hopes* (Trenton, NJ: African World Press, 1992), 202.

43. The fullest treatment of Buganda's interregnum politics is Karlström, "Cultural Kingdom in Uganda."

44. "Museveni Breached Agreement—Mmengo," *Monitor*, 15 May 2010; "Wikileaks: Kabaka's Views on Museveni," *Monitor*, 7 September 2011.

45. Mutibwa, *Buganda Factor in Uganda Politics*, 251–52.

46. "President Museveni's remarks before handing over Ebyaffe to Buganda Kingdom's delegation on April 15, 2014, at State House Entebbe," The State House of Uganda, 16 April 2014, http://www.statehouse.go.ug/media/presidential-statements/2014/04/16/president-musevenis-remarks-handing-over-ebyaffe-buganda-ki.

47. "Highlights of China-Uganda Relations," *New Vision*, 5 March 2014.

48. *Towards a Free and Democratic Uganda* (Kampala: Authority of the National Resistance Movement, [c. 1986]), 1.

49. *Towards a Free and Democratic Uganda*, 4.

50. See Neil Kodesh, *Beyond the Royal Gaze: Clanship and Public Healing in Buganda* (Charlottesville: University of Virginia Press, 2010).

51. Yoweri Museveni, *Ten-Point Programme of NRM* (Kampala: National Resistance Movement Publications, 1986), 26–27.

52. Museveni, 5–7.

53. "Deaths in Uganda Forest Protest," *BBC News*, 12 April 2007, http://news.bbc.co.uk/1/hi/world/africa/6548107.stm; "Ugandan Plan for Forest Suspended," *BBC News*, 22 May 2007, http://news.bbc.co.uk/1/hi/world/africa/6680637.stm; "Is the Mabira Saga a Govt [sic] Trick to Divert Citizens' Attention?," *Monitor*, 1 October 2010.

54. "Mmengo Opts for Court in Battle of Land Bill," *Monitor*, 1 December 2009; "Campaign against the Land Bill Was Misplaced," *New Vision*, 9 December 2010; "Reactions to Land Law," *New Vision*, 7 January 2010.

55. "Kayunga Becomes Battle Field as Youths Take On Cops," *Monitor*, 10 September 2009; "Gunfire Rocks Bulange as Besigye Blames Museveni," *Monitor*, 12 September 2009; "Kayunga Fiasco: How It Could Impact on 2011 Polls," *Monitor*, 12 September 2009.

56. "CBS Told to Move out of Bulange," *New Vision*, 22 January 2010; "Mmengo Rejects Government Terms on CBS," *New Vision*, 1 February 2010; "State House: CBS Radio Must Apologise," *Monitor*, 30 March 2010.

57. Frederick Golooba-Mutebi, "Settling the Buganda Question," *Transition*, 106 (Side B) (2011), 10–25.

58. Florence Brisset-Foucault, "Re-inventing a Royalist 'Public Sphere' in Contemporary Uganda: The Example of Central Broadcasting Services (CBS)," *Journal of African Cultural Studies* 25, no. 1 (2013): 72–87.

59. "'Walk to Work' in a Historical Light—Mamdani," *Monitor*, 24 April 2011; "Number of Injured in Kampala Riots Shoots to 84," *Monitor*, 29 April 2011; "Police Arrest Mao as Besigye Jets In," *Monitor*, 11 May 2011.

60. Charles P. Mayiga, *King on the Throne: The Story of the Restoration of the Kingdom of Buganda* (Kampala: Prime Time Communication, 2009), 274.

61. Mayiga, 418.

62. Mayiga, 274.

63. "Fire Destroys Kasubi Tombs," *Monitor*, 17 March 2010; "Abaganda batandise okukungubaga Amasiro (Aba Gavumenti bagenze e Mmengo)," *Bukedde*, 20 March 2010; "Mmengo esazeewo," *Bukedde*, 23 March 2010; "Kabaka: Bagenda kumunaaliza mu Masiro," *Bukedde*, 24 March 2010.

64. Following the fire, I spent several days purposely roaming the streets of Kampala, conducting informal and semi-structured interviews. In local restaurants, taxis, mosques, and churches, I observed extensive conversations regarding the tombs. During the following weeks, in Bulemeezi (Luweero) and Mpigi, communities were similarly concerned.

65. Copies in author's possession, Kasubi Video/33/002 Kasubi Grounds, 18 March 2010.

66. "Three Killed as President Museveni Forcefully Enters Kasubi Tombs," *Monitor*, 18 March 2010; "Army Explains Shooting," *New Vision*, 18 March 2010.

67. Copies in author's possession, Lukiiko Recordings Anonymous, Lukiiko Session, 10 March 2010: "Olwaleero twandibadde tetwogera, nga tukulukusa bukulukusa maziga kubanga bulijjo tugamba nti, 'Kabaka alimukabya amaziga ndimukaabya musaayi.'"

68. Copies in author's possession, Lukiiko Recordings Anonymous, Lukiiko Session, 10 March 2010:

> Omukulembeze waffe tumwagala nnyo naye lwaki atuteetera okulowooza nti tetumwagala, n'akulembeza abajaasi mu maaso. Nzi ndabye ku bakulembeze abababaddewo, Amin yavuganga n'akagali.

Twayagala Museveni nga newalinnye twagalawo naye lwaki essawa eno akulembera magye nga bwe kyabadde? Yandisoose wa ssabasajja oba wa katikkiro n'amugamba nti, "Nga Kitalo nnyo!." Naye n'olyoka ojja n'okuba amasasi ate n'ogamba nti osaasire, ng'eno emirambo bwegigwa. Olwo osubidde nti b'ogenze okusaasira bakulowoozamu kiki? Mmwe[!] abali wano beyasindise, mutegeeze His Excellency nti ensonga eno etuluma nti lwaki omuntu gw'oyagala okusooka kumukuba miggo ng'ogenda okusaasira? Bwe waba waliwo ensonga President gy'alina ku Buganda aginnyonnyole kubanga twali tumwagala nnyo naye tetumanyi nsonga etutuusa awo. Ssabasajja Kabaka awangaale!

69. "Museveni Speaks Out on Kasubi Tombs Fire," *New Vision*, 21 March 2010.

70. Peterson, "Introduction: Heritage Management."

71. Viera Pawliková-Vilhanová, "Swahili and the Dilemma of Ugandan Language Policy," *Asian and African Studies*, 5 (1996), 158–70.

72. "Fire Destroys Kasubi Tombs"; "Ebibuuzo ku muliro gw'e Kasubi," *Bukedde*, 21 March 2010; "Effujjo mu Masiro," *Bukedde*, 23 March 2010; "Ab'e Masaka nabo bakungubaze," *Bukedde*, 26 March 2010; "Basabye eyayokezza Amasiro asaanewo," *Bukedde*, 26 March 2010; "Kasubi yalese bangi bazirise," *Bukedde*, 28 March 2010; "Ebiwanuuzibwa ku kwokebwa kw'Amasiro e Kasubi: Kibuuka Omumbaale munyiivu, akooye myuziyamu," *Bukedde*, 28 March 2010; "Buganda gwe mutima Yuganda," *Ggwanga*, April 2010.

73. For further discussion on the biography of the 1950s prophet Kibuuka, see Jonathon L. Earle, "Political Theologies in Late Colonial Buganda" (PhD diss., University of Cambridge, 2012), 257–63.

74. While the climbing of trees at Kasubi looked remarkably similar to practices during the 1950s, I was unable to fully identify the extent to which possessed interlocutors made the historical connection.

75. Copies in author's possession, Kasubi Recordings Anonymous, Kasubi, 20 March 2010:

> Leader: Lebuleebu, abange leebu leebu
> People: Kalipuko—twakedde nkya kulebuka
> Leader: Lubaale wa maanyi ng'akola luno
> People: Kalipuko—twakedde nkya kulebuka

76. Copies in author's possession, Kasubi Recordings Anonymous, Kasubi, 20 March 2010.

77. Copies in author's possession, Kasubi Video/34/004 Kasubi Grounds, 18 March 2010: "Lijja lilondoola; Nebwobeera ng'oli."

78. "Investigating Kasubi Fire: Masaka Traditional Healers Launch Own Probe," National Television, Kampala, 21 March 2010, http://www.youtube.com/watch?v=ft4g6CxF9Rc&feature=youtube_gdata, (accessed 23 March 2010): "Emyaka amakumi ana. Yayonoonye ebintu byaffe era tumaze okumukwata. Bwannema sijja kudda ku jjoba."

79. "Tulina okulaga amaanyi nga ffe abakkiriza mu buwangwa okukwata omulabe oyo."

80. "Ebyafaayo by'Amasire g'e Kasubi," *Ggwanga*, March 2010, 5.

81. "Okwokya Amasiro kitujjukiza ebyaliwo mu 1966," *Bukedde*, 26 March 2010.

82. Copies in author's possession, Kasubi Video/34/00A Kasubi Grounds, 18 March 2010.

Contributors

CÉCILE FEZA BUSHIDI is currently a postdoctoral researcher and lecturer in dance and art history at Yale University. She is a graduate of the School of Oriental and African Studies, where she earned a PhD in history. Previously, she held fellowships at NYU Center for Ballet and the Arts, the University of Cambridge, and the Institute of Historical Research, University of London. Her current research interests cover dance history, dance historiography, and performance theory. As a performance artist, Cécile is involved in independent dance and theater projects.

JONATHON L. EARLE is Associate Professor of African History and Chair of African and African American Studies at Centre College. His first book, *Colonial Buganda and the End of Empire: Political Thought and Historical Imagination in Africa* (Cambridge University Press, 2017), was short-listed for the Bethwell A. Ogot Book Prize. His most recent work has appeared in the *Journal of African History* and *History in Africa*.

HARRY FIRTH-JONES studied history as an undergraduate student at the University of Leeds, including a year abroad at the University of Leiden. While researching his dissertation at the National Archives in London, he discovered a cache of letters written by white settlers in Kenya, requesting repatriation during decolonization. These form the basis of the chapter he has coauthored with Will Jackson, included in this volume. He now lives in London and works at the Foreign and Commonwealth Office.

ANDREA MARIKO GRANT is Lecturer in Social Anthropology at the University of Cambridge. Her work explores popular culture and religious change in Rwanda, as well as memory and the creation of postgenocide archives. Her work has appeared in *Africa: The Journal of the*

Contributors

International African Institute, *Journal of Religion in Africa*, and *Journal of Eastern African Studies*, among others.

WILL JACKSON is Associate Professor in Imperial History at the University of Leeds. He works on settler colonialism, race, and intimacy in east and southern Africa during the twentieth century. His first book—*Madness and Marginality: The Lives of Kenya's White Insane*—was published by Manchester University Press in 2013. Since then he has published on aging, childhood, friendship, and the emotions. He is currently working on a history of whiteness in southern Africa during the late nineteenth and early twentieth centuries.

RACHEL KING is Lecturer in Cultural Heritage Studies at the Institute of Archaeology, University College London. She is the author most recently of *Outlaws, Anxiety and Disorder in Southern Africa: Material Histories of the Maloti-Drakensberg* (Cambridge Imperial and Post-Colonial Studies Series, Palgrave Macmillan).

NAKANYIKE B. MUSISI is Associate Professor at the University of Toronto. She is a former Director of Makerere Institute of Social Research at Makerere University, Kampala. Her research interests are in gender, colonialism, missionary work in Uganda, social change, and education. With Jean Allman and Susan Geiger, she coedited *Women in African Colonial Histories* (2002). Her articles have appeared in *Signs: Journal of Culture and Society*, *Journal of African History*, *History in Africa*, *Gender and History*, and in edited collections.

KALALA NGALAMULUME is Associate Professor of Africana Studies and History at Bryn Mawr College. He specializes in the social history of medicine in Africa, history of public health, urban history in Africa, and francophone West Africa. He has published in the *Journal of African History*, *Cahiers d'études africaines*, *African Economic History*, and *Oxford University Bibliographies*. His first book, *Colonial Pathologies, Environment, and Western Medicine in Saint-Louis-du-Sénégal, 1867–1920*, was published in 2010 (Peter Lang). He is coeditor with Paula Viterbo of *Medicine and Health in Africa: Multidisciplinary Perspectives* (Michigan State University Press, 2010).

Contributors

YOLANA PRINGLE is Senior Lecturer in the History of Medicine at the University of Roehampton. Pringle has research interests in the history of psychiatry and mental health, humanitarianism, and global health, with a regional focus on East Africa. Her first book, *Psychiatry and Decolonisation in Uganda*, was published in 2019. She is currently working on a history of mental health care in contexts of political violence in Africa, funded by the H. F. Guggenheim Foundation.

SIMON TURNER is Associate Professor of Archaeology, Ethnology, Greek & Latin, and History at the Saxo Institute of the University of Copenhagen. His research interests include gender, refugees, ethnic conflict and genocide, and diaspora. His articles have appeared in such journals as the *Journal of the Royal Anthropological Institute*, *Ethnos: Journal of Anthropology*, and *Conflict and Society*.

Index

acclimatization, 7, 94
Achebe, Chinua, 6, 219
affect, 1, 3–4, 14, 18, 20, 34, 36–38, 44, 50–57, 64n97, 168–69, 198; and the affective, 3, 6, 10, 11, 14, 17, 18, 36, 38, 57, 69, 92; "affective turn," 2, 3, 86n10; raiding affects, 9–10, 47, 50
Africa: anxiety about postcolonial Africa, 14, 23, 115, 158–60, 218–19, 223–24; imagining/inventing Africa, 7, 9, 42, 80–83, 97, 145, 149, 158
African Union, 151, 210, 211, 212
agency, 9–10, 20, 36, 37, 40, 47, 57, 136–37
Ahmed, Sara, 4
Algeria, 146, 218
Amin, Idi, 222–23, 224, 228
anger, 11–12, 117, 118, 154
anthropology: anthropological approaches to anxiety, 3, 4, 16, 18, 19, 168–69, 196–99. *See also* ethnography
anxiety: as an analytical lens, 5–6, 9, 11–12, 15–19, 21, 24, 34–35, 57–58, 66–67, 69, 94, 118–19, 146, 159–60, 169; and anticipation, 8, 13, 15, 116, 196–99, 200, 203; anxiety disorder, 92; definitions of, 1–2, 7, 16–18, 92–93, 116, 196–99; embodied nature of, 4, 5, 17, 18, 80–83, 209; multidirectional/multifaceted nature of, 4, 14, 16, 168–69; and narratives, 5, 6, 12, 19, 22, 84, 130, 169; as a political tool, 3, 10–11, 38–39, 57, 66, 187, 210; as subjective experience, 3, 5, 15, 17, 18, 19, 34, 37, 92; vernaculars of, 17–19, 116–17, 137–38, 201–2, 219, 222. *See also* anthropology; archaeology; colonial anxieties; emotions; fear; future; history
apartheid, 146–47, 150
Appadurai, Arjun, 197
Apter, Andrew, 82
Arcangeli, Alessandro, 66
archaeology, 4–5, 20, 33–35, 36–38, 57

bandits, 38–40
Basutoland, 37, 50–53
Beatty, Andrew, 19
Berckmoes, Lidewyde, 201
"black peril," 76–77, 156
Bloch, Ernst, 12, 168, 198

Blundell, Geoff, 47
bodies, 7–8, 12, 15, 16–17, 20–21, 38, 40, 65–69, 75, 77, 82–84, 86n9, 87n14, 124, 130, 177, 217, 220, 226
borders, 50, 53–55, 73, 171, 208
Bornstein, Erica, 184
Botswana, 17
Bourdieu, Pierre, 197, 199, 209, 213
Bourke, Joanna, 16
Branch, Daniel, 161
Buganda. *See* Uganda: Buganda kingdom
Burundi, 15, 22–23, 174, 195–214; 2015 crisis in, 195–96, 210; ethnic and political tensions in, 199–203, 210. *See also* Nkurunziza, Pierre

calm, 11, 14, 23, 82, 118, 169–70, 182, 187, 218, 221–22, 225–26, 231–34
Challis, Sam, 45–47, 63n70
churches, 22, 66, 119, 167–68, 204, 212, 216n36, 220; and the state, 170–87
citizenship, 168
climate, 7–8, 12, 94, 95
clitoridectomy, 73–74
Cole, Jennifer, 169
colonial anxieties, 2, 6, 8, 10, 12–13, 16, 65–67, 71, 144–45, 219
Comaroff, Jean, 39
Congo, 11, 13, 81, 100, 101, 146, 158, 174
constructivism, 2, 3, 5, 42, 57, 60n38, 66
control, 4, 10, 73, 118; colonizers' perceptions of, 13, 38, 40; of disease, 7, 98; of raiders, 45, 47, 53–56; by Rwandan state, 168–69, 171–72, 174, 175, 177, 184, 201; sexual, 123, 128
Cooper, Elizabeth, 15, 16
Cooper, Frederick, 146
Copeland, Lyndsey, 18
Côte d'Ivoire, 99, 101–7
COVID-19, 13, 93
crime: fears about, 71, 73, 83; criminality, 13, 35, 38–40, 42, 44, 158
Cullen, Poppy, 147–48

dance, 9, 20–21, 65–85; as protest, 68–69, 73–74, 83–84; as soothing, 67, 68, 80–83, 84; as spectacle, 82–83, 84
Dangarembga, Tsitsi, 219

245

Index

Ddiba, Father J., 221
death, 7, 93, 97, 119, 129, 137–38, 153, 155, 176, 197, 209, 219–20, 224, 228
Decker, Alicia, 223
decolonization, 6, 13, 22, 146–48, 152, 157–58, 159–61
de Luna, Kathryn, 15, 18
despair, 23, 196, 199, 209, 212, 213
development, 4, 22, 68, 80, 167–72, 173, 176–77, 179–80, 182, 184–87
deviance, 38, 39, 57, 58, 62n59
Dewey, John, 19
Di Nunzio, Marco, 15
disaster, 8, 97, 102, 103, 117
disease, 7–9, 13, 21, 67, 68, 72, 80, 83, 93, 94–109, 145
dissent, 39–40, 177, 188n6, 230–31

Ebola, 13, 93
economy, 4, 41, 79, 168, 170–72; economic instability, 14, 93, 222–24; economic interests, 73, 78, 83, 84, 102, 124, 157, 225
Eldredge, Elizabeth, 51
emotional communities, 5, 10, 34, 94, 95
emotions: as an area of academic study, 2, 3–5, 8–9, 11–12, 15, 16, 17, 19, 33–34, 36–37, 67, 92, 93, 168, 196–99; negative, 15, 16, 18, 67, 87n14; as residing in interactions, 1, 36–37, 65–66, 92
Englund, Harri, 186–87
environment, 7–9, 21, 22, 34, 69, 81, 84, 94, 102, 108, 145, 147
envy, 11–12, 168
epidemics, 13, 92–109
Ethiopia, 15
ethnicity, 43, 50, 57, 173, 174, 199–201, 203, 210, 222
ethnography, 2, 4, 16, 17–19, 23, 34, 37, 69, 146, 196, 201, 218, 219–20
expectation, 13, 15, 38, 69, 78, 79, 94, 129, 197

faith, 131, 184–86, 211–12
Fanon, Frantz, 218
Fassin, Didier, 16
fear, 6, 11–12, 76–77, 84, 95, 165n59, 196, 219–20; distinction between fear and anxiety, 16, 17, 18, 116, 147, 157, 196–97, 199, 202, 212
Fischer-Tiné, Harald, 2
Fleisher, Jeffrey, 4, 34, 37
Fujii, Lee Ann, 170
future, 6, 12–15, 23, 34, 38, 40, 108, 116, 146, 148, 151, 159; of Burundians, 196, 198, 201–15; of Rwandans, 168–69, 172–73, 177, 179, 185–87; study of, 197; unknowability of, 12, 23, 196–99, 210

gender, 21–22, 75, 115–38, 156–57, 177, 223
genocide, 17, 167, 202, 206–7
Ghana, 10
González-Ruibal, Alfredo, 40
Guha, Ranajit, 8, 16, 147, 159

Habyarimana, Juvénal, 172, 173, 174, 186
Hage, Ghassan, 197, 213
Hamilton, Kenneth, 126, 127, 131
Harris, Oliver, 36
healing, 11, 127, 174, 221–22
helplessness, 3, 148
heritage, 226, 229
history, 2, 3, 6, 7–8, 16, 42, 65–66, 92–93, 115, 146, 161, 220, 221, 223–24
HIV/AIDS, 13, 93
Hoad, Neville, 131
Hobsbawm, Eric, 38–39
homosexuality, 22, 119, 124, 126–27, 137, 138
hope, 12, 15, 22, 147, 168, 177, 169, 196–214, 216n36, 227
Huggins, Chris, 183
Hugo, Pierre, 155
human rights, 168, 186, 200–201
Hundle, Anneeth, 223
Hunt, Nancy Rose, 11

indefiniteness, 8
influenza, 13, 93
irrationality. *See* rationality (and irrationality)

Jansen, Stef, 198, 213
jealousy, 135
Jolly, Pieter, 42

Kagame, Paul, 167, 168, 170, 172, 176, 177, 205, 213
Kaggwa, Apolo, 118, 122, 220–21
Kennedy, Dane, 145–46
Kenya, 9, 13, 20–21, 22, 65–80, 83–85, 144–61, 174, 229; independence of, 13, 22, 146, 147–54, 161; land, 13, 67–68, 70–72, 73, 75–76, 77, 79, 83, 84, 147–48, 150, 154, 160, 165n54. *See also* Mau Mau
Kimmel, Michael, 134
Kiwanuka, Semakula, 117, 119, 120, 128
Kleist, Nauja, 198
Knight, Daniel M., 198
Kus, Susan, 37

land, 53, 138, 145, 159, 160, 165n54, 225; Kenya, 13, 67–68, 70–72, 73, 75–77, 79, 83, 84, 147–48, 150, 154, 160; Rwanda, 183–84, 187; Zimbabwe, 144
landscape, 9, 34, 47, 49, 54, 80, 82, 84, 144–45;

Index

affective, 10, 14; of anxiety, 20. *See also* environment
language, 7, 16, 17–18, 79, 84, 145, 152, 156, 199, 220, 225, 229. *See also* anxiety: vernaculars of; linguistics
Laszczkowski, Mateusz, 3
Lesotho, 43
linguistics, 18, 43, 54, 60n38, 69
Livingston, Julie, 17
Longman, Timothy, 186
love, 18, 124, 126, 228

Madagascar, 37
Mallen, Lara, 47
Maloti-Drakensberg Mountains. *See under* South Africa
marginality, 4, 15, 35, 41, 128, 134–35, 147
Marriott, McKim, 17
Marshall, Ruth, 185
masculinity, 10, 21–22, 115–19, 125–26, 128, 133–37
material culture, 1, 34–35, 36, 37, 41–47, 66, 226
materiality, 4–5, 67
Mau Mau, 148, 150–53, 156, 160
Mayiga, Charles Peter, 225
Mazzarella, William, 4
McLisky, Claire, 11
media, 109, 175, 177, 195, 200–201, 205, 212; newspapers, 34, 100; radio, 191n54, 200, 225, 226
mental illness, 17, 92, 149, 156
missionaries, 10, 11, 14, 21, 44, 66, 115–38, 174, 220–21, 226; obsession with sexual practices, 126–27
Miti, James, 130, 221
modernity, 6, 66, 81, 160, 171, 183, 225
moods, 10, 11, 182, 199, 200–201, 210
mourning, 74, 78–79, 83, 227
Mukasa, Hamu, 221
Mulira, Eridadi, 11, 219, 221
Museveni, Yoweri, 14, 23, 217, 222–25, 227–31
music, 18, 66, 72, 80–81, 174
Mutibwa, Phares, 223–24
Mwanga II (of Buganda), 10, 14, 21–22, 115–38; accusations of sodomy, 119, 123–24, 127

Nardocchio-Jones, Gavin, 161
nationalism, 10, 39, 147, 224, 225
nervousness, 11, 18, 156, 218–19
neurasthenia, 7–8, 22, 145–46, 156
neurochemicals, 2
newspapers, 34, 100. *See also* media
Ngai, Sianne, 11, 12, 168
Nigeria, 82
Nkurunziza, Pierre, 22, 199, 205, 213
Norman, Neil, 4, 34, 37

Obote, Milton, 217, 222–24, 225, 231
O'Neill, Kevin, 185
outlaws, 9, 20, 34, 35, 38–39, 40–47, 57

panic, 96–97, 117, 121; moral, 66–67
p'Bitek, Okot, 91n68, 219
Peckham, Robert, 2, 9
Peterson, Derek R., 229
plague, 93, 101
police, 47–57, 73, 74, 77–78, 150–54, 158, 171, 195, 203
politics: anxiety as a political tool, 3, 10–11, 38–39, 57, 66, 187, 210; political authority, 3, 35, 38, 118, 120, 136, 182, 225, 232; political instability, 35, 41–43, 44–47, 50, 54, 56, 67–68, 73–74, 115, 119–22, 150–56, 195, 199–203, 210, 217, 218, 222–23, 226–34
power, 3, 4, 10, 14, 20, 22, 37, 38, 53, 56, 83, 158; in Burundi, 200–201; emotional, 36; and Kenyan settlers, 67, 71; in Mwanga II's Buganda, 117, 118, 124, 128, 129, 134–35, 138; in postcolonial Buganda, 217, 221, 225, 228–29, 231; of Rwandan government, 168, 169, 171, 174, 177, 184, 187
Pratten, David, 15, 16
prestige, 6, 8, 67, 86n10, 147–53, 158
prostitution, 18
protest, 23, 49, 69, 71, 74, 83, 96, 217–18, 219, 225, 227–34
psychiatry, 6, 8, 17, 92, 219
psychoanalysis, 1, 17
public health, 21, 94, 98–101, 107–8

quarantine, 14, 21, 94, 97–108

race, 6, 9, 10, 11, 13, 16, 21, 22, 38, 42–44, 67, 69, 77, 83, 93–94, 108, 122, 146–48, 152, 157
radio, 191n54, 200, 225, 226
Ranger, Terence, 39
rationality (and irrationality), 3, 7, 8, 16, 65, 93, 117, 122
Ray, Carina, 10
rebellion, 12, 47, 52–53, 56, 119, 121, 148, 207, 210, 213
Reeves, Madeleine, 3
refugees, 196, 198, 199, 203–5, 210, 213, 216n36
Reid, Richard, 14, 115, 119
Reinkowski, Maurus, 2
religion, 15, 22, 23, 37, 66, 120, 122, 124, 135–36, 167–68, 175, 186–87, 196
Reyntjens, Filip, 172
roadblocks, 13–14, 144, 160, 206
rock art, 34, 37, 41, 43, 45–47
Roscoe, John, 18, 130, 219–20
Rosenwein, Barbara, 3, 17, 94

Index

rumors, 40, 96–97, 132, 170, 200–202, 226
Rwanda, 14, 15, 17, 22–23, 167–87, 195–96, 200–206, 209, 210, 213; Hutu revolution, 173–74; postgenocide development, 14, 22, 168, 170–72, 183–85, 201; postgenocide religious landscape, 172–77, 186–87. *See also* genocide; Habyarimana, Juvénal; Kagame, Paul

safari, 9, 21, 67–70, 79–83, 84
Sartre, Jean-Paul, 219, 234n6
Schoenbrun, David, 222
Scott, James, 39
security, 34, 42, 44, 45, 68, 79, 99, 147–53, 159, 160, 168, 176, 201, 204–5, 227
segregation, 9–10, 21, 67, 71, 73, 79, 83, 93, 94, 108
Sekimwanyi, Haji, 221
Senegal, 8, 13, 21, 92–109
sensibilities, 5, 9, 38, 57, 202
sensory experiences, 18, 68, 80
sensuousness, 4, 34, 37
sex, 10, 89n43, 118, 122–38, 141n64. *See also* "black peril"; sexuality
sexuality, 21–22, 116, 118, 124, 126, 129, 129–37, 138
Shadle, Brett, 87n10, 89n43, 155
Sierra Leone, 93, 95, 98, 99, 100, 103
social lives, 4, 15, 18, 19, 36, 120, 122, 169, 197, 205
sociology, 16, 69, 91n68
somatic, 17, 19, 65
Sørensen, Tim Flohr, 36
South Africa, 33–58, 93, 97, 146–47, 150, 154, 155, 159; Maloti-Drakensberg Mountains, 9, 35, 37, 42–44, 45, 47–48, 49, 52, 54; raiding movements, 9–10, 35, 47, 50. *See also* apartheid; outlaws; rock art
space(s), 5, 6, 9–12, 13, 20, 21, 34–35, 45, 47, 57, 68–70, 71, 73, 77–80, 84–85, 119–25, 152, 155, 158–59, 217
spirit possession, 23, 217, 226, 229–31
Stanard, Matthew, 13
Staples, Amy, 81, 90n62
state (the), 3, 13, 14, 22, 34, 39, 148, 157, 160, 168–69, 172–73, 181–82, 183–84, 185, 186, 188n6, 217, 218, 223, 234
Stewart, Charles, 198
Stoler, Ann Laura, 3, 38, 67, 88n17
structural adjustment, 4
subjectivity, 5, 9, 15, 18, 19, 34, 37, 92, 197
surveillance, 14, 50–53, 98, 102–3, 129, 135, 168
Swanson, Maynard, 97

Tarlow, Sarah, 4, 36
Taussig, Michael, 97

temporality, 6, 12–15, 20, 22–23, 148, 158–59, 168–69, 198, 209
Thiong'o, Ngũgĩ wa, 219
Thum, Gregor, 2
Tiberendwa, Ado K., 115
time, 12–15, 17, 24, 95, 148–49, 168, 196, 197, 211, 220, 225
trauma, 17, 182; traumatic histories, 83, 115
tropical neurasthenia. *See* neurasthenia

Uganda: Acholiland, 67, 68, 69, 80, 82–83; Buganda kingdom, 14, 21–22, 23, 115–38, 217–34; homosexuality in contemporary Uganda, 22, 13; Kasubi Tombs, 11, 23, 217, 226–31, 234; missionaries in, 116, 118, 124–29, 130–36, 220, 221, 226; National Resistance Movement (NRM), 14, 224, 228; place of kingdoms in, 222, 224, 228, 234; political instability in postcolonial Uganda, 14, 222–26; Uganda Martyrs, 116, 130–31. *See also* Amin, Idi; Museveni, Yoweri; Mwanga II; Obote, Milton
uncertainty, 4, 15, 16, 19, 34, 38, 50, 145, 146, 147, 181, 196–99, 202, 210, 216n32, 218, 219–20
uneasiness, 15, 16, 66, 115, 196
universalism, 2, 5
urban elites, Rwandan, 171–72, 183
urban poor, 95, 97, 108–9, 183; residential segregation, 93, 108

Vallgårda, Karen, 11
Vaughan, Megan, 131
violence, 13, 15, 22, 57, 83, 147, 160, 173, 195, 202, 208, 210, 218, 225; fear of, 8, 11, 13, 22, 52, 89n43, 126, 147–48, 150, 155, 157, 158–59, 202
vulnerability, 4, 8, 14, 117, 122, 145, 149, 152–56; of the colonial enterprise, 2, 7–8, 12, 77, 102, 108, 145

Wagner, Günter, 75
war, 4, 52–53, 100, 121, 127, 144, 145, 160, 173, 196, 199–201, 206–7, 213, 223, 228
Whyte, Susan Reynolds, 19
worry, 18, 34, 94, 219
Wyndham, Richard, 144–45

yellow fever, 8–9, 21, 92–109; imposition of quarantine, 97–108; as a "white man's disease," 95–96
youth, 72, 124, 129, 182, 195, 201, 227, 229

Zimbabwe, 13, 144, 158, 160, 184, 219